THE REST
OF
THE ELEPHANT

Perspectives on the Mass Media

John D. Stevens
William E. Porter

University of Michigan

PRENTICE-HALL, INC., ENGLEWOOD CLIFFS, N.J.

Library of Congress Cataloging in Publication Data

STEVENS, JOHN D.   comp.
    The rest of the elephant.

    Bibliography: p.
    1. Mass media—United States.   I. Porter, William
Earl, joint comp.   II. Title.
P92.U5S7   301.16'1   72-8804
ISBN 0-13-774596-6
ISBN 0-13-774588-5 (pbk.)

FOR VICKY AND JEFF, JIM AND LISA

PRENTICE-HALL INTERNATIONAL, INC., *London*
PRENTICE-HALL OF AUSTRALIA, PTY. LTD., *Sydney*
PRENTICE-HALL OF CANADA, LTD., *Toronto*
PRENTICE-HALL OF INDIA PRIVATE LIMITED, *New Delhi*
PRENTICE-HALL OF JAPAN, INC., *Tokyo*

CONTENTS

PREFACE   v

INTRODUCTION   1

SECTION ONE
THE MEDIA AND THEIR AUDIENCES   7

WORLD AFFAIRS NEWS AND ITS AUDIENCES   16
John P. Robinson and James W. Swinehart

COMMUNICATING WITH THE URBAN POOR   24
Carl E. Block

HOW ONE TV STATION SERVED ITS BLACK AUDIENCE   34
Nicholas Johnson and Kenneth Cox

SECTION TWO
THE BUSINESS OF BUSINESS   39

THE MEDIA BARONS AND THE PUBLIC INTEREST   49
Nicholas Johnson

WHAT NEWS COSTS AT NBC   56
Alan Pearce

CIRCULATION DISASTER AMONG CHICAGO NEWSPAPERS   64
Brian Boyer

WHY NEWSPAPERS ARE MAKING MONEY AGAIN   69
Staff of Business Week

DECLINE OF THE DOWNTOWN MOVIE PALACES   81
Robert Kraus

SECTION THREE
HOW THE WORK GETS DONE   87

SHERIFF WHO?   89
Lee M. Rich

PLANNING TO SHOOT A MOVIE   102
John Gregory Dunne

HOW THE NEWS GETS INTO THE PAPER   107
Theodore M. Bernstein

CORRIDOR OF MIRRORS   115
Thomas Whiteside

THE MAN WITH THE PENCIL OF LIGHT   142
Richard L. Tobin

SECTION FOUR
THE JOURNALIST AND HIS COMMITMENTS   147

THE REPORTER AS ACTIVIST   152
J. K. Hvistendahl

THE "NEW JOURNALISM" IS SOMETIMES LESS THAN MEETS THE EYE 158
W. Stewart Pinkerton, Jr.

THE BLACK PRESS IN TRANSITION   .   165
L. F. Palmer, Jr.

ADDITIONAL READING   179

INDEX   181

PREFACE

We hope this book does at least two things. The first is to provide meaningful observations on all the mass media, without segregating each in its own cubicle. We have tried to integrate our comments and conclusions *across* the mass media. We think there are four main reasons why the mass media are like they are, and those reasons correspond to the sections of this book: audiences, economics, working processes, and ethics.

Second, we have tried to combine the advantages of an original book (unity and direction) with those of an anthology (contrasting viewpoints and special expertise). We selected the reprint material carefully from among hundreds of worthwhile articles, books and speeches, and then we condensed them; naturally, we take responsibility for any inadvertent shifts in meaning which might result from our editing. We are grateful for the permissions to reprint these works.

We are also grateful to many hundreds of students in Journalism 201, Social Role of the Mass Media, during the last half-dozen years, whose comments and questions have helped shape our own thinking.

Although John Stevens was primarily responsible for the first and fourth sections and William Porter for the second and third, both authors share the conclusions throughout the book.

J. D. S.
W. E. P.

Ann Arbor

INTRODUCTION

Oneofthe bearded clichés about learning is the parable of the blind men and the elephant, which depicts the problem of generalizing about the whole beast from the feel of a leg or the tail or the trunk. We'd like to revive this story one more time because it provides the simplest way to explain the need for one more book about the mass communication media. This book is about the rest of the elephant.

Aspects of the media that have been little analyzed will be discussed. The first section is about the audiences of the mass media. Most of the analysis of the relationship between the individual and the media to which he attends has been moralistic and curiously abstract. It could be summarized as saying that the stuff on the tube and in the newspapers ought to be better, and that people would have better taste and would be nobler creatures if it were. (The first director-general of the British Broadcasting Company, Sir John Reith, developed the BBC exactly on that premise.) Too often the response of media managers to such a pious oversimplification has been, "We just give the people what they want." (American broadcasters and moviemakers have been saying that for 40 years; publishers for a much longer period.) Of late such arguments have been heated by growing concerns as to what extent media are responsible for violence in the society.

No one can fault the wish that the artistic and moral level of both producers and consumers were higher, but this point of view ignores the central fact that different media perform different functions for different

1

people—and different functions for the same people at different times. The audiences select their mass media. Not only can you not make an elephant drink, but if he is balky, you will have the devil's own time just getting him to the water.

The beginning point for an analysis of any medium must be efficiency: whom does it reach and what is done with it? We shall give some answers in terms of specific situations. Even though considerations of economics and ethics underlie some of the discussions, the first consideration is with demonstrating that the media-audience relationship is two way and that the search for more efficiency continues to shape it.

Since the size of the audience equals the amount of income for the media, the next subject to be examined will be the media as businesses. The critical problem is the threat implied by growing population concentration, making significant the demonstration that people who live in big cities don't buy newspapers or go to movie houses the way they once did. That's one part of the elephant, but so is the fact that the media, generally, are thriving. The death throes of the general-interest magazines and the (generally poor) big-city dailies are loud and long and often are interpreted as symptomatic of their industries. But they aren't. The steady infusion of the "smart money" from conglomerates and corporations into newspapers, magazines, book publishing houses, movie studios, broadcast stations, and cable television systems is the best indication of their general economic health.

The third major section of this book deals with communications technology. The guy who flips a switch to light his TV set gives no more thought to the electronics of television than he does to the workings of the electric utility. If the TV show includes an elephant act, he will not give much thought to the hours that went into the pachyderm's training, either. Why should he?

Many use mass communications in the same unthinking way: the teenager with the radio screwed into his ear while reading a paperback book, the New York subway strap-hanger, insulated from all those others by his copy of the *Daily News,* the lonely oldster half-seeing the shadows on the screen that vaguely suggest human company. There are people back there somewhere producing all this stuff, presumably, but essentially it is something magically present in the air or left on the doorstep.

Of course, some users are certain that communication professionals are bad guys who connive to manipulate and distort. This belief is an article of faith among those at either end of the political spectrum; there is disagreement about what these evil folk are trying to do (reinforce the system and make it more repressive, says the left; destroy the system, says the right), but there's agreement about their responsibility.

This position contains an assumption as naïve as the vague unconcern of the first group discussed—the unconscious consumer. It likewise disregards any of the implications of elaborate organization and complicated processes. It holds that the producer has complete and easy control of the product, both in content and tone, and therefore can be held totally responsible for it.

This simply is not true. The process, for example, of getting a news story from Teheran into the pages of a newspaper in Nebraska calls for the coordinated, skilled activity of many specialists working at high speed, and the requirements of the system affect the story's length, clarity, accuracy, and its chances for use. All told, they probably mean more than either the reporter's judgment or his skill as a writer. Realistically, then, any analysis of the media designed to explain their role in society must take into account the structure and processes of the mass communication system.

The final section deals with the individual professional and particularly the newsman. The popular view of his job always has been singularly narrow, a one-dimensional stereotype which reached its apogee in the B-grade movies of the 1940's. It has been uniquely American (in no other country are journalists even minor folk heroes), simultaneously favorable and patronizing. In the stereotype the journalist has a singular drive to seek out The Truth with a rocklike integrity which makes him refuse to be co-opted or intimidated. He is a useful man, in societal terms, but he is not very bright—and he is remarkably insensitive. The stereotype has been about all we've had. Remarkably few studies have been made of the social origins of newsmen or of what motivates or satisfies them. Two trends of the last decade force attention on the individual journalist in the system today.

The first is a serious challenge to the idea that the newsman has to be objective, that he is a kind of neutral instrument for observation and notation. No one seriously regards real objectivity as possible, since all reporting comes through filters, but the training process—originally in the newsroom under the apprentice system, then in journalism education—has tried to establish the outlines of "objectivity" as a part of the professional psyche. The key test traditionally has been the reporter's conscious *attempts* to be objective.

But there is a new kind of journalist who sees his job as too important to be handcuffed by such arbirtrary guidelines, who sees journalism as a powerful engine for social change and proposes to use it that way. This attitude is clearly related to the concept of a larger role in policy making. Together, they pose a problem for those who own the media and control them at the top levels, and they suggest that mass communication in the future will be different from that of the past. The speed at which the revolution comes is much more difficult to predict than its inevitability. A violently changing world has brought new demands upon the mass media. The financial structure has moved to help meet them, providing the equipment of new technology and opening up new audiences which are also new markets; in part, in response to the technology, the structures and processes through which the media function are beginning to change.

The other is a closely related movement referred to by phrases ranging from "the democratic newsroom" to "reporter power." The lack of a consensus name is not surprising, since there is a lack of consensus about its objectives, even among the activists in the cause. They appear to agree, at least, that working newsmen should have some say in the selection of news executives and in policy decisions. Beyond that, cultural variations set in.

On the European continent (where the movement originated as early as 1951), for example, there is much interest in protecting the staff member against abrupt changes in the publication's political line. This is not an issue in the United States. For the last half-century, the thrust of innovation in journalism has been from the United States toward Europe; this movement to protect the journalist reverses the trend.

Traditionally, in this country the news professions have suffered from a steady outward migration of journalists, most of whom leave within the first five years on the job. In a sense, because many are bright and highly motivated, this is more costly to the society—because of what they might have produced—than to the media, which are geared to this replacement of novitiates. Another large group leaves in their middle and late forties, after perhaps 15 years in the field. This is the time when first-raters sometimes desert the media for positions around the fringes of the news business —in public relations, government, or (far more rarely than most realize) the teaching of journalism. The departure of this group cripples the media badly, for they represent, not lost potential, but high-level daily competence.

There is evidence that suggests that most professional newsmen come into the field because they see it as important, socially useful work. Most come from middle- or upper-middle-class, educated families, as every one of the sparse studies of the social origins of U.S. journalists has shown, although there is a kind of wistful folklore which holds that the best are poor boys who fought their way up. (Gay Talese fed the myth in *The Kingdom and the Power* in a discussion of the New York *Times* staff, but he was preoccupied with Abe Rosenthal and James Reston and forgot to notice the sons of bankers, plantation owners, small businessmen, physicians, and ministers who were their colleagues.) "Scratch a journalist," Leo Rosten said in *The Washington Correspondents,* "and you find a reformer." Most do not come into journalism either for status or for money; they come in to help bring about change. And sometimes they leave it when they realize that's a hard thing to do.

One of the reasons for the exodus of such people from journalism is their growing perception of the kind of reality described at the beginning of this book: the mass media are, inevitably, businesses which must respond to the ground rules of profitability, and most jobs within them are anchored in the efficient performance of routine. This perception develops early in the job, and one either drops out immediately or does well and moves upward rapidly, finding satisfaction in new challenges. Sooner or later even the ablest journalist bumps against a ceiling, not only because there is little room at the top, but because all important decisions come from the top down. This is traditional in all kinds of bureaucracies (certainly in newsrooms around the world), but it may be poorly suited to satisfying members of a profession which constantly is being upgraded in intelligence, sensitivity, and social concern.

The ultimate and greatest need is a better professional in mass communications. He is not only the best hope of the business, but in many ways the hope of the world. He is the only one who can make the elephant perform the way we all would like.

SECTION ONE
THE MEDIA AND
THEIR AUDIENCES

Each communication—a whispered word, a story in the morning newspaper, a network television show—is aimed at a specific audience. A professional communicator can slant a message so that it will be understood, or at least heeded, by that audience. If others "eavesdrop" on the message, it may be a bonus, but success is measured on the ability to reach the target audience.

Advertisers understand this best. An editor has limited feedback about his publication. He hears comments from his friends, reads letters, and talks with his staff; but an advertiser's sales figures are a much more sensitive barometer of success—and his definition of "success" is also clearer.

A young man smitten with love could reach more girls by running his "Ode to Lucinda" on CBS during prime time, but even if he could afford this method of communication, it might miss his target audience. Lucinda might not be watching. Not only would it be more efficient, but it would be more effective if he delivered his message in person—to say nothing of being more pleasant.

If you want to share your secret for getting chickens to lay more eggs, you probably could reach most of the nation's poultry raisers by buying time on *Flip Wilson* or a full page in *Life* magazine, but it is an inefficient way to reach your audience. More than 99 per cent of the people you reach couldn't care less about chickens. Run your story in a journal for poultrymen, even if it has only a few hundred readers. They will be the *right* few hundred.

Not only that, but the more specialized an information source, the more the users believe it. A pediatrician may read medical stories in the newspaper and watch medical shows on television, but he probably will not be influenced by them. For professional information, he will turn to books and specialized magazines. An endorsement of a new technique or medicine in a general medical journal will carry less weight with him than will similar praise in a pediatrician's journal. On the other hand, he does not look to that specialized journal to provide him endorsements of plays or political candidates.

Each publication or program must attract a unique audience, and then it must perform enough of a service for each member of that audience to hold him. There is virtually no overlap in audiences for a classical music and a teeny-bopper radio station in the same city, any more than there is between the subscription lists for *Mademoiselle* and *Field & Stream*.

In no medium is the trend toward specialized audiences more apparent than in magazines. Some 8,000 commercial magazines have a combined circulation of 400 million. The same person may subscribe to several magazines, but no two magazines attract the same kinds of audiences. While such circulation giants as *Look* and *Saturday Evening Post* have folded in recent years, others (especially those concentrating on sports and leisure) have been booming. Advertisers want specialized audiences; they can buy large, undifferentiated audiences at a cheaper per-thousand rate on TV.

Reader's Digest remains the exception. In 1971, as it marked its 50th anniversary, the *Digest* could boast that nearly 30 million copies were purchased every month in 13 languages. From its first issue (when the editors copied many of the articles by hand from magazines in the New York Public Library), the magazine has sought to provide something for everybody in every issue. Few readers seem aware of, or are bothered by, its conservative bias; they are equally oblivious to the open secret that the *Digest* pays for many of the articles, places them in other publications, and then reprints them.

Reader's Digest was one of the last holdouts among general magazines against carrying advertising. In 1954, a research firm showed a sample of the magazine's readers a copy of the Canadian edition (which contained ads) and the American (which did not); 81 per cent preferred the magazine with ads, which began appearing in April, 1955. Many magazines are purchased primarily *for* the ads, not in spite of the ads. *New Yorker* is a good example. Ads place high in readership studies of newspapers, too, although not as high as comics, which consistently lead the field.

Blondie remains as she has for many years, the queen of the comics, appearing in an estimated 1,600 papers around the world. Comparative figures for strips are difficult to come by in the notoriously closed-mouth and competitive syndicated feature field; however, it is estimated that

Peanuts and *Beetle Bailey* appear in about 1,200 papers each and are among the runners-up to *Blondie*. (College students often find it hard to believe that *Blondie* is more popular than *Peanuts,* and, of course, with college students she is not.) Humor or gag strips clearly are more popular than adventure or continuing strips, both in this country and abroad.

The comics audience is wide and varied, but as with most media usage, it is heavier at the higher income and higher education levels. For example, two out of three men who are college graduates read at least one strip a day.

How do comics capture and hold such a wide readership? Part of the secret is internal consistency within a strip. It is this internal consistency which permits one's eye to move without wincing from Camp Swampy to the prehistoric landscape of *B.C.,* to Okeefenokee Swamp to Dagwood's suburban bungalow. What happens within each of these environments *is* consistent; we know what to expect. Another factor which makes them popular is their simplicity, in both word and style. Almost all readers *can* handle more difficult presentations; it is simply that they do not want to do so all the time.

All the media must think about "secondary audiences," too. Television producers know that few new series will make it past the first year; therefore, they count on later sales of the show by syndicates to individual stations for daytime showing. Only shows with strong female appeal run in the early daytime hours and only those with kid-appeal re-run in the late afternoon.

Hollywood has turned out few films based on football or baseball, and one reason has been that the producers count on sales in foreign nations, where these American games are unknown. As movie makers saw television sales become more important, they began planning appropriate lengths and themes for TV audiences; in some cases, they even shoot alternate scenes or endings—one for movie audiences and another for TV.

Book authors always have eyed book club sales, condensations, and film rights, and many of them have written books with these outlets in mind. Paperback rights of more than $400,000 have been paid to Jacqueline Suzanne, Irving Wallace, Mario Puzo, and Elia Kazan.

Industries which invest heaviest in research turn the largest profits, but the communications industries are the exception to this general business rule. They invest comparatively little and still turn higher profits than most industries. The American Newspaper Publishers Association, on behalf of 207 member daily papers, spent only $6.2 million on research in 1967, of which nearly half was on advertising and less than 10 per cent on how to improve the news and editorial product. Some individual newspapers and broadcast stations do study the demographics (age, sex, income, etc.) of their audiences, primarily for the benefit of the ad sales staff. While most stations make a cursory effort to survey the likes and dislikes of their readers every three years at license renewal time, many broadcasters do not want to know who is watching. For example, the producer of one innovative news program on a public TV station admits he has never surveyed his audience; he prefers to answer such questions with anecdotes about being recognized on the street by bus drivers. But that hardly suffices for data.

The section of the record industry which produces popular hits finds it cannot do market research in any traditional sense because audience tastes change too rapidly. Before a surveyor can determine the demand from a subaudience, convey the information to the record company, and the company produce such records, the audience wants something else. As a result, the companies developed an alternate strategy, namely, over-production. They will record almost anything, dump it on the market, and then put all their promotion behind the one or two winners. Companies release 300 or more singles a week, knowing full well that only a handful will be hits, but those hits will mint money. They can tolerate this inefficiency because it costs only a few thousand dollars to do a recording—a drop in the bucket, compared with the costs of a failure in most of the media.

For example, audiences for both books and magazines have been demanding more and more nonfiction during the last quarter-century. In 1947, before the paperback deluge, a survey of American best-sellers over the century showed that 17 of the first 20 had strong religious overtones, and only about 10 per cent were primarily of topical interest. Sex was an important element in less than 10 per cent. Paperbacks changed this, of course, especially the percentages dealing with topicality and sex. But an even greater shift was toward nonfiction, including the "instant books" which appear within a few days of almost any major news event. The biggest selling book of all time (excluding the Bible) is Dr. Benjamin Spock's baby book. It has sold twice as many copies as the best-selling novel *Peyton Place*.

Peyton Place has, in fact, outsold all the novels of Dreiser, Fitzgerald, Hemingway, Faulkner, and Melville combined. The second most popular novel is Erskine Caldwell's *God's Little Acre*. Seven of the next eight spots are filled by the hardboiled novels of Mickey Spillane. In terms of total sales by author, *Publisher's Weekly* places twentieth-century novelists in this order: Erle Stanley Gardner, Spillane, and Caldwell. Fourth place belongs to Charles Schulz and his *Peanuts* books, followed by John Steinbeck, John O'Hara, Pearl Buck, and James Michener.

Nevertheless, media producers must constantly consider the sensitivities of their audiences. Just as the TV networks edit out the strongly sexual scenes from movies, so do newspapers in direct quotes use ellipses in place of vulgarities. The New York *Times* bowdlerized the text of the Walker

Report in its own pages but put its imprint on a paperback book which contained all the obscenities. The Supreme Court has recognized in recent years that different standards of obscenity can be applied to the use of the same material by different audiences.

The coming of network television about 1950 killed network radio, except for brief newscasts and sports events, and turned radio into a local medium—often with higher profits than before. TV also killed the half-century love affair of the working class with the movies. Small screens drove out big screens in the United States during the 1950's and in Europe during the 1960's. In this country, moviegoing is about one-third what it was in 1948. Any prime-time TV show which draws as few viewers as all the movie theaters in the United States draw for all their showings in an entire week is in serious trouble.

Today's movie audience is young (nearly half of it is under twenty and three-fourths under forty), well-educated, and affluent enough to pay the steep ticket prices, prices which doubled during the 1960's. A survey by the Motion Picture Association of America confirmed that of those who attended college, one-third call themselves regular movie goers, while only 9 per cent of those who did not finish high school so label themselves.

Today's film audience will not lay out $3 or so to see formula entertainment; if they want that, they can stay home and watch television. Filmmakers have no choice but to give them what they want; certainly they know they can never lure the lower classes back to the theaters, not even if they instituted 5-cent admissions and gave away free china every bank night.

Are those who stay home satisfied with what is on the tube? Network officials are fond of quoting statistics to show that they are, but then if you ask a Chinese peasant, he almost certainly will say he likes rice. He has never tasted beefsteak, but he knows he likes rice better than going hungry. With millions of persons throughout the world, television viewing is about as habitual as eating. During certain hours, they "watch television," pretty much whatever comes on. They even are reluctant to switch channels.

There are many ways to describe the TV audience—more homes have sets than have refrigerators, children spend more time watching than any other activity except sleep, the average set is on six hours a day, more people see a rookie shortstop in a World Series game than saw Babe Ruth in his entire career—but they all boil down to its mind-boggling size. No book, not even the best-selling paperback, will ever reach as many persons as the lowest ranking network show, a dubious distinction almost always reserved for a news or public affairs program.

One sometimes suspects that the networks set up circular arguments to justify their reliance on the ratings for making programing decisions. For example, in the fall of 1971, CBS devoted an entire evening to news and public affairs programing, airing *Sixty Minutes* and documentaries on Picasso and Mexican-Americans. The one evening depressed the entire week's ratings, and the president of CBS-TV announced, "We wanted to see what audiences will do and we found out. They defect to entertainment in droves. Absolute disaster."

My World and Welcome to It, a television series based on the works of humorist James Thurber, picked up two major Emmys in 1970—two months after NBC canceled it. The show was named best comedy series and its star, William Windom, best comedy actor of the year. It was canceled for the usual reason, namely, low ratings, since it was attracting *only* 18 million viewers.

"The frustrating part," said Danny Arnold, the producer, "is that you can never find out who made the decision to cancel. Everybody says, 'Gee, it was a great show and I, personally, loved it and think it should have stayed on'."

In a rare move, CBS replayed the series in the summer of 1972.

One Sunday evening in 1969, CBS televised the Royal Shakespeare Company's production of *Midsummer Night's Dream* and was outdrawn by both *Bonanza* and *Movie of the Week* on the other channels. In fact it only attracted 23 per cent of the audience, but put another way, those 20 million viewers would have filled the Globe Theater for 10,000 performances.

Within an hour of the assassination of President Kennedy, 90 per cent of the American population had heard the news; still, some studies suggest television's impact may be less than its reach. For example, researchers have found that half of the people cannot recall one item from a network newscast they watched a few hours ago; even with prompting on headlines, many still cannot recall a single story.

Children select their TV fare disturbingly like adults; that is, they praise quality shows but watch *kitsch*. Studies indicate kids prefer to watch reruns of such bearded comedies as *The Munsters* or *Gilligan's Island* to *Sesame Street* and *Captain Kangaroo,* such cartoons as *The Flintstones* or *The Archies* to *Hot Dog* or *Children's Television Workshop*. They may watch the quality programs to please their folks, but in their heart of hearts, they would rather be entertained. With the rapid increase in multiple-set homes, the children are making more and more of thir own program decisions, which may bode ill for all the grandiose plans for upgrading children's TV offerings.

The three TV networks have been caught up in the numbers game of trying to reach the maximum audience all the time, and their overall Nielsen rating ends each year in a virtual dead heat. Here is how it went for five years:

Season	CBS	NBC	ABC
1967–68	20.9	19.0	16.7
1968–69	20.3	20.2	15.7
1969–70	20.0	20.1	16.6
1970–71	19.6	19.7	17.5
1971–72	20.5	19.3	18.6

Even the networks are starting to pay attention to the demographics of audiences for individual shows. One network dropped *Dark Shadows,* a horror–soap opera, from its late afternoon schedule, not because of low ratings (they weren't), but because the show was attracting children instead of housewives. Such network stalwarts as Ed Sullivan, Red Skelton, and Lawrence Welk were canceled because they were reaching too many in the Geritol and too few in the Ripple generation.

Not only have television sets become, quite literally, our modern baby-sitters, but they also have become the central focus of life for millions of people throughout the world. For them, the question is not whether to watch television tonight, but rather, which program will I watch in which hour? Regardless who might come to visit, the set stays on. As Norman Cousins, former editor of *Saturday Review,* once wrote: "Few things are more terrifying in this world for some persons than an open hour if the TV set is out of order. Their relaxation reflexes have been conditioned by the turning of knobs."

Television, while it has some local programs, is essentially a national medium; however, cable television may make local programing practical—even within neighborhoods.

Cable *may* change everything; but that is not the same as saying that it *will.* Cable communication is still in its infancy, but by 1972 about 10 percent of American homes were on cables and about half of the local franchises for cable systems were held by conventional broadcasters, publishers, and phone companies—all with vested interests in minimizing the effects of the cable revolution. It would be tragic if the 20, 40, or more new channels (Akron has a 64-channel system) end up by giving us little more than the 8 P.M. show from each of the three networks, but on five or six channels simultaneously.

The President's Task Force on Communications Policy Report, issued in 1969 after being suppressed for two years, envisioned a "wired nation" with coaxial cables tying homes with other homes, homes with businesses, and both with computers and other networks. Politics and economics are greater restraints on such a development than is technology.

Cable communication has the potential for being far more than a delivery system for television programs. The same cables can carry music, radio, computer data, shopping information, facsimile newspapers, and person-to-person messages. They also can read gas, water, and electric meters and can carry "yes-no" opinions back from a home to some central polling place, thus opening up the possibilities of instant referenda. Shades of Marshall McLuhan's Global Village!

But for the most part, the public has not been much interested in cable. One reason is that it was born in remote areas and small towns. It was not until 1971 that the Federal Communications Commission issued guidelines that permitted the cautious introduction of cable systems into areas close to major TV markets, and then only under restrictions designed to minimize competition with existing over-the-air broadcasters.

The two cable companies franchised in Manhattan each provide a pair of public access channels, one for users with a one-time or last-minute message and the other for groups reserving a regular time slot. Users must bear most of the production costs, although the cable firms provide limited studios, cameras, and technical assistance. With half-inch videotape equipment and volunteer help, production costs are within reach of most potential users. During the first year of access, few radical groups or politicians demanded time; the audiences were too small for them to fool with. Series which were aired included sign-language tapes for the deaf and news and entertainment for the elderly. Young filmmakers found a showcase. Single-shot programs included parts of a medieval festival at the Cloisters, three long-time residents telling how much cleaner and safer the city used to be, nationality groups celebrating holidays, and a woman claiming that "homosexual plastic surgeons" had botched her face lift.

An indication of how small some of the audiences were came when a tape featuring a lecture about an exhibit of Picassos at the Museum of Modern Art was aired without sound and no one called to complain.

Open-access channels have sparked more reaction in smaller cities. Perhaps that is natural, since citizens there are used to dealing on a personal basis with officials and issues and community involvement is a tradition. Contracts with the two Manhattan cable companies require them to decentralize their operations into 10 subdistricts by 1975, and each will be able to originate programs for that neighborhood. That may create the kind of community interaction which other towns already have.

Most of the 6 million American families which had laid out the installation and monthly fees to receive cable television by early 1972 did so because they wanted a clearer picture. They either were in fringe areas, distant from conventional stations, or they were in cities where skyscrapers interfered with reception. The cable systems provided some exclusives, ranging from weather information, to extra movies, to sporting events, to coverage of local governmental meetings. But most of these people paid for a better picture, not for more variety in their fare. They were comfortable, if not satisfied, with the programs the networks were serving up. Three kinds of rice were enough.

Americans, of course, invest sizable amounts of money as well as time in their media. They spend about as many dollars on radios and television sets and their repairs as they do on books, magazines, and newspapers, and about twice as much as they pay for tickets for movies, cultural events, and sports. The typical middle-class adult spends three hours a day with TV, a couple of hours in the earshot of radio (although often while driving, eating, or doing something else), 20 minutes with his newspaper and 10 minutes with a magazine. If he reads any books (and only one in four adults reads even one book a year) or sees any movies, he probably reads or sees several.

The higher an individual's education, the more he relies on magazines and books; those on the lower end of the educational scale hardly use them at all. *Psychology Today* magazine asked its readers (three-quarters of whom are college graduates) which medium provided the most reliable information on racial and urban problems. TV, newspapers, and radio *combined* received fewer votes than either magazines or books.

Like the peasant with his rice, most persons have difficulty criticizing their media, even when they feel vaguely dissatisfied with them. Often the criticism is aimed too low, as at typographical errors. In an average newspaper column there are 10,000 letters. Since there are seven possible wrong positions for each, there are 70,000 chances for error and several million for transpositions in each column. The Sunday edition of the New York *Times* contains twice as many words as James Joyce's novel of heroic proportions, *Ulysses*. (A possibly apocryphal story says the publisher of the *Times* once started reading on Sunday morning and was still at it on Thursday night.)

You can add pages to a newspaper, magazine, or book if you have important news or analysis to present. You likewise can make a movie a few minutes longer, but broadcasting is in a much less flexible format. You present the same number of words and images in any five-minute broadcast, whether it is a big news day or a dull one. Walter Cronkite reminds audiences that network newscasts cover only a small proportion of stories (and those in much briefer form) than what a newspaper can fit on its front page alone.

Some criticisms aim too high. For example, those who criticize local newspapers for not giving them enough details about foreign affairs or science miss the basic fact that a newspaper is trying to carry a little something for everybody. To expect one paper to provide enough specialized information for all specialists at a cost of 15 cents a day is ridiculous. Those who want such details should expect to purchase other media, or at least other newspapers.

Newspapers still seek saturation coverage of their own city and region, but they don't care about the people beyond. In fact, distant subscribers probably cost the daily paper more than they bring in. The United States, almost uniquely, has no true national newspaper. The New York *Times,* the *Christian Science Monitor,* and the *Wall Street Journal*—taken together—have a daily circulation of less than 3 million (of national newspaper circulation of about 62 million daily). Looked at another way, these papers have a smaller total circulation than some individual newspapers in Great Britain, Japan, and the Soviet Union. But for impact in an individual community on local issues, there is no substitute for the local newspaper.

The mass-appeal newspapers of the world have built their circulations on entertainment and sensationalism. By far the largest in the United States is the New York *Daily News.* This tabloid outsells the *Times* two to one, and when you think how many libraries subscribe to the *Times* and not to the *News,* that figure becomes even more impressive. But the *News* has been going through an identity crisis. With the demise of all but two city rivals, the *News* added suburban, middle-class readers and department store and quality shop advertising. While its editorial mix has continued to emphasize entertainment, the editors have been paying more attention to news. The trick is to hold onto its subway strap-hangers while serving this new middle-class clientele. Whether it can do so is still an open question.

In the following article, two University of Michigan researchers discuss some general notions about audiences, and then turn to the kinds of news material that may or may not reach various segments of the public. Their focus in on world affairs news, but most of what they discuss has broader implications.

WORLD AFFAIRS NEWS AND ITS AUDIENCES *

John P. Robinson and *James W. Swinehart*

In its 30 years of existence, the field of mass communications research has hardly had time to develop into a fully integrated area

* Condensed from *Television Quarterly* 8:2 (Spring 1968). With permission of the journal and the authors.

of scientific inquiry. Nevertheless, some findings have appeared with enough consistency and regularity to be accorded serious consideration. Five of these seem particularly relevant to the topic of this paper:

> The personal contacts within a person's immediate milieu generally have more influence on his beliefs and attitudes (especially deep-rooted attitudes) than do the mass media.
>
> Historically speaking, the quality that has moved any communication medium into the "mass" category is its conveyance of superficial rather than serious news matter.
>
> Subtlety and implicit arguments are less effective than straightforward explicit appeals in changing audience attitudes and beliefs.
>
> Those members of a mass audience who are already best informed and most interested in a topic are most likely to pick up information on that topic conveyed through the mass media. But just as important is the reverse: those people who are relatively uninformed and uninterested (usually the vast majority for any given topic, such as foreign affairs) are likely not to encounter such information in the media or, if they do, are likely to "tune out."
>
> The content of prime-time television programs reflects the mentality of the average American better than any other mass medium. The typical citizen finds bread-and-butter issues far more relevant than almost any news about national or international affairs.

It would be inaccurate to give the impression that such findings do not require considerable qualification. Not one of them is known at a level of detail sufficient to adequately explain the processes through which media information is absorbed (or perhaps more appropriately, not absorbed) by the public. Some of the above findings are derived from studies of captive audiences, usually college students, far brighter and better informed than the average American.

We should make clear at the outset that this paper is concerned not with the effects of day-to-day presentations of news events (on which the present media do a remarkable job, given their practical constraints) but with their cumulative impact on mass audiences over time. Our primary assumption is that adequate comprehension of international events requires an understanding of the abstract and complex concepts employed by the media to convey news most efficiently. While television has made tremendous strides in giving international events more visual impact on the public, it is impossible for a TV broadcast to fill in the large information gaps that still exist in public perceptions of the world. Consider the difficulty of trying to convey an understanding of a shift in cold-war alliances, such as has happened between Russia and China, to an audience only half of whom know that China has a Communist government.

Thus when we note that the *New York Times* devotes five times as many words to a major international news story as does a TV network news broadcast, we are trying to make the point that, while "a picture may be worth a thousand words," no number of pictures can provide an adequate context for understanding international news to the uninformed viewer. The individual viewer may see the King of Greece arrive at the Rome airport but have no idea what he really represents or even why he's there. Nor can the TV news program afford to alienate its more interested and knowledgeable audience by repeating information needed by its less aware viewers.

Most available research fails us badly with regard to long-range considerations of media impact. Many studies on mass communications deal with the impact of a single film or program about a topic of little importance to the audience. Almost nothing is known about the long-range or in-depth effects of the media, and in this state of near-vacuum the pronouncements of a Marshall McLuhan can often gain unwarranted acceptance.

Mass Media Content and Audiences

Our focus is on the information conveyed by television. However, TV functions in an informational environment with other media, which both supplement and compete with information conveyed on television. On an average day television reaches the same proportion of Americans as do newspapers (about 80 per cent of the U.S. population); about 65 per cent listen to radio sometime on an average day, but only 16 per cent read a magazine.

However, as a news medium, television's role is far less impressive. While news is a prominent feature of good (but not prime) TV time, TV as a news source falls to third place on the average day, behind newspapers and radio. Less than half of the population watches a TV news program on an average day. Moreover, TV functions mostly as a headliner; a hot news story on television is given 175 words perhaps one-fifth the length given to the same story on the front page of the *New York Times*. TV news producers and editors have to assume that the viewer interested in more detail or background can find this in the printed media.

Studies of media usage generally find that the best-educated and most literate segments of the population rely far more on the printed media than on the broadcast media. However, in magazines—the most "demanding" of the media in terms of reading skill, personal effort, and news content—only a small proportion of the total non-advertising space is devoted to news of any kind; and of course, not all news deals with foreign affairs. Even within a news magazine such as *Time* or *Newsweek,* where world affairs articles constitute less than one-fifth of the magazine's news content, such articles comprise probably the least engrossing reading for the average subscriber. Nevertheless, magazines (or in some cases, books) are the most likely source of the background material for the person interested in an interpretation of world events.

Newspapers devote a much smaller proportion of their space to world events than do news magazines, although there is wide variation between the *New York Times* and the *Decatur Democrat.* Most of the space given to foreign affairs in the average newspaper concerns actual hostilities or potential armed conflict between nations, with little interpretive treatment or background. Consistently, readership studies show that the public would not mind if even less space were devoted to international matters. A parallel finding holds true for actual readership of foreign affairs stories in the paper, i.e., the percentage of newspaper space devoted to world affairs is far larger than the percentage of readers who read these articles. People who do read newspaper stories about international affairs are likely to read about them in magazines as well.

The medium most affected by television is now approaching the end of its initial period of readjustment. Radio is still popular among the TV isolates, those few who are too poor to have access to TV and those fewer still who feel too sophisticated to own one. Like television, however, its major news function is to provide headlines which, unlike television, it does at almost any time of the day or night. Radio's major non-advertising function is now as background, especially musical background.

Television, the latest and largest medium (in terms of time the average American spends with it), devotes precious little time to critical examination and analysis of world events. However, when it does focus on serious matters, TV appears to score highly. A prime-time interview with Walter Lippmann—which may draw only ten per cent of the available audience—appears in the same number of living rooms as an average issue of *Time,* and many of these viewers probably don't read news magazines.

On the other hand, exposure does not constitute communication. News stories which receive prominent attention on prime-time television may be scarcely perceived by the public at large. Even Presidential addresses on television, preempting prime-time shows on all networks and dealing with as vital a topic as nuclear disarmament, are recognized or recalled by only about half of the adult population a month after they are given.

Educational television was instituted to more fully realize the informational potential of the television medium. Unfortunately, educational television has limited reach outside major urban areas, and even in the cities its programs do not fare well in terms of audience size (usually well under five per cent of the total TV audience for programs broadcast in prime time). Data from a Harris Survey indicate that in New York, where ETV is on a standard VHF channel, regular viewers of educational TV (the approximately 20 per cent who use it at least once a week) tend to be highly educated. These regular ETV viewers are seven times as likely to watch a program on ETV as the average commercial TV viewer.

We have sketched the approximate numbers of people who may use the various media and the likelihood that they will encounter material dealing with international affairs. Two further elements are needed to put these data into proper perspective. The first deals with the educational background and attitudes of those who use the medium; these are discussed in some detail below.

The second consideration may be just as important: how does one become involved in the use of a medium? Some communications researchers feel that TV and newspaper use involves casual choice of content whereas magazine or book reading reflects a more deliberate choice. We suggest a different division, with book reading and TV viewing in the category of deliberate choice of content, and magazines and newspapers in the category of casual choice of content. With books and TV, the consumer knows what he's getting into; the magazine reader may also, to a lesser extent, and the newspaper reader to a still lesser extent. However, we still need to know how much TV viewing is planned by the viewer in advance on the basis of *TV Guide* listings, newspaper TV listings, ads for specific programs, or simple recall of the times at which certain regular programs are broadcast. An individual may actively seek programs of interest, may just tolerate those which happen to appear on a channel he is watching, or may actively avoid certain kinds of programs. We feel this choice-vs.-chance viewing distinction is extremely important in trying to set realistic expectations for enlarging the audience for foreign affairs programs. If any sizable proportion of viewing is unplanned, this will obviously limit the payoff one might expect from listings and ads and "promos" used in advance of specific programs.

One common rule of thumb about mass media audiences is that the educational composition of the audience is directly reflected in the size of the audience. The smaller the audience, the more likely its members are to be relatively well educated. Thus the relatively small audience for general news magazines is indicative of their appeal to the better-educated; this proposition is equally true when applied to the less popular TV network documentaries and panel discussions.

Who Gets What Message

By its nature, narrative accompanying the television pictorial display can convey far less analytic information per unit of time than printed media. The script for a half-hour documentary can be read by a knowledgeable person in the subject area in less than ten minutes. Moreover, the viewer does not have the opportunity to check a point which he has missed. For these reasons, when aiming at all but the elite audience it would be well to concentrate on making no more than two or three major points in a TV program, to make them as explicit as possible, to repeat them with slightly different phrasing, and to make them behaviorally relevant (for example, showing the viewer with whom he can communicate to effect desired change).

Such suggestions need some modification if a series of programs is planned—a strategy to be recommended in view of some discouraging evidence on the effects of single programs. Data from a large sample of high school students showed that the "CBS National Citizenship Test" (a one-shot program) did effect changes in attitudes and information, but only directly on the issues covered in the program; attitudes and knowledge about related issues were not affected. Moreover, the direct effects of the program had all but disappeared six months later. In other words, these high-school viewers appeared to retreat to their pre-exposure positions over time in those areas where they had changed originally.

A repeated finding of attempts to convey information through educational or political campaigns is that those who already are best informed are most likely to pick up the information given in the campaign. Moreover, such campaigns appear to be even less successful in changing entrenched attitudes than in conveying information.

Although it is true that the public is becoming better-educated, many social commentators appear overly optimistic about what this portends for the future make-up of media audiences. However, when looking at the most critical set of media users—those who have gone to college, whether graduating or not—it is important to note that the projected rise in this segment's proportion of the total U.S. population is only from 16 per cent in 1960 to 21 per cent in 1980. This hardly constitutes enough of a change by itself to effect a dramatic rise either in general television programming or in that segment of the population adequately informed about world affairs.

As of the moment, television has many advantages over the other news media. It is seen as more credible. It reaches large segments of the public who have trouble understanding foreign news in the newspaper and who receive no news magazines. Its typical documentaries (although not high rating programs) draw larger audiences than typical news magazines, and it appears to be the most popular public new medium.

On the other hand, television fails to provide the interpretive or editorial framework necessary for the public to adequately understand most international events. The relatively infrequent documentaries on international topics usually draw less than half of the audience drawn by a typical light entertainment show in the same time slot. In the documentaries, only a few of the points made can be absorbed by the vast majority of viewers and these points have to be repeated and kept simple if they are to have any impact. The typical documentary will probably be missed or ignored by the majority of those who are most informed about the international issue in question. This elite in fact looks down its nose on TV generally.

If a broadly stated objective is "to increase public understanding of international events," it may be necessary to segment the total "public" into sub-publics and to direct different levels of programming to each. Regarding topics, formats, and treatments likely to attract and retain a mass audience and assuming that one of the objectives is to increase the size of audiences for foreign affairs programs, it is obvious that this cannot be done without supplementing the present audience of well-informed people with other persons who have previously rejected the opportunity to view such programs. This latter group also has tended to reject other kinds of public information programming, but several programs have managed to attract large numbers of these people. The CBS audience-participation programs on driving and health will serve as examples. Three characteristics of these programs stand out: they involve viewers actively rather than passively, they were seen as offering information which was personally relevant, and this information was seen as of practical use.

Perhaps a cynical strategy (at least in the eyes of those who hold to a romantic view of our democratic society) would be to aim foreign affairs programs mainly at elites and to essentially expect only minimal response from others. The former are already most cosmopolitan in orientation, most interested in international affairs, and most likely to act in response to a program (e.g., writing to a congressman). Such an approach implicitly assumes that it would be naïve for television to attempt to bring the vast majority near the levels of orientation of the better-educated. Indications are that foreign-policy decision makers are tuned in disproportionate numbers to programs such as the *Today* and *Tonight* programs, network documentaries and "intellectual ghetto" discussions on topics of interest, and the efforts of educational television. While it is not realistic to expect half or even a quarter of these influentials to view a particular foreign affairs program, they will soon hear about it through word-of-mouth, if the program has something unique or interesting to contribute. It might further help this process in the future if newspapers and magazines were to more actively supplement TV foreign affairs programs with constructive criticism and reviews after broadcasts.

There are several shortcomings and even dangers in forsaking the mass audience, however. Not the least of these is that there already seems to be a substantial, if not increasing, feeling of resentment toward "eggheads" and "professors" by the less-educated. A monopoly of programs beamed at the better-educated audiences could serve to create even greater apathy or distrust of government foreign policy among those who can't follow what's happening. It is obvious that somehow these "unreadables" must be reached.

The urban poor—both black and white—comprise one large segment of the presumed "unreachables." The economic attractiveness of an audience will largely determine how well it is served by the media. Gunnar Myrdahl, the Swedish social scientist who has been a devoted analyst of the American scene, insists that the basic rift in society is not black-white but rich-poor. He uses the term "underclass" to describe those on the lowest rung. In the following article, a professor in the School of Business and Public Administration at the University of Missouri assesses the job the media are doing in reaching this underclass.

COMMUNICATING WITH
THE URBAN POOR *

Carl E. Block

The compassion of the American public for those in poverty has been building to the point where many individuals and groups are sufficiently moved to want to take action to help reduce the suffering that is evident to all. This public consciousness has been particularly aroused by the efforts of individuals like David Caplovitz and Daniel Moynihan through their skill in interpreting the needs of the poor for us. Most of this attention has been directed toward such critical subjects as unemployment, malnutrition, crime, inadequate housing, discrimination and the like. These efforts certainly have been enlightening; however, little attention has been given to a subject which is quite fundamental in dealing effectively with all of these problem areas. It is the issue of communication.

This research project has provided a means of exploring several aspects of communicating with the poor. Particular attention has been given to the use of the mass media, although other channels of communication also have been considered.

One aspect concerned the economic behavior of these people. This phase included the determination of the media exposure patterns generally, an analysis of their search for product information preceding the purchase of selected consumer goods as well as a study of their food buying habits. As a result, 350 interviews taking approximately 40 minutes each were conducted in the inner-city of St. Louis in August 1968. The average annual household income among those surveyed was $2,382 or approximately $608 per household member.

Human communication is a topic that must be studied in some specific context. That is, one has to study the transmission and reception of information via various channels regarding some definite topic or set of topics. The context used for analyzing the subject of

* Reprinted and condensed from *Journalism Quarterly* 47:1, Spring 1970, with permission of the author and journal. © Copyright by *Journalism Quarterly* 1970.

"communicating with the urban poor" is a market environment with attention drawn specifically to the availability and use of consumption facilitating information.

This context was selected because most of the facets of poverty have been discussed in terms of economic deprivement. Actually, modern technology has brought unparalleled abundance to the market place which provides new want-satisfying opportunities to all consumers. This same technology, however, has made the consumer's choices more difficult. Faced with almost infinite product variation, considerable price differentiation, the added complexities of trading stamps, the subtleties of cents-off deals, the average shopper hardly can be expected to choose wisely, much less the ghetto resident. The consumer's job is further complicated by the fact that prices tend not to be uniform in different stores even of the same chain, and many vary daily.

Given this orientation, one might ask a very basic question: to what extent is the social and economic deprivation of ghetto residents reflected in their contact with the consumer market through the mass media? That is, are these people as deprived of information concerning the selection of goods and services as they are of the goods and services themselves?

The results of this study indicate that the mass media do reach the poor; however, this does not mean that they have as much access to various types of information as do most people nor does it imply that the messages they receive through the traditional channels of communication are in the most usable form for them. What does seem evident is that to achieve optimum effectiveness in communicating with these people through the mass media, the advertiser must understand their media exposure patterns and their information usage patterns.

Ownership of radio and television sets is at a high level even among very low income households. This in part may be due to compensatory consumption: the overindulgence in selected consumer goods as an attempt to compensate for the more general deprivation they experience. Nevertheless, the 84.1% rate of radio ownership and the 83.5% television ownership level found here are still approximately 10% below the national average.

Slightly more than 70% of those interviewed claimed that they were regular television viewers while only 58.3% showed similar regularity in their radio listening habits. The 246 interviewees who claimed to be regular television viewers spent an average of 3.7 hours each day watching television. The average time spent listening to the radio was not determined in St. Louis; however, another study found that the residents of a Negro ghetto in Pittsburgh spent 5.5 hours daily listening to the radio.

Specific time exposure patterns of the two media also varied. As would be expected, morning radio listening (particularly before 9 A.M.) is much more popular than morning television viewing. Radio listening then drops off from its morning high to a lower early afternoon level while television viewing picks up at this time. Attention given to both radio and television then falls off somewhat in the late afternoon, but both broadcast media attract large audiences among these low income persons during the evening hours. Even with these variations, the total reach of the broadcast media is extensive and exceeds that of the print media in this ghetto area.

Program interest patterns showed considerable variation between the two broadcast media. As was anticipated, radio drew most attention as a source of music and secondly as a means of keeping informed on news, weather and sports. Only incidental interest was expressed in other radio programming. Interest in television programming was concentrated in four areas. The greatest interest was in soap operas with 24% of the 246 regular television viewers mentioning that they watch this type of program often. News, weather and sports followed closely behind as did interest in adventure programs (excluding westerns) and comedy programs. Despite the fact that the total reach of the print media in this low income area is less than that of radio and television, its reach is still substantial. Nearly ⅔ of these St. Louis residents read or at least look at a newspaper almost every day with about 40% claiming to read at least one magazine every week.

One discouraging discovery made with respect to this area of concern is that nearly 40% of those interviewed said that they either did not read at all (7.2%) or read less than one hour per week (31.8%). In effect this means that these people are almost completely cut off from a wealth of information that could be very valuable to them personally. In addition, only about 20% of those contacted read eight hours or more per week (i.e., more than an hour per day average).

Based on the results of this study, television and newspapers are the two most effective modes of communication for reaching the urban poor. Both of these forms of mass media have high rates of exposure and involvement among those interviewed. It will be recalled that over 70% of the respondents claimed that they were regular television viewers and approximately two-thirds of the interviewees read or at least look at a newspaper almost every day.

Newspapers and television were also listed as the two most useful sources in helping these individuals choose a product, that is, help them to get the most for their money. And, although personal contact may appear to be a very desirable means of communicating with these economically deprived people, they themselves do not place as high a value on this type of exchange as one might expect. In fact, when given a hypothetical situation regarding the purchase of a television set, over 60% said that they personally would not ask anyone for advice before buying such an item. These people consider newspapers the best single source of product information with television the next best source. Advice from friends followed television as a source of product information while radio was ranked fourth, store window signs fifth, advice from sales clerks sixth, magazines seventh. Advice from social workers was considered the least desirable source of such information.

Even though both groups placed newspapers and television at the top of their respective lists of helpful sources, 40.7% of the white interviewees indicated that newspapers would be the most useful source of product information and 16.9% mentioned television; only 25.5% of the Negroes listed newspapers as their choice and 24.1% said television would be the best source. Advice from friends ranked third among the Negro respondents as the most useful source, while this source was ranked sixth by the white group. Nearly 24% of the Negroes mentioned personal sources in general as the most useful in providing product information, while only about 15% of the white respondents mentioned such sources. Of these personal sources, the white people favored advice from social workers almost exclusively, while the Negroes considered advice from friends much more important than advice from either social workers or sales clerks.

It seems reasonable to suggest that these results might reflect a certain element of anti-establishment bias on the part of the Negroes. At least as one examines selected aspects of this latter response pattern, it appears possible. The sources mentioned most frequently by Negroes following their listing of newspapers and television are advice from friends, radio, store window signs and magazines, all of which may be separated to some extent from the white establishment. That is, these sources may have a rather personal orientation for them. These black residents often listen to Negro oriented radio stations, shop at stores in their immediate neighborhood (some of which are Negro operated) and read *Ebony* magazine. According to the National Advisory Commission on Civil Disorders, this reflects a distrust and dislike by the black person toward the white-oriented media resulting from false portrayal of what goes on in the ghetto.

The evidence obtained in this study shows that those who watch little or no television are less likely to read newspapers than are the moderate to heavy television viewers. . . . Again, those who watch little or no television are less likely to read magazines than those who have greater exposure to television.

No such relationship was found between radio listening habits and either magazine or newspaper readership. And, no significant relationship was discovered between radio listening and television viewing behavior either.

As was anticipated, formal education and reading habits are definitely related. For instance, of those who completed high school, 47.4% read at least three hours each week, but less than eight hours. Of those interviewed who completed only seven or eight years of formal education, the reading level was generally lower. In this latter group, only 33.3% read at least three hours each week, but less than eight hours. Among the less educated group 43.3% read less than one hour per week while only 15.8% of the high school graduates did so little reading.

The attention given to general interest magazines exceeds that given to news magazines by at least three to one among those respondents having less than a high school education. This changes significantly as formal education increases. Of those who completed high school or who have more than 12 years of formal education, news magazines gain considerably in popularity.

Whatever the interrelationship generally between level of formal education, time spent reading and grocery store patronage, it appears to be quite clear in this case that those who have the greatest exposure to the printed word are the more price conscious.

Of these low income respondents, the men generally spend more time reading than do women. More specifically, 44.6% of the men surveyed claimed to read at least three hours each week, while only 33.3% of the women had this degree of involvement in reading. In addition, approximately 35% of the women read less than one hour per week, whereas about 25% of the men showed such a limited amount of reading.

Variation in media use patterns was related to racial differences among the respondents in four instances. Two of these occurrences deal with the respondents' association with certain specific communication vehicles, e.g., certain magazines. The other two concern respondent attitudes toward various forms of the mass media in general. The findings presented generally confirm Leo Bogart's conclusion regarding the importance of racially related differences in explaining consumer media experiences. Based on the results of a Bureau of

Advertising study, Bogart concluded that variation in mass media exposure is ordinarily not related to race. Additional evidence presented in the Bureau of Advertising report as well as the findings of this study strongly suggest that other variables, particularly education, are more helpful in explaining the observable differences in the media experiences of these ghetto residents.

Specifically, from the St. Louis study it seems reasonable to conclude that low income black people are attracted to Negro-oriented media but not to the exclusion of other forms of mass media. Both Negro magazines and Negro radio have drawn the attention of significant numbers of the poor black people of St. Louis.

In regard to attitudes, the black respondents in this study were much more favorably inclined toward broadcast advertising than the white subjects. Respondents were asked, "What do you think of most radio and television commercials—would you say in general they are entertaining, informative or annoying?" Approximately 27% of the white people answered entertaining or informative, while nearly 58% of the Negroes responded with one or the other of these positive connotations.

Yet, as mentioned earlier, the Negroes generally tend to favor personal sources of product information more than the whites. Even though this greater emphasis on personal sources of information arose in a consumer product context, isn't it possible that this relationship could prevail in additional contexts? For instance, Negro residents of this ghetto area may not be sufficiently affected by job want ads, as an impersonal source, to encourage them to inquire about employment opportunities. In fact, it may take some form of personal contact not currently available or characteristic of the "traditional establishment."

The results of this study show that the mass media do reach the urban poor. This should provide sufficient evidence to encourage greater interest in the use of the mass media as a means of channeling much needed information to the poor on a number of subjects which directly affect their well-being.

An Indianapolis study found that blacks and whites watched about equal amounts of television but that blacks read less of the morning newspaper. About as many blacks as whites read something on the front page, but four times as many whites read all the page-one stories; blacks read markedly fewer opinion-oriented, sports, and society articles. Traditionally, blacks have looked to their own papers to provide such information. They have to, since many white papers, especially weeklies, still carry little about their black communities. For example, a 1968 survey by *American Press* magazine found that one-fourth of its editor-readers never ran photos of blacks, almost one-third never covered black social events, nearly one-third did not carry black engagements, and only about half ran black obituaries.

Social news still is the backbone of the black press, editors of black papers told Henry LaBrie III, a University of Iowa communications researcher, during extensive interviews in the summer of 1971. They rated editorial pages a distant second in importance.

The failure of white dailies to report the daily activities of blacks drew sharper criticism from the National Advisory Commission on Civil Disorders (the Kerner Commission) than did their actual coverage of the 1967 racial disorders. The commission's report included this admonition:

> Most newspaper articles and most television programming ignore the fact that an appreciable part of their audience is black. The world that television and newspapers offer to their black audience is almost totally white, in both appearance and attitude. . . . Far too often, the press acts and talks about Negroes as if Negroes do not read the newspapers or watch television, give birth, marry, die, and go to PTA meetings. Some newspapers and stations are beginning to make efforts to fill this void, but they have still a long way to go.

At least three other types of minorities are served poorly by the mass media, and two of the three have developed an alternate press. The first is alienated youth; the failure of the media to serve their needs led to the blossoming of the underground press. The second is people who cannot read English or who feel more comfortable reading another language. Although the foreign-language press is a shadow of its former self (its heyday was the early twentieth century with its waves of new immigrants), there still are 400 foreign-language papers, circulating 2 million copies a week in this country, to say nothing of the thousands of hours of radio broadcasts on local stations in languages other than English.

The third is not so well defined; it is the educated elite. If it has its own press, it consists of high-brow magazines, learned journals, some FM radio stations, and a few television specials. The 1970's even saw the birth of a publication called *Intellectual Digest,* which seems almost on the face of it a contradiction in terms—somewhat akin to a book entitled *Philosophy Made Simple.* Too many intellectuals assume there is some sort of conspiracy by media owners to avoid a vast reservoir of original talent. Cursed as they are by an unquenchable demand for more and more material, the mass media will always be short of the original and fresh; besides, the media already are devoting more time and space to intellectuals and their interests than their numbers justify. Certainly anyone entering college is already atypical (or to quote a certain vice-president, "effete intellectual snobs") and should remember that the mass media are just that—mass.

The ultimate solution to serving minority audiences, of whatever kind, may lie in technology. Certainly technology is moving us toward consumer control of the media. In the past, the user has largely had to take or leave what the media served up, but with the wiring of cities for cable communication and the prospects of low-cost visual cassettes which he can play in his living room, the way is opened for selection of news and entertainment when and where the viewer wants it.

Cartridge television, after proving its feasibility as a sales and training device, next proved profitable in hotels, where guests were willing to pay extra to see a feature film in their rooms. In 1972, viewers went on sale in retail stores, and a subsidiary of Columbia Pictures began setting up distributors around the country to rent cassette films, including *The Bridge on the River Kwai, High Noon,* and *I Am Curious (Yellow).* Rentals were $3 to $6, and each tape has a locked rewind system to prevent it from being played more than once.

Providing yet another way to see old movies may be of limited social value, but those same viewers can see cassettes prepared by any kind of interest group. If nothing else, cassettes go one step further in shifting control over programing from the senders to the receivers.

Although the growth in quantity and diversity of information has been so great that it has outstripped growth in population, Gross National Product, energy consumption, and other indicators, there has been little increase in man's capability to process more information. The individual simply has to become more selective, even in choosing the channels of such information. An intelligent, middle-aged businessman may realize that he might acquire some useful information if he listened to a teeny-bopper radio station on his way to work, but he decides the odds are better if he listens to a station which programs for adults. Communications research indicates that most of us seek information corresponding with our preexisting points of view, and when we encounter information which does not, we tend to misinterpret or distort it. On the other hand, studies of reading habits indicate that involved political activists end up exposing themselves to opposition arguments, not because they set out to read the other side, but simply because they read more and get this exposure in the process.

The point is that with all the competition for attention, a medium (including an individual program or edition) has to deliver something which the consumer considers of value. He may know why he considers it valuable ("Will it rain on my fishing trip tomorrow?" "Wait till I drop that into the lunch room conversation tomorrow!") and he may not ("I never thought of that before" "That's pretty funny").

Women told researchers in the 1940's that they received help with their own everyday problems from listening to radio soap operas, and more recently adults have told survey-takers that they learn much about medical and police practices from their favorite TV series. Perhaps they were giving socially acceptable excuses for the time they spent with radio and television, but clearly TV teaches some things, whether it sets out to do so, as in the documented success of *Sesame Street,* or incidentally. To give two examples of the latter, studies have found that people know much more about weather patterns and pressure systems than they used to, and the explanation seems to be the TV weathermen. Children also are better informed about the socioeconomic status of occupations portrayed on TV than about similar occupations not seen regularly on the tube.

The fact that our news media deliver information does not mean that many people understand or remember what they have been told. Never underestimate an individual's ability to ignore or misconstrue information. In 1966, only 30 percent of the population could identify the Vietcong as South Vietnamese Communists. In 1968, one-third of a national sample had heard of the Kerner Commission report, and a year later less than one-third could identify Ralph Nader or Martha Mitchell.

The media provide their audiences not only with entertainment and facts (the temperature, the vote in Congress, the baseball score), but they also provide them with opinions in the form of editorials, columns, and reviews.

Renata Adler, when she was a critic for the New York *Times,* said that reviewing a movie for a potential ticket-buyer was much like "reviewing" a new candy bar for someone standing in front of a counter with a dime clutched in his palm. It did not help him much to tell him whether you liked it or not; the important thing was to describe the ingredients. Although most of us rely on the media for such details, some persons are willing to pay dearly for tailor-made opinion. There are those who supplement their incomes by attending plays (price: $25 plus the ticket) for other people and then telling them enough so that they can discuss the plays at cocktail parties.

The media, in turn, often rely on syndicates which provide columns, features, and even editorials. Syndicated material is relatively cheap, so cheap in fact, that the average daily can purchase 15 syndicated columns for half what it would cost them to employ one good local columnist. Some newspapers devote up to one-third of their news space to such stuff.

Few readers can distinguish between local and syndicated material, just as few viewers differentiate the early-evening network news show from the locally produced late-evening version.

Media owners are understandably chary about taking positions on controversial issues. Those who agree usually do so quietly, and those who disagree do so angrily. Opinion content was the historical *raison d'être* for newspapers, but today only about half the weeklies regularly publish editorials and even one-fourth of the dailies do not endorse a presidential candidate. Many of the editorials on general topics are purchased ready-written from syndicates in the same way that many ministers purchase their sermons. Station owners are carrying more editorials, but seldom are these very meaty. Opinion programs are not profitable; they create enemies, and they may lead to trouble with the FCC about fairness.

Both the print and broadcast media always have sought to serve their audiences. The women's magazines of the 1890's led the fight for women's rights and for such legislation as the Pure Food and Drug Act, and the muckrakers of the next decade exposed working and sanitary conditions in all sorts of industries. More recent examples include radio call-in shows, the "Action Line"-type columns and programs which seek to play ombudsman for those who write in, and much more reporting of consumer affairs.

Newspaper editors have been trying hard to involve readers. As Don Carter told the Associated Press Managing Editors Association in his 1971 presidential address:

> We have coaxed [the reader] to write more letters, provide us guest columns, ask us more questions through "Action Line" and similar features, encouraged him to call us by telephone and have called him, in turn, to seek out his views. We have surveyed his preferences through numerous readership studies and distributed the information among ourselves so that we can tailor our products to meet his changing wishes.
>
> We want our reader to feel that the newspaper is not just to be accepted, but to be argued with, responded to, and made to feel that it is a part of his family—a part he cannot do without.

Most newspaper readers say they are fairly satisfied; but, one must keep in mind the Chinese peasant and rice analogy. In 1965, a sample of all regular readers of daily papers published in a Midwestern state were asked this question: "Taking the whole paper into account, how do you rate the [name of newspaper]: as an excellent paper? good? fair? poor?" Twenty-three per cent said excellent, 55 per cent said good, 19 per cent said fair, two per cent said poor, and 1 per cent had no opinion. Other questions in the same survey determined that the general esteem in which a specific newspaper was held by its readers was highly related to its perceived fairnss and to its accuracy.

The black audience has felt particularly frustrated about its treatment on the airwaves, and this discontent has been channeled into two related efforts:

1. Increasing black ownership and control of broadcast facilities. Blacks own fewer than 20 radio and no TV stations, and since few are for sale, there is not likely to be any dramatic increase in ownership of conventional broadcasting stations; however, many black groups are determined to bid for the hundreds of cable television franchises with their thousands of channels which will be assigned in the next few years. As a minimum, racial groups want to make

sure there is provision for a channel or two in each system which is set aside for anyone who feels he has a message to deliver. What makes these black groups think they will get any better shake in the distribution of these new channels than they did of the old? The first reason is that they have capital now which they did not have in the 1920's and 1930's. The second was expressed by one of the black activists: "With cable, they have to run the line through *our* part of town. We can control a line better than we can an air-wave." Another technological development which may help minorities in distributing programs to interested members of the audience is the television cassette.

2. Forcing present broadcasters to provide more minority programing and jobs. The principal ground upon which an individual or group may challenge the renewal of a station's license is that it has failed during the preceding three years to serve the needs and interests of its audience. Such groups as the Office of Communication of the United Church of Christ and the Citizens Communication Center have presented well-documented challenges to more than 50 stations serving areas which include substantial numbers of minority citizens, charging either that they have not been served or that the coverage was unfair. Not many licenses have been lifted but citizen groups have used the challenges as levers in bargaining with station owners, several of whom have met demands for black programs and for hiring more black employees.

One of the first stations to be challenged by citizens' groups was WLBT in Jackson, Mississippi. When, after four years of debate and litigation, the FCC finally renewed the TV station's license, two members of the commission outlined in their dissent the treatment of blacks on the station:

HOW ONE TV STATION SERVED ITS BLACK AUDIENCE *

Nicholas Johnson and *Kenneth Cox*

The second major charge against WLBT was its failure to serve the Negro community in its coverage area. No policy of the Communications Act is more fundamental than the Commission's require-

* Reprinted and condensed from 14 FCC2d 431 (1968).

ment that broadcast stations serve the particular needs and interests of the communities to which they are licensed. The FCC has refined and reaffirmed this command over and over again through the years, most recently in its "1960 Report and Statement of Policy" which vigorously reasserted and elaborated the obligation of licensees:

> . . . to take the necessary steps to inform themselves of the real needs and interests of the areas they serve, and to provide programing which in fact constitutes a diligent effort, in good faith, to provide for those needs and interests.

We have already seen how WLBT ignored the needs and interests of Negroes as far as controversial political issues were concerned. Not unexpectedly, its service to, and presentation of, Negroes on its other programing also reflected the assumption that its service was to be directed only to those people in its coverage area who happened to be white. This assumption is rather difficult to square with the requirements of the "1960 Policy Statement" in view of the fact that 47 percent of the people living within the station's coverage area are black.

The majority does not dispute the petitioners' description of WLBT's presentation of programs aimed at the Jackson Negro community. It concedes that "Negro participation per se [whatever "per se" means in this context] in WLBT's locally originated programing was limited." It was, in fact, limited to almost zero. "The record indicates," the majority recites, "that during [the 1961–64 renewal period] there were no Negro appearances on the programs 'Teen Tempos,' 'Romper Room,' and 'Youth Speaks,' and that religious programing of special interest to the Negro community was limited to one program, 'Voice of Good Will.' " (The latter was a 15-minute religious program broadcast at 6:45 a.m.)

The majority agrees with petitioners on the facts regarding Negro participation in WLBT programing during the renewal period. Nevertheless, it rejects their contention that WLBT failed to provide adequate service to Jackson Negroes and opportunity for their use of its facilities. Lack of Negro participation in programing, the majority explains, is not by itself "determinative." "Other factors must enter into our consideration of the matter." Precisely what these other factors might be, however, is not specified in the majority's opinion.

After attacking the monitoring study, the majority then says that the church failed to prove its contention that WLBT habitually flashed a phony "Sorry, Cable Trouble" sign on the screen whenever unwanted, prointegration items were shown on network television programs. In the first place, this was not alleged by petitioners in their original pleading. It was, in part, the basis for the misrepresentation issue which this Commission put into the case as the result of its investigation into the operation of the station. On this issue the burden of proof—or, more properly, the burden of going forward with the evidence—was put upon the Broadcast Bureau. The majority asserts that intervenors' allegation—that a 1955 appearance by then-NAACP General Counsel (and now Supreme Court justice) Thurgood Marshall on Arlene Francis' "Home" show was cut by WLBT and a "Sorry, Cable Trouble" sign substituted—was "unfounded." The majority's assertion is not true. The allegation was not disproven. It would not even be accurate to say that it was denied.

A newspaper reported that Fred Beard, the White Citizens' Council member who was station manager of WLBT from 1953 to 1965, had publicly bragged of using the cable trouble ploy to keep the distinguished Negro lawyer off the Jackson station. Mr. Beard's only response was that the paper "misquoted" him. He did not say the newspaper report was fundamentally wrong. He did not specify any way in which the report misquoted him. Counsel for the church did not press the matter, unfortunately, so there is no way of knowing precisely what was erroneous about the report—assuming that Beard was telling the truth when he said he was misquoted. (Given his well-documented penchant for making pious misrepresentations to the Commission, a fact which will be dealt with later in this opinion, there is ample reason to treat with at least a grain of salt WLBT Manager Beard's guarded claim that he was "misquoted" in this case.) But it certainly cannot be said that the allegation was disproven.

In fact, even the version offered by Beard is damaging enough in itself. For Beard admits that he did cut that portion of the "Home" show which carried Miss Francis' interview with Mr. Marshall (and not, as the Examiner claimed in his initial decision, the entire show). Beard claims that he substituted a rerun movie, rather than a "Sorry, Cable Trouble" notice. No one, however, denies that Beard was deliberately preventing Negroes from appearing on his station. And he thus admits he took this step in order to prevent the people of Jackson from seeing a Negro—this man who had risen to the position of distinction and respect even then held by Mr. Thurgood Marshall. The majority seems to suggest that there have been some changes made on channel 3 in Jackson. Whereas there was once only one Negro religious program there are now three. Whereas Negroes formerly participated in none of the station's regularly scheduled local origination shows, they now participate—at least the record shows one such occasion—in one of those programs, "Teen Tempo." ("Romper Room" has been discontinued, thus avoiding the possibility of integrating small Negro children into this show.) Courtesy titles are now in vogue when WLBT announcers refer to Negroes, and WLBT announcers no longer indulge their preference for the terms "nigger" and "negra."

One may or may not be impressed by this new spirit of brotherhood in Jackson. But it has only occurred since WLBT's Washington counsel advised its principal owners, the Murchison brothers of Texas, that their license to operate this several million-dollar television station was in serious jeopardy. It is indefensible for the Commission to consider such evidence of decisive significance.

This case has everything. A racist television station in Mississippi. An offended citizenry that actually takes the expensive and frustrating course of involving itself in the license renewal process. A church as a party. Negroes protesting the programing abuse received by that nearly 50 percent of the people in the station's viewing area who are black. A landmark, first-impression decision by the U.S. court of appeals awarding "standing" to such parties. The station's misrepresentation to the Commission over the years. The Commission's contortions to keep the public out entirely, then to place upon them an impossible burden of proof, then to reverse long-held precedents and ignore the clear suggestions of the court as to the standards to be applied. This disappointing saga has now ended with a finding by this Commission that the station has been serving "the public interest" and is entitled to a regular three-year license renewal. We are disturbed at the majority's willingness to go to such great length to protect a licensee with a very bad record. It has sanctioned obstruction and procedural harassment which can only discourage and defeat citizen intruders so bold as to venture to exercise rights guaranteed them by law. Indeed, it would appear that the only way in which members of the public can prevent renewal of an unworthy station's license is to steal the document from the wall of the station's studio in the dead of night.

Not everyone considers citizen-group challenges desirable. Certainly most broadcasters do not, but then neither does Clay T. Whitehead, director of President Nixon's Office of Telecommunications Policy. He told broadcast executives in 1971 that he (and presumably he was speaking for the Administration) favored longer periods for TV licenses, which would be renewed almost *pro forma* for any station making a "good faith effort" to serve its community. He would not make program categories, percentages, or formats considerations in renewals. He said such changes would "add stability to your industry and avoid the bitter adversary struggle between you and your community groups." Leaders of such groups agreed that the changes would end the struggle all right—by ruling out valid protests before they could be filed.

For now, at least, audiences can exert direct pressure on broadcasters through the licensing process, which is more than they can do about the other media. Buying or not buying a book or a movie ticket is a fairly direct "vote," but writing a letter, answering a survey, or supporting an advertiser offer but very indirect controls over the other commercial media.

SECTION TWO
THE BUSINESS
OF BUSINESS

In one respect, a newspaper, magazine, broadcast station, movie production company, or a book publishing house is exactly like a foundry or a hot dog stand: if it does not show a profit, it goes under.

The linkage of the mass media with profit-oriented private enterprise is almost total, and is greater in the United States than anywhere else in the world. In many nations, political parties, trade unions, and ideological groups subsidize the print media, but such support is almost unknown here. Both U.S. wire services are entirely supported by private money. Except for Reuters in Great Britain, almost all other wire services of the world are either government-owned or subsidized. Worldwide, broadcasting is almost always a government monopoly, although some nations have both public and private networks. The United States has 500 noncommercial radio and more than 150 noncommercial television stations, but they operate on shoestrings and have depressingly small audiences.

Many nations offer tax and other advantages to their filmmakers, something the United States has not done. Even university presses are expected to pay their own way. But movies and books are different from the other media in at least two important economic ways:

1. They do *not* sell their services to advertisers, who in effect "rent" the audience for their commercial messages.

2. They are nonsequential. They cannot count on subscribers who agree to purchase the product in advance. Each book or movie title must be sold on its own merits.

It may be instructive to look at the critical factor of editorial independence, since worrying about where every dollar is coming from is one of the restraints that can do a good man in. The publication or station with its bills paid may have the greatest independence of all. No newspaper has been firmer in resisting any hint of advertiser pressure than the immensely profitable *Wall Street Journal,* by any definition one of the great newspapers of the world. Some corporations, such as American Can, have financed elegant corporate magazines, and others, such as Xerox, have sponsored quality television shows with no thought of selling more goods. For the author who is convinced that none of the commercial book publishers recognizes his genius, there has always been a thriving vanity press, in which he can pay to have his words printed. Occasionally a magazine, newspaper, or network will produce something for the sheer artistic hell of it. For example, CBS News has from time to time given its staffers great freedom in developing specials and documentaries, and the *Christian Science Monitor* gave a reporter a year and a half to develop a single series of stories. In the early 1950's, *Life* magazine was an extraordinarily prosperous showcase for photojournalism. Only a a small part of its space was devoted to text pieces, some of which were curiously out of key with the rest of the magazine. Islands of scholarly analyses of the Peloponnesian Wars were completely surrounded by picture spreads of the Korean War or sex kittens in black-lace lingerie. An authentic intellectual, Emmet John Hughes, was text editor, and when a professorial interviewer asked him for an estimate of the readership of *Life's* articles, Hughes replied cheerily "less than five per cent. *Life* carries the articles *I* like." In effect, the magazine was rich enough to give one editor, at least, complete freedom of expression.

Generally, however, the piper does indeed call the tune. The French government since the days of Charles de Gaulle has manipulated the activities of ORTF, the state-financed monopoly network, to the incumbent party's political and electoral advantage. Government-financed media generally need not be that heavy-handed, however, since the fear of offending the powers is endemic, and it produces blanket caution which may as effectively strangle freedom as direct intervention. The British Broadcasting Corporation was notorious for its skittish avoidance of controversy or possible bad taste as long as it was a monopoly; the best thing about commercial television in Great Britain may be what it has done for the BBC. The state-operated Italian television system, RAI, goes even further than the BBC ever did to avoid criticism. All reporting of political crises (which are almost continual, of course) has to be approved, in effect, by a special committee made up of representatives of the major parties. Furthermore, the television format is rigidly set: spokesmen for each of the parties appear serially in front of the same microphone and read statements—but their voices are not heard. Their lips move vigorously but silently while an announcer reads, voice over, an approved summary. One of Italy's most distinguished journalists has compared Italian politicians on television to fish in an aquarium. Their mouths move, but they don't talk.

In contrast to such nonsense, public television in the United States is bold and independent indeed, but it still has a long way to go. Although one of the primary reasons for its existence is the providing of an alternative to commercial television, the noncommercial variety is heavily dependent upon handouts from those who do make money from broadcasting. The networks have contributed substantial sums to such stations as Channel 13 in New York, and other noncommercial stations use both studios and electronic equipment donated by the commercial world (a marvelously all-purpose act which provides help to the needy and both a righteous feeling and a useful tax write-off for the donor). To media which cannot earn their own way, even grateful good manners can be a powerful restraint.

Good manners is not likely to be a factor in the relationship between the medium and the advertiser who buys time or space. That relationship is businesslike, sometimes to the point of being grim. It also is the form of media support which has had the worst press (in exposés ranging from novels through movies to journalism textbooks) and which probably would be considered most threatening to media integrity. Yet there are good reasons for considering advertising, all told, the best of all forms of media support.

Before analyzing why, it might be well to look at the rough dimensions of advertising's involvement in U.S. media. Despite the spectacular rise of television, print still gets the dominant share of advertising figures, with newspapers in the lead. In rounded-out figures, 1970 looked like this:

Total expenditures by advertisers were around $18 billion.

Newspapers received around $5 billion, about 30 per cent of the total.

Television received around $3 billion, about 20 per cent.

Magazines received about $1.5 billion, about 8 per cent.

Radio received about $1 billion, about 7 per cent.

Direct mail, billboards, the business press, and other forms totaled about $7 billion.

An unlimited potential for control would seem to be represented by those figures, particularly when one remembers that they refer to all the support for broadcasting and around 70 per cent, on the average, of the magazine and newspaper business. But there are several reasons why they also represent a certain kind of freedom.

In the first place, there are few cases any longer in which an advertiser tries directly to kill or distort editorial content. If he succeeds in muscling content, he not only loses his dignity but also will probably find himself a case history in a liberal magazine or a journalism textbook. He is more likely to demonstrate his displeasure by angrily pulling his advertising out of the offending medium (as, in a famous case, General Motors canceled everything with the *Wall Street Journal* and Dow Jones), but if the advertising has been intelligently placed originally, he soon realizes that he needs the medium more than it needs him, and he comes back after his temper cools. There are more advertisers than media. A metropolitan newspaper probably has only one advertiser which could wound it mortally by pulling out and staying out—the leading department store. But as the experience of newspaper strikes has indicated, there is a life-and-death symbiosis here. Without the newspaper, the store suffers too.

Although it is difficult to prove, there seems to be a historical decline in advertisers' attempts to impose negative sanctions. They are much more likely to be successful at planting materials which improve their image or even tie in with their advertising. Food and real estate sections and, to some extent, business pages of newspapers are notorious for this, but even the most prestigious consumer magazines may carry advertiser plants.

Second, marketing is not yet an exact science. Advertisers, being human, sometimes buy time or space for irrational reasons—perhaps because they like to do it and to hell with anybody else. The Firestone company sponsored a televised version of the *Firestone Hour* despite miniscule ratings until the networks refused to carry it any longer. Why? Because TV watchers do not like to change the dial and its low ratings were dragging down adjacent programs. Advertisers are also human enough to advertise in a medium because "everybody is advertising there" or to associate with media they admire. There has been a long tradition, for example, of consumer magazines buying the back page of the first section of the New York *Times* to advertise themselves—not to sell copies, but to sell their own advertising space. On the face of it, this is somewhat irrational, since almost any potential advertiser and his agency are constantly targets for personal selling by experts who are among the highest-paid people in the business. Nicholas Samstag, who was for many years the promotion director of *Time*, once explained his magazine's regular full page in the *Times* by saying, "Well, the official reason we run it is that it may reach some potential customers our salesmen do not, but that's nonsense. The real reason is that if we don't, the brass calls up and says plaintively, 'Why is it *Newsweek* has ads in the *Times* and we don't?' "

There is a similar tradition in Detroit, where morning radio newscasts have been sponsored by companies such as Great Lakes Steel and Inco—companies which sell only to the motor companies and have no consumer products at all. It is remotely possible that they may swing a multimillion dollar deal because a General Motors executive is persuaded while shaving—but only remotely.

Irrationality can work both ways, of course. Major campaigns have been canceled because a board chairman's wife mentioned casually that she doesn't like a particular publication any more. Advertising is especially sensitive to the swings of the economy. The company whose sales are off, say 5 per cent, will often reduce its advertising budget by 15 per cent, even though what it needs is more advertising, not less.

Publications become "hot," (popular with advertisers and ad agencies) for no discernible reason—and then cool down, sometimes to the point of disaster. *Look* magazine went through a classic cycle, attaining a popularity with advertisers in the 1950's that not only made it the talk of Madison Avenue but even led to an article in *Harper's* trying to explain it. *Look's* own executives, when they stopped counting money long enough to talk about it, ascribed it to everything from "high editorial quality" to a new color-printing process. Neither editorial quality nor printing perceptibility changed, but within a few years *Look's* success was much more modest, and within 15 the magazine was dead. There is some explanation of the decline, as we shall see a little later, but both rise and fall were demonstrations of the relative freedom for the editorial operation provided by the money from a multiplicity of adverisers buying time or space for a multiplicity of reasons. Most advertising is placed by agencies which try to make sound judgments, based on research and in behalf of clients who do not try to second-guess them for idiosyncratic reasons. But there is enough slack to give an editor room and time to be something of his own man.

The third kind of financial support comes directly from the consumer, from the sale of the product to the audience. In mass communications, this means books, records, and theater motion pictures. The open market can give the man who succeeds in it a heady satisfaction, but it also can be brutal. In the long run, there probably is no more depressing process for most media professionals than finding a market and holding it.

The system works best when costs can be kept low and the margin of profit high enough to provide a sense of freedom of maneuver. For many years the book publishing business was a classic model. Both the labor and the materials of book manufacturing were small enough parts of the total cost that publishers could afford to do many things well. They paid writers very high rates. They established and built into national importance magazines which were primarily designed to publicize their own books: *Harper's,* the *Atlantic,* and the now-dead *Scribner's* all began this way, with the serialization of the house's publications as a staple of their content. When outside advertisers wanted to buy space in *Harper's,* the Harper brothers at first indignantly refused. In that era book publishers owned extensive printing plants and employed the most expert printers and lithographers; it was a comfortable business.

And it remained so for a long time. In the 1930's, bolstered by the success of the Modern Library and an occasional best seller, Bennett Cerf could afford the taste and courage to publish James Joyce's *Ulysses,* knowing it meant a long expensive court fight and modest sales. Alfred Knopf, a talented egocentric, published literally hundreds of writers he thought important with no hope of making money, particularly Europeans in translation, including every ponderous volume of a prolific but deservedly forgotten Norwegian named Sigrid Undset.

The economic vise is squeezing such good-hearted enterprise. The book publisher is in a cost bind which requires a substantially higher gross; he might get this by greatly increasing his prices, but his instincts and some experience convince him that trade books are a luxury, and that people will pay only so much; he therefore, like most businesses, moves toward the classic pattern of trying to make more money by taking a lower percentage profit on greatly increased sales. This inevitably drives him in the direction of taking fewer chances, and all but closes the possibility of publishing books he knows in advance to be losers. That category includes almost all first novels and books of poetry and short stories, even by name writers.

From 1966 to 1970, the sales of books grew by 50 per cent from about $2 billion to $3 billion, but during the same period, most publishers agreed they simply published too many titles (over 30,000 in 1970) for their own good. "Basically we sell more books and make less money," W. Bradford Wiley, chairman of John Wiley & Sons and president of the American Association of Publishers, explained.

The same period saw a heady round of mergers in the book business, and more and more observers doubted that a publisher could stay small and orient himself to quality alone. Ballyhoo became a more important part of the book business, and it produced such synthetic formula best-sellers as *Valley of the Dolls* and *The Exhibitionist.* One of the favorite tools was planting writers in the talk-show–gossip-column subculture. It was said that an appearance on *Tonight* was translated into thousands of sales around the country the next day.

An 80-year-old poet with a regional reputation recited some of his poems about Indians on the *Dick Cavett Show* and suddenly found himself a national celebrity. Orders for his books rolled in so fast that they exhausted the stocks of the university press which had published him, and a commercial publisher signed him—a rare tribute to any poet, since books of poetry are notorious money-losers. (The exceptions are "pop" poets such as Rod McKuen.) This octogenarian poet had been writing and reciting his poems for decades, but a few minutes on a late-night talk show made all the difference.

Ironically, it was the demand for appearances by the author of a best-selling sex novel that led to the exposure in 1969 of a funny publishing hoax. A *Newsday* staffer had 25 of his friends write separate chapters, each with an "unremitting emphasis on sex," about a suburban home-wrecker. He warned his contributors that any signs of literary merit would be edited out, and he was as good as his word. The book was published under the title *Naked Came the Stranger* by a reputable publisher. The pseudonymn was Penelope Ashe, identified on the book jacket as "a demure Long Island housewife." The book shot to the best-seller lists and movie companies bid for the rights. When the true editor revealed the hoax, it only increased the book's sales and drew more inquiries from moviemakers.

A sure sign of change in the book business came in 1972 when Bantam Books, a paperback publisher, signed Irving Wallace to a $2.5 million contract for his next three novels and one autobiographical book. Thus Bantam attained rights in advance to negotiate and share in book-club, serial, and foreign-language rights, rights which in the past almost always were owned by hardcover publishers.

On completing the deal, Wallace said, "What these figures say to me is there are enough people out there who read me. The publishers made sure of that. They had a big market investigation before they signed." Market survey or no, Bantam could read the sales figures from Wallace's earlier books: 70 million copies of 15 books.

High volume, low margin, and increasing attention to marketing considerations have emerged as dominant principles of direct selling in this society. They have made possible remarkable economic development, but they constitute a set of restraints when applied to mass media which often affect the tune more than any imposed even by a single piper.

We can sum up the most important characteristics of the financial support system for each of the media in Table 1.

One thing which the table does not convey, however, is a sense of change—and historically the most important fact about media economics is that the constant drive for better support has meant great change. The trends, much simplified, might be set out as listed on page 47.

TABLE 1.   COMPARISON OF SIX MASS MEDIA BY SUPPORT AND FOCUS

	Content Focus	Prime Function	Support	Kind Advtg	Share Total Advtg Dollars	Trend
Newspapers	Local & national	Inform	⅔ advtg ⅓ user	80% local 20% natl	30%	Steady %; more local advtg
Magazines	National	Inform or entertain	⅔ advtg ⅓ user	All natl	7% genl 4% trade	More specialization content
Television	National & local	Entertain	All advtg	70% natl 30% local	20%	Rapid increase in % advtg revenue
Radio	Local	Entertain	All advtg	30% natl 70% local	7%	Localization
Books	National	Inform & entertain	All user	—	—	Absorbed by conglomerates
Movies	National	Entertain	All user	—	—	Low budgets; aim at special audiences
					Remainder mail, outdoor, other media	

Newspapers. Head-to-head competition has declined almost to the vanishing point; only 45 cities had competitive dailies in 1972. The total number of dailies has remained stable at around 1750, although there has been a steady pattern of some folding and new ones beginning. The greatest number of casualties have been in the area of metropolitan dailies, while most new dailies have been suburban, some converted weeklies or shopper newspapers. There has been a growing tendency toward small chains—five to fifteen papers within a single geographic area.

Radio broadcasting. Network radio has disappeared except for news and special events. The number of elaborately staffed metropolitan stations seeking a broad general audience also is in decline; the trend is all for finding, and capitalizing on, specialized audiences. The range is remarkable, particularly in FM: all-talk stations, all-news stations, rock and roll, ethnic stations, particularly for black audiences, background music stations, "good music" stations, and others.

Television broadcasting. The primary phenomenon has been growth, growth in dollar income and percentage of total advertising expenditures, now showing some signs of stabilizing. The number of commercial stations is stable at around 600, since almost all channels which are financially viable are assigned. There has been a remarkable *lack* of change in audience seeking (i.e., programing) or corporate structure.

Big change probably is on the way, however, with the rise of cable television and a potential explosion of new channels on the dial. Present station owners are trying to acquire cable properties; the FCC is debating various aspects of problems of regulation, including copyright; foundations are concerned with the nature of cable franchises.

Book publishing. Many changes have occurred throughout the industry. The number of bookstores has shrunk, but paperbacks are distributed through a whole new system, with thousands of outlets served by wholesalers (generally magazine distributers) and selling on consignment. The rise of book clubs has also helped kill the retail bookstore. The "nonbook," designed by formula to be a sure thing and backed with heavy outlays for promotion has been developed, increasing emphasis upon picking winners every time. In corporate structure, the movement by publishers has been to contract printing and manufacture and the disposition of any physical property. Since 1965, most major book houses have become part of large conglomerates.

Magazines. The most important trend has been the rise of specialization and the decline of mass circulation, general-appeal consumer magazines. In 1952 there were six general-interest weeklies; 20 years later there was one survivor, *Life,* and it was in serious financial difficulty. The total number of magazines published rose during the period, however, and the total dollar gross for all magazines climbed steadily. The decline of general consumer magazines was not due to a decline in circulation—*Colliers, The Saturday Evening Post,* and *Look* were at the highest circulations in their history when their terminal illnesses appeared—but to an increase in costs, both in production and mailing, and the loss of advertising revenue as advertisers put their money elsewhere, particularly into television and specialized magazines. While *Look* died and *Life* teetered on the edge, *Sports Illustrated* and *TV Guide* prospered.

One overall trend since about 1965 has involved all the media. Many communication properties have merged into larger corporate groups. Most of these have grown up through the success and enterprise of a single company which has bought other, smaller companies in the same field, and so essentially have retained communications orientation. Thus the Los Angeles *Times* organization (known now as the *Times-Mirror* Corporation) owns, in addition to that spectacularly successful newspaper, an important book publisher (New American Library–World), a substantial forest-products operation, a distinguished map-making company (Denoyer-Geppert), and the country's best-known suburban daily, Long Island's *Newsday.* The New York *Times,* which until the last years of the 1960's owned a great newspaper and operations ancillary to it and one "good-music" broadcast station, by the middle of 1971 was part of a combine which included such improbable enterprises as *Golf Digest,* the Microfilming Corporation of America, the Ocala (Fla.) *Star-Banner, Family Circle* magazine, Quadrangle Books, and the Teaching Resources Corporation.

A kind of consensus pattern has emerged: almost everybody has a big-name newspaper or magazine, a string of little-known but highly profitable afternoon papers, some broadcasting stations, a book publishing house, and a company working on new technology in education, such as programed learning. Such a pattern provides hedges against overdependence upon a vulnerable major sector (for example, a metropolitan newspaper) and a preliminary base in the most promising fields for expansion (such as learning technology), yet at the same time keeps the enterprise within the general communications area and promotes high-level corporate homogeneity and economies of scale. Most do not wander far afield in their acquisitions, although CBS and NBC, which got into conglomerate building early, have curious branches, as Nicholas Johnson points out in the article which follows. There seems to be another symptom of CBS's movement to a more indiscriminate corporate character in the appointment of a new president in the fall of 1971. Charles Ireland, at the time of his designation, was a classic corporate manager who cheerily admitted that he knew nothing about broadcasting but was willing to learn and who further made it clear in an early interview that he felt his primary job was to make the network turn a better profit for the stockholders. Both admirers and detractors of Ireland's predecessor, Frank Stanton, the epitome of the aggressive, committed men who built the media, must have felt a sense of loss.

The problem with ownership of media by conglomerates is that the book publisher or newspaper is likely to be judged by the same standard of profitability that is applied to the oil refinery or girdle factory. If it doesn't make enough money some year, the stockholders of Shoes-Ships-&-Sealing Wax, Inc., may decide to get rid of it and invest the money in more oil rigs or girdle machines. ("You mean we have a man in Latin America who went two weeks without even writing for the paper?")

To at least one of the articulate and highly competent critics of media corporate structure in the United States today, worrying about the future is a superfluous fantasy. Nicholas Johnson, a Commissioner of the Federal Communications Commission and a proud gadfly of big media, sets out forceful arguments against the present patterns of ownership.

THE MEDIA BARONS AND
THE PUBLIC INTEREST *

Nicholas Johnson

Before I came to the Federal Communications Commission my concerns about the ownership of broadcasting and publishing in America were about like those of any other generally educated person.

Most television programming from the three networks struck me as bland at best. I had taken courses dealing with propaganda and "thought control," bemoaned (while being entertained by) *Time* magazine's "slanted" reporting, understood that Hearst had something to do with the Spanish-American War, and was impressed with President Eisenhower's concern about "the military-industrial complex." The changing ownership of the old-line book publishers and the disappearance of some of our major newspapers made me vaguely uneasy. I was philosophically wedded to the fundamental importance of "the marketplace of ideas" in a free society, and a year as law clerk to my idol, Supreme Court Justice Hugo L. Black, had done nothing to weaken that commitment.

But I didn't take much time to be reflective about the current significance of such matters. It all seemed beyond my ability to influence in any meaningful way. Then, in July, 1966, I became a member of the FCC. Here my interest in the marketplace of ideas could no longer remain a casual article of personal faith. The commitment was an implicit part of the oath I took on assuming the office of commissioner, and, I quickly learned, an everyday responsibility.

Threats to the free exchange of information and opinion in this country can come from various sources, many of them outside the power of the FCC to affect. Publishers and reporters are not alike in their ability, education, tolerance of diversity, and sense of responsibility. The hidden or overt pressures of advertisers have long been with us.

But one aspect of the problem is clearly within the purview of the FCC—the impact of *ownership* upon the content of the mass media. It is also a part of the responsibility of the Antitrust Division of the Justice Department. It has been the subject of recent congressional hearings. There are a number of significant trends in the ownership of the media worth examining—local and regional monopolies, growing concentration of control of the most profitable and powerful television stations in the major markets, broadcasting-publishing combines, and so forth. But let's begin with a look at the significance of media ownership by "conglomerate corporations"—holding companies that own, in addition to publishing and broadcasting enterprises, other major industrial corporations.

During my first month at the FCC I studied the cases and attended the meetings, but purposefully did not participate in voting on any items. One of the agenda items at the July 20 commissioners' meeting proposed two draft letters addressed to the presidents of International Telephone and Telegraph and the American Broadcasting Company, ITT and ABC, Messrs. Harold Geneen and Leonard Goldenson. We were asking them to supply "a statement specifying in further detail the manner in which the financial resources of ITT will enable ABC to improve its program services and thereby better to serve the public interest." This friendly inquiry was my first introduction to the proposed ITT-ABC merger, and the Commission majority's attitudes about it. It was to be a case that would occupy much of my attention over the next few months.

There wasn't much discussion of the letters that morning, but I read carefully the separate statements filed with the letter by my two responsible and experienced colleagues, Commissioners Robert T. Bartley and Kenneth A. Cox, men for whom I was already feeling a respect that was to grow over the following months.

Commissioner Bartley, a former broadcaster with the deep and earthy wisdom one would expect in a Texas-born relative of the late Speaker Sam Rayburn, wrote a long and thoughtful statement. He warned of "the probable far-reaching political, social and economic consequences for the public interest of the increasing control of broadcast facilities and broadcast service by large conglomerate corporations such as the applicants." Commissioner Cox, former lawyer, law professor, counsel to the Senate Commerce Committee, and chief of the FCC's Broadcast Bureau, characterized the proposed merger as "perhaps the most important in the agency's history." He said the issues were "so significant and far-reaching that we should proceed immediately to designate the matter for hearing."

Their concerns were well grounded in broadcasting's history and in the national debate preceding the 1934 Communications Act we were appointed to enforce. Precisely what Congress intended the FCC to do was not specified at the time or since. But no one has ever doubted Congress' great concern lest the ownership of broadcasting properties be permitted to fall into a few hands or to assume monopoly proportions.

I do not believe that most owners and managers of the mass media in the United States lack a sense of responsibility or lack tolerance for a diversity of views. I do not believe there is a small group of men who gather for breakfast every morning and decide what they will make the American people believe that day. Emotion often outruns the evidence of those who argue a conspiracy theory of propagandists' manipulations of the masses.

On the other hand, one reason evidence is so hard to come by is that the media tend to give less publicity to their own abuses than, say, to those of politicians. The media operate as a check upon other institutional power centers in our country. There is, however, no check upon the media. Just as it is a mistake to overstate the existence and potential for abuse, so, in my judgment, it is a mistake to ignore the evidence that does exist.

In 1959, for example, it was reported that officials of the Trujillo regime in the Dominican Republic had paid $750,000 to officers of the Mutual Radio Network to gain favorable propaganda disguised as news. (Ownership of the Mutual Radio Network changed hands once again last year without any review whatsoever by the FCC of old or new owners. The FCC does not regulate networks, only stations, and Mutual owns none.) RCA was once charged with using an NBC station to serve unfairly its broader corporate interests, including the coverage of RCA activities as "news," when others did not. There was speculation that after RCA acquired Random House, considerable pressure was put on the book publishing house's president, Bennett Cerf, to cease his Sunday evening service as a panelist on CBS's *What's My Line?* The Commission has occasionally found that individual stations have violated the "fairness doctrine" in advocating causes serving the station's economic self-interest, such as pay television.

Virtually every issue of the *Columbia Journalism Review* reports instances of such abuses by the print media. It has described a railroad-owned newspaper that refused to report railroad wrecks, a newspaper in debt to the Teamsters Union which gave exceedingly favorable coverage to Jimmy Hoffa, the repeated influence of the DuPont interests in the editorial functions of the Wilmington papers which it owned, and Anaconda Copper's use of its company-owned newspapers to support political candidates favorable to the company.

Economic self-interest does influence the content of the media, and as the media tend to fall into the control of corporate conglomerates, the areas of information and opinion affecting those economic interests become dangerously wide-ranging. What *is* happening to the ownership of American media today? What dangers does it pose? Taking a look at the structure of the media in the United States, I am not put at ease by what I see.

Most American communities have far less "dissemination of information from diverse and antagonistic sources" (to quote a famous description by the Supreme Court of the basic aim of the First Amendment) than is available nationally. Of the 1500 cities with daily newspapers, 96 percent are served by single-owner monopolies. Outside the top 50 to 200 markets there is substantial dropping off in the number of competing radio and television signals. The FCC prohibits a single owner from controlling two AM radio, or two television, stations with overlapping signals. But it has only recently expressed any concern over common ownership of an AM radio station and an FM radio station and a television station in the same market. Indeed, such ownership is the rule rather than the exception and probably exists in your community. Most stations are today acquired by purchase. And the FCC has, in part because of congressional pressure, rarely disapproved a purchase of a station by a newspaper.

There are few statewide or regional "monopolies"—although some situations come close. But in a majority of our states—the least populous—there are few enough newspapers and television stations to begin with, and they are usually under the control of a small group. And most politicians find today, as Congress warned in 1926, "woe be to those who dare to differ with them." Most of our politics is still state and local in scope. And increasingly, in many states and local communities, congressmen and state and local officials are compelled to regard that handful of media owners (many of whom are out-of-state), rather than the electorate itself, as their effective constituency. Moreover, many mass media owners have a significant impact in more than one state. One case that came before the FCC, for example, involved an owner with AM-FM-TV combinations in Las Vegas and Reno, Nevada, along with four newspapers in that state, seven newspapers in Oklahoma, and two stations and two newspapers in Arkansas. Another involved ownership of ten stations in North Carolina and adjoining southern Virginia. You may never have heard of these owners, but I imagine the elected officials of their states return their phone calls promptly.

The principal national sources of news are the wire services, AP and UPI, and the broadcast networks. Each of the wire services serves on the order of 1200 newspapers and 300 radio and television stations. Most local newspapers and radio stations offer little more than wire service copy as far as national and international news is concerned. To that extent one can take little heart for "diversity" from the oft-proffered statistics on proliferating radio stations (now over 6000) and the remaining daily newspapers (1700). The networks, though themselves heavily reliant upon the wire services to find out what's worth filming, are another potent force.

The weekly newsmagazine field is dominated by *Time, Newsweek,* and *U.S. News.*

What we sometimes fail to realize, moreover, is the political significance of the fact that we have become a nation of cities. Nearly half of the American people live in the six largest states: California, New York, Illinois, Pennsylvania, Texas, and Ohio. Those states, in turn, are substantially influenced (if not politically dominated) by their major population-industrial-financial-media centers, such as Los Angeles, New York City, Chicago, and Philadelphia—the nation's four largest metropolitan areas. Thus, to have a major influence in *one* of those cities is to have significant national power. And the number of interests with influence in more than one of these markets is startling.

Most of the top fifty television markets (which serve approximately 75 percent of the nation's television homes) have three competing commercial VHF television stations. There are about 150 such VHF commercial stations in these markets. Less than 10 percent are today owned by entities that do not own other media interests. In 30 of the 50 markets at least one of the stations is owned by a major newspaper published in that market—a total of one-third of these 150 stations.

In addition to the vast national impact of their affiliates the three television networks each *own* VHF stations in all of the top three markets—New York, Los Angeles, and Chicago—and each has two more in other cities in the top ten. RKO and Metromedia each own stations in both New York City and Los Angeles. Metromedia also owns stations in Washington, D.C., and California's other major city, San Francisco—as well as Philadelphia, Baltimore, Cleveland, Kansas City, and Oakland. RKO also owns stations in Boston, San Francisco, Washington, Memphis, and Hartford—as well as the regional Yankee Network. Westinghouse owns stations in New York, Chicago, Philadelphia *and* Pittsburgh, Boston, San Francisco, Baltimore, and Fort Wayne. These are but a few examples of today's media barons.

There are many implications of their power. Groups of stations are able to bargain with networks, advertisers, and talent in ways that put lesser stations at substantial economic disadvantage. Group ownership means, by definition, that few stations in major markets will be locally owned. (The FCC recently approved the transfer of the last available station in San Francisco to the absentee ownership of Metromedia. The only commercial station locally owned today is controlled by the San Francisco *Chronicle*.) But the basic point is simply that the national political power involved in ownership of a group of major VHF television stations in, say, New York, Los Angeles, Philadelphia, and Washington, D.C., is greater than a democracy should unthinkingly repose in one man or corporation.

For a variety of reasons, an increasing number of communications media are turning up on the organization charts of conglomerate companies. And the incredible profits generated by broadcast stations in the major markets (television broadcasters *average* a 90 to 100 percent return on tangible investment annually) have given FCC licensees, particularly owners of multiple television stations like the networks, Metromedia, Storer Broadcasting, and others, the extra capital with which to buy the New York Yankees (CBS), Random House (RCA), or Northeast Airlines (Storer). Established or up-and-coming conglomerates regard communications acquisitions as prestigious, profitable, and often a useful or even a necessary complement to present operations and projected exploitation of technological change.

It would be foolish to expect any extensive restructuring of the media in the United States, even if it were considered desirable. Technological change can bring change in structure, but it is as likely to be changed to even greater concentration as to wider diversity. In the short run at least, economics seems to render essentially intractable such problems as local monopolies in daily newspapers, or the small number of outlets for national news through wire services, newsmagazines, and the television networks. Indeed, to a certain extent the very high technical quality of the performance rendered by these newsgathering organizations is aided by their concentration of resources into large units and the financial cushions of oligopoly profits.

Nevertheless, it seems clear to me that the risks of concentration are grave.

Chairman Philip Hart of the Senate Antitrust and Monopoly Subcommittee remarked by way of introduction of his antitrust subcommittee's hearings about the newspaper industry, "The products of newspapers, opinion and information, are essential to the kind of society that we undertake to make successful here." If we are serious about the kind of society we have undertaken, it is clear to me that we simply must not tolerate concentration of media ownership—except where concentration creates actual countervailing social benefits. These benefits cannot be merely speculative. They must be identifiable, demonstrable, and genuinely weighty enough to offset the danger inherent in concentration.

This guideline is a simple prescription. The problem is to design and build machinery to fill it. And to keep the machinery from rusting and rotting. And to replace it when it becomes obsolete.

America does have available governmental machinery which is capable of scotching undue accumulations of power over the mass media, at least in theory and to some extent. The Department of Justice has authority under the antitrust laws to break up combinations which "restrain trade" or which "tend to lessen competition." These laws apply to the media as they do to any other industry.

But the antitrust laws simply do not get to where the problems are. They grant authority to block concentration only when it threatens *economic* competition in a particular economic *market*. Generally, in the case of the media, the relevant market is the market for advertising. Unfortunately, relatively vigorous advertising competition can be maintained in situations where competition in the marketplace of ideas is severely threatened. In such cases, the Justice Department has little inclination to act.

In general, I would urge the minimal standard that no accumulation of media should be permitted without a specific and convincing showing of a continuing countervailing social benefit. For no one has a higher calling in an increasingly complex free society bent on self-government than he who informs and moves the people. Personal prejudice, ignorance, social pressure, and advertiser pressure are in large measure inevitable. But a nation that has, in Learned Hand's phrase, "staked its all" upon the rational dialogue of an informed electorate simply cannot take any unnecessary risk of polluting the stream of information and opinion that sustains it. At the least, the burden of proving the social utility of doing otherwise should be upon him who seeks the power and profit which will result.

It seems appropriate to comment, "yes, but. . . ." Bigness is not always badness. Some of the enterprises which have been most energetic in developing bigness are on everybody's list of the best: The New York *Times,* the Washington *Post,* and the Los Angeles *Times* are among the top five newspapers in the country. The broadcasting stations once operated by Time, Inc., were among the best and most socially responsible in the country, employing large, professional news staffs.

Whether you are talking about networks or local stations, it is much cheaper to fill air time with game shows and reruns of movies and comedy series than it is with news and special events. Money invested in such programing is often only partly retrievable through advertising revenue. In the following article, a British economist who spent a year studying the organization and costs of news and sports programing at NBC, discusses the budgeting process during 1970, a fairly recent typical year.

WHAT NEWS COSTS AT NBC *

Alan Pearce

News and sports programming is very expensive. It is also an essential part of the broadcasting business. Many in network broadcasting's top management regard news as the cornerstone of everything they do. Sports programming is given to provide a balanced schedule, and also because the network affiliates demand it. NBC—the subject of this article—spends over $100 million every year on news and sports programming for the Television Network, the Radio

* Reprinted and condensed from *Broadcast Management/Engineering* 8:1 (January 1972). © Copyright by Broadband Information Services, Inc., 1972.

Network, and the owned television and radio stations. These news and sports program costs exclude what NBC calls "overheads"—that is, money spent on top executive salaries, plus the running costs of all the other departments such as sales, corporate planning, research, business affairs, press and promotion, etc. In return for the $100 million or so investment in news and sports programming, the NBC News Division fills 25 percent of the regular television network programming schedule, between 75 and 80 percent of the radio network's programming, between 21 and 22 percent of local programming by the owned television stations, and 25 percent or more of total programming by the owned radio stations.

How the NBC News Budget Is Made

Because the News Division is not operated as a profit center, advertising revenue earned by news and sports programming goes directly to the Television Network, the Owned Television Stations, or the Radio Division, including its six owned AM/FM stations. In return the Television Network, the Owned Stations, and the Radio Division, have to pay all of the News Division's costs. The NBC Television Network pays approximately 75 percent of the total costs of news and sports; the Owned Television Stations Division takes roughly 18 percent; and the Radio Division provides 7 percent of total costs. In fact, the Enterprise Division picks up a small proportion of costs (less than one percent) because it receives income from sales of NBC news and sports material sold abroad. Although the costs of news and sports are shared, control of the capital budget is exercised through the Television Network Division in conjunction with the News Division, and not through the owned stations or the Radio Division. The owned stations and the Radio Division are treated like customers of the News Division, whereas the relationship between the News Division and the Television Network is much closer because the network pays the bulk of the bills; in return the network gets whatever it can from advertising sales to offset its costs of news and sports.

The sum to be spent on news and sports in any given year is not chosen as an amount of money, to be followed by decisions on what the News Division is going to do with it. The News Division decides what it wants to do and then decides how much money it will cost. If the costs are too high, the News Division negotiates with top management, and the contributing divisions, and a compromise is reached. On the whole, however, the budget is a reflection of past experience.

Part of the budgeting process is like trying to foresee calamity. The president of the News Division is supposed to be a responsible journalist and also a responsible officer of the company. In an emergency, he is allowed to rape the balance sheets of the three operating divisions that contribute to his overall budget, so long as he does it responsibly.

In the fall of any given year, the News Division goes to corporate management and tells them how much will be needed to cover news and sports in the following year. There are certain known costs like labor, equipment, office rent, and the regularly scheduled program bdugets. Then comes the unknown element—forecasting the calamities that occur regularly in world news. Officers of the News Division do not look into a crystal ball and try to determine what will happen, but they do thorough research as to what is likely to happen and there are usually a number of known events.

For 1970 NBC decided that the News Division could spend $103 million on news and sports coverage in that year. This is a percentage breakdown of how the money was spent:

	%
Sports programming	42.2
Regularly scheduled news programming	37.1
Other news programming	7.5*
Departmental costs	13.2
Total	100.0%

*Percentage breakdown of other news:

	%
Moonshots	.8
Political programming	2.5
Unscheduled news	2.5
Planned specials	2.3
Total	7.5%

Source: NBC News Divisions Business Affairs.

From the above budget breakdown, it can be seen that there are two elements of cost—departmental and show costs. The show costs wind up against a particular program and many of these costs will be examined in this article. Departmental costs include the administrative overheads that cannot be assigned to a particular program but are assigned to the Division in general, the unliquidated portion of the cost of the overseas bureaus, and any other non-program costs that cannot be put into a particular program budget.

The remainder of this article will be devoted to breaking the costs of news and sports down into particular programs or types of programs. The costs of programming will be examined under the headings of the separate divisions, beginning with the Television Network, then going on to the Owned Television Stations, the Radio Division, and finally taking a look at the costs of sports programming.

The Cost of Regularly Scheduled News on the NBC Television Network

The most important regularly scheduled news programs aired by the NBC Television Network are:

The NBC Nightly News. A seven-day-a-week, year-round, half-hour, early-evening news program. The whole of NBC's News Division has been built around this program, which was formerly known as *The Huntley-Brinkley Report.* The weekly budget in 1970 was $137,-800. Total cost for the full year: $9,037,600.

The Today Show. A five-day-a-week, year-round, early-morning, two-hour, news and general features program. The weekly budget in 1970 was $99,736. Total cost for the full year: $5,186,272.

First Tuesday. A monthly, two-hour, news magazine. The monthly budget in 1970 was $264,145. Total cost for the full year (there were only eleven programs because of the mid-term election program which came on the first Tuesday in November): $2,905,595.

Meet the Press. A weekly, half-hour, news interview program, aired on Sunday of each week throughout the year. The weekly budget in 1970 for a show coming from Washington was $5407; for a show coming from New York it was $6844. Average weekly show cost was $6000. Total cost for the full year: $312,000.

The show budgets are prepared by the News Division's business affairs office in conjunction with the Television Network's business affairs office. In order to keep track of the weekly, monthly, and annual expenditures, a business manager, or unit manager, is assigned to each program; in some cases two business managers are assigned. The main function of the business or unit manager is to act as a cost controller. He attempts to administer the budget as efficiently as possible.

Non-regular News Programming

As we have seen, there were in 1970 four main elements of programming in this category: moonshots, political programming, unscheduled news, and planned specials.

1) *Moonshots.* There was, of course, only one moonshot in 1970, the Apollo 13, which developed a fault and could not land on the moon. NBC carried special Apollo 13 programming from April

11 to April 21. The total cost was $831,000. Moonshot budgets have been reduced recently due to greater pool coverage; that is, greater cooperation between the three networks who might pool their resources, and also by presenting less ambitious coverage. The Apollo 11 shot, which landed the first men on the moon in July 1969, had an ambitious programming budget totalling over $1.5 million.

2) *Political programming.*   The News Division budgeted 2.5 percent of its total annual budget of $103 million for 1970 to political programming because there was a midterm election. Most of the budget money was spent on the election return program broadcasts on November 3 and 4.

3) *Unscheduled news.*   This accounted for only 1.9 percent of the total News Division budget in 1970, but it is the most unpredictable category and it is in the area of unscheduled news that the budget is most likely to be exceeded. Unscheduled news is the most highly priced news, because: a) it is unlikely to attract any advertising, since it goes on the air on an emergency basis; b) it displaces other regularly scheduled programs; c) there is often a considerable advertising loss due to the preemption of other programming; d) very often the programs do not lend themselves to advertising, for example, the assassinations of President John F. Kennedy, Dr. Martin Luther King, and Senator Robert Kennedy, or a Presidential Press Conference, or special war coverage in the Middle East or South East Asia.

As examples: On May 10, 1970, the NBC News Division put on an unscheduled program entitled "Our House Divided." It cost $87,-000 to make the program, but the pre-emption costs—the loss of advertising in the programs it replaced—amounted to $144,000. The News Division is not responsible for pre-emption costs, but they have to be borne by the Television Network. "A Conversation with the President," broadcast on July 1, 1970, cost NBC News only $12,000 in production costs because it was pool coverage, but the Television Network lost $57,600 in pre-emptions.

4) *Planned specials.*   These represented 2.3 percent of the total news budget for 1970. They vary enormously in cost, ranging from only $29,000 for a show like "The Loyal Opposition," to $750,000 for one like "From Here to the 70's," which was 2½ hours long. Sponsorship of planned specials varies. Usually the non-controversial ones like "The Everglades" or "The Great Barrier Reef" earn money, while documentaries on drugs like "Trip to Nowhere" lose heavily. In fact, one NBC documentary, "Migrant: An NBC White Paper," shown on July 16, 1970, cost $168,190, and led eventually to a great

loss in advertising revenue. Coca-Cola, a company that was criticized in the program, eventually withdrew its advertising from NBC and placed it with the other two networks.

Departmental Costs of the Television Network

Departmental costs represent 13.2 percent of the total News Division budget at NBC and the largest proportion of these costs are picked up by the Television Network. Departmental costs consist of administrative overheads that cannot be assigned to a particular program, the unliquidated portion of the cost of overseas bureaus, and other non-program costs that cannot be put into a particular program budget.

News Programming on Owned Television Stations

The NBC Owned Television Stations Division is responsible for 18 percent of the annual news and sports budget at NBC. In 1970 this amounted to roughly $19 million, $14 million for programming and $5 million for operations and engineering.

WNBC in New York was responsible for 35 percent of the $19 million budget; KNBC in Los Angeles was responsible for 25 percent; WMAQ in Chicago picked up 20 percent; and WRC in Washington, D. C. and WKYC in Cleveland each had 10 percent of the total Owned Television Stations Division annual news budget.

As an example of a news program budget at the owned station level, WNBC's "Sixth Hour News," since renamed "News 4 New York," cost a total of $3,366,000 in 1970.

News Programming in the Radio Division

NBC Radio Division takes 7 percent of the News Division's annual budget. This news is divided between the Radio Network, which broadcasts between 30 and 40 hours a week and between 75 and 80 percent of that is news and sports rogramming, and the six owned AM/FM radio stations—WMAQ in Chicago, WKYC in Cleveland, WNBC in New York, WJAS in Pittsburgh, KNBR in San Francisco, and WRC in Washington, D. C. These stations vary the amount of news and public affairs programming used because some of them have a mostly music format while others have much more news and sports and talk-show programming. At a very minimum, however, NBC-owned radio stations have 25 percent of news and sports programming content.

Radio news can, of course, be done much more cheaply than it can on television. Radio does not need all the engineering and film crewing that television requires, nor does it need stagehands, make-up, production personnel, and complicated studio facilities. Content and production is much simpler on radio, and this is reflected in the radio news programming budgets. The only factor of budgeting that is just as costly is administration; it costs almost as much to administer the radio network and the owned stations as it does to administer the television network.

The Radio Network's news operation cost almost $5 million in 1970, and nearly $4 million was spent on covering news for the owned stations. About 60 percent of radio's news costs were attributable directly to programming costs, and 40 percent for supporting costs.

"News on the Hour" is NBC Radio Network's most important news program. The direct operating costs were $20,000 a week in 1970, making a total for the year of $1,040,000. If an allocation were made for supporting services, then the budget would be something in the order of $40,000 a week, making a total for the year of $2,080,-000.

Sports Programming

Sports programming at NBC comes under the authority of the News Division. Sports is probably the highest priced programming on television; it represented 42.2 percent of the News Division's budget of $103 million in 1970 and provided only one-third of the Division's total network programming contribution.

The biggest slice of the sports programming budget goes to rights costs—these are the fees paid to the football, baseball and basketball leagues, and the money paid to golf, tennis, and other sports tournament organizers, for the privilege of broadcasting their events on a regular basis. Consequently rights cost NBC News Division 34 percent of the $103 million budget; the other 8.2 percent goes to program costs.

In 1970 NBC paid $11 million for a limited football season, excluding Super Bowl costs and the all-star game. In 1971, the same season will cost $12 million in rights. In addition NBC paid $2.5 million rights costs for the Super Bowl.

NBC's contract with the baseball league is for $50 million rights payments over a three-year period ending after the 1971 season. This means that NBC pays between $16.5 and $17 million a year for baseball rights.

By comparison rights costs for college basketball, golf, tennis, and other sports are minor. A major golf tournament can cost as much as $250,000 for rights, down to $50,000 for a minor tournament. NBC paid the NCAA $1.4 million over two years for college basketball.

The rights for Wimbledon Tennis from England in 1970 came to $60,000.

Although rights costs are very high due to the intense competition between the three networks, program costs for sports events are also quite high due mainly to the type of sophisticated coverage that the viewer demands. An average sports pick-up, that is the cost of sending a mobile unit to cover a ball game, costs $40,000. The Super Bowl, however, needs a $125,000 pick-up because it requires more cameras.

Obviously, a corporation has to be both big and wealthy to afford such outlays, and the networks contend they can afford it only because of the profits from their wholly owned stations and from their sideline business of developing and marketing entertainment series. The federal government has been looking askance at both these aspects and threatening to force the networks to concentrate on delivering programs, not making them or running their own stations. If the networks lose these sources of income, they no doubt will economize, and the most obvious place to economize is in news and sports. This is a sort of counterargument for the position which Commissioner Johnson put forth.

It is the same kind of argument which newspaper publishers make to justify monopolies. Some of the best papers in this country are in competitive situations, and so are some of the worst. There are excellent papers in one-newspaper towns, and there are awful ones. Washington, D.C., has two fine newspapers, but is that because they are intensely competitive? If so, why hasn't competition had that same effect on the two dailies in Boston or in San Francisco? Incidentally, the general low quality of journalism in those two cities refutes the old adage that a city gets the kind of papers it deserves.

A. J. Liebling wrote essays on the press for many years for *The New Yorker*. He was an astute, if cynical, observer. He was fond of comparing the news content of a paper to the free lunch that saloonkeepers once provided their patrons. When the barkeeps got together and did not put out the cold cuts and cheese any longer, they found that the customers still drank as much beer and the management pocketed the additional profit. Liebling accused publishers of cutting back on news expenditures to the same end. He insisted the publisher provided a bit of news and features out of the same sense of guilt that made the saloonkeepers continue to set out some stale pretzels.

It is a colorful metaphor, but there is not much evidence to back it up. The news hole has not changed much over the years, and expenditures for news and features have skyrocketed. There *has* been a sharp rise since Liebling's time in the number of papers which make no pretense of providing news. These are the shoppers which exist solely as an advertising medium and which are either given away or provided on a pay-if-you-wish basis to every resident of a town or section of a city.

There is a thread of argument in the communications business that competition, in fact, serves the society badly because it concentrates attention upon reaching the largest audience and therefore drives content and news selection constantly toward the lowest common denominator. The obvious example is the three major television networks. It would be difficult to find anywhere in mass communications a more competitive situation—and a more steady movement away from innovation and experimentation toward mass pablum.

The point is not whether Nicholas Johnson is wrong. The correlations between abstractions and reality have not been sufficient to settle the argument in either direction, and they make more difficult the evaluation of various systems of media support.

The decline in the number of metropolitan daily newspapers is often cited, not only as a portent of a growing trend of noncompetition, but as a sign of terminal illness in the whole newspaper field. There are other bad signs: the evidence that young people do not much attend to papers; the survey reports which have indicated, over the last 20 years, a growing reliance among the general public upon television as the primary source of news, and much talk both within and without the field about a credibility problem. There is no question that some segments of the newspaper business are in trouble that will only get deeper.

An example in microcosm is set out in the article which follows. It comes from the *Chicago Journalism Review,* one of the journals of media analysis and criticism which were founded in the late 1960's.

CIRCULATION DISASTER AMONG CHICAGO NEWSPAPERS *

Brian Boyer

The way Chicago newspapers figure their circulation successes, 1969 was another big year for the *Chicago Sun-Times*. The flagship of Field Enterprises steamed closer to the *Chicago Tribune's* commanding armada by losing only 15,000 copies a day. The *Tribune*

* Reprinted from *Chicago Journalism Review,* January 1970. © Copyright by *Chicago Journalism Review,* 1970.

lost 30,000 readers. At the rate they are going, in 20 years the *Sun-Times* will lose 300,000 readers and the *Tribune* 600,000, giving them roughly equal circulations of 150,000 in a neck and neck race to disaster.

However, at losing Sunday circulation, the *Tribune* is in a class by itself. "The World's Greatest Newspaper" lost 86,576 Sunday subscribers last year, a rate fast enough to bring it to zero in 12 years. The Sunday *Trib* has lost 435,000 readers in the past two decades —more newspapers than most publishers would ever dream of printing.

The *Sun-Times* and the *Tribune* are not the only newspapers that are in trouble, of course, *Chicago Today* (formerly the *American*) has lost 513,000 Sunday and 230,000 daily buyers since 1950. The *Daily News* is down about 90,000. The four papers have lost more than 500,000 weekday readers in the years between Presidents Eisenhower and Nixon. It hardly seems possible that all of them can survive the Seventies, although the most likely candidate for an early death, *Today,* may continue to be maintained by the Tribune Corporation as a fighting brand, a spoiler directed at the *Sun-Times.*

The usual reasons given for these declines include saturation television, the developing rigor mortis of the central city and the life-styles of the burgeoning suburbs.

American Research Bureau figures show that in 1955 (the earliest available figures), only 560,000 households were tuned in on the 10 P.M. news. The A. C. Neilsen Co. and ARB figures now indicate that about 1,500,000 households watch the evening news, and increase of about 300 per cent. Many people watching television news feel that newspapers have nothing for them, and if they feel that way, they're right.

Because newspaper managements are usually conservative in business as well as in politics, they have not been able to respond to television's challenge. Canny promotion by book publishers, which once were threatened by motion pictures in the same way that newspapers are by television, has capitalized on the competition. Books sell better after movies have been made from them. If newspaper publishers recognized that television news acts as an advertisement for their product and developed new formats for it, readers wouldn't be so indifferent to them.

Television hasn't hurt newspaper circulation more than the move to the suburbs has. People who read newspapers want to learn about what happens where they live, and 1,000,000 more people reside in Chicago's suburbs now than in 1960. The Chicago dailies don't cover their news, and only the *Tribune* makes any real attempt to. The policy is probably responsible for the *Trib's* retail trading zone circulation increase of 125,000 since 1950, to 325,000. But in light of the fact that the suburban population has grown 2,000,000 in that time, the numbers increase has been a real as well as a percentage failure.

Circulation that has grown belongs to the suburban community newspapers, but even that hasn't been nearly what one would expect. Some 100 weekly, bi-weekly and small dailies sell to about 600,000 households in the suburbs, about twice as much as they did 20 years ago.

Chester Hayes, director of the Suburban Press Association, said that the big increase in suburban newspapers is expected in the next decade. He is not displeased that the dailies are unable or unwilling to cover news outside of the city limits where 3,500,000 people live.

"The largest individual segment of the population is now suburban," Hayes said, "and the *Tribune,* which does the best out here, doesn't have nearly 50 per cent of the circulation it should have.

"The daily newspapers are going to have to change if they're going to survive. I don't know how, though, and neither do they. But we've got at least two newspaper readerships—city and suburban."

But despite appearances, television and the move to the suburbs may not be the most important reasons why newspaper sales are dropping. Circulation experts say that the fundamental causes are higher prices, the collapse of public transportation and the growth of expressways, new life styles by the young and, in Chicago at least, the distribution mess.

It's almost forgotten, but the crime syndicate supplied the muscle for the newspaper circulation wars that killed at least seven men in one year. The price that publishers eventually paid for their final peace has caused them trouble ever since.

In the agreement that the publishers wrote, news stand operations had to carry all dailies on an equal basis, including promotion and display. This seemed like a good idea at the time, but it severely limited the advertising and promotional efforts of any newspaper, since a good campaign would send a buyer to the same stand where other papers were equally displayed. The way it worked out, effective advertising sold the other guy's newspaper, too.

In other cities, newspapers control their own delivery systems, and the newsboy is the best sales device anybody has ever found. But not in Chicago, where home delivery people are almost always independent wholesalers. The kid who carries the *Tribune* also carries the *Sun-Times,* and the publishers didn't trust him to work in their individual best interests. So they agreed that delivery people could not solicit subscriptions. (Except for *Today,* which has its own delivery network in the city.)

This has resulted in separate sales and delivery systems, and accounts for the fact that while newspapers in other cities have as much as 90 per cent of their sales home delivered, the ratio in Chicago is about 50 per cent.

It also meant that circulation came down to the newsstand dealer whose operations were traditionally linked to the syndicate. Until former Police Supt. O. W. Wilson came to Chicago, there were some 10,000 newspaper-selling and book-making corner stand operators on Chicago's streets. The crackdown on the bookies reduced the number of green stand dealers to about 3,000 whose number will be 300 fewer by the end of the year. Seeing that circulation is a reflection of distribution, not the other way around, the friendly corner book-maker was the best friend Chicago newspapers ever had. O. W. Wilson was the worst.

For reasons which include lack of imagination and sweetheart deals with wholesale distributors, the publishers have not been very aggressive about opening up new sales points in such places as parking lots, grocery stores and gasoline stations. Yet these are all key institutions in the suburbs, and one way the newspaper effectively can get into the suburban market. Their sole stroke of inspiration has been the machine vendors, which have the disadvantage of being handy coin purses for petty thieves.

It's tempting to blame outside forces for the drop in circulations, but probably more honest to look for the trouble in the newspapers themselves. The psychology of the 55-year-old male executive still shapes the editorial product when half of the population is under 30, and just plain not interested in what he has to offer. The *Tribune* has lost the most circulation not only because it had the most circulation to lose; its public has been disappearing. On a proportional basis, the *Sun-Times* has fared better, because it covers more of the news that young readers want, because it is in touch with the mood of the last half of the 20th Century, and because it usually does a better job of backgrounding the events that television news brings to public attention.

There are readers out there, and the phenomenon of the "underground" press is one indication of how many there are. In Los Angeles, the *Free Press* has swelled its weekly circulation to about 120,000 with an offering of pornographic personal advertisements for the middle-aged and the good and bad news about drugs and radical politics for the young. The *Chicago Seed* has a paid bi-monthly circulation of 40,000 that is expected to rise to 50,000 or more by the summer, because it gives young readers what they are interested in on the political, drug and cultural scene and because of its aggressive street-hawker distribution system. One example of its vigor is *Fortune Magazine's* estimate that an underground newspaper has a pass-on readership of about 8-to-1, compared with the daily pass-on rate of about 2.3-to-1. It doesn't mean that the underground editorial product is always good, but it is interesting. And for the most part, Chicago's dailies aren't very interesting any more.

The largest single drop in newspaper readership has been with the multiple buyer—the person who once bought two or more papers to find out what each of them had to say. News products used to be fundamentally different from each other, like the *New York Daily News* is fundamentally different from the *New York Times*. This is not only fun for the reader, it sells more papers. Despite the homogenized appearance of the news that Chicago's dailies offer (if one newspaper reports it they all do; if one doesn't none do) there are lots of different ways of looking at the world. A vigorous press is a diversified one.

One can't escape the feeling that Colonel McCormick, Hearst and the original Marshall Field were infinitely better newspapermen than their more cautious descendants. A lot more people than today wanted to know what their newspapers had to say. If this isn't the case, then the days of the city daily are numbered, and there's not much that anybody can do about it.

There is a grim persuasiveness about the facts and figures in Boyer's article—although the Chicago situation has improved somewhat—but it must be put along side other equally solid data based upon a different vision of the newspapers' future.

Nobody knows how profitable newspapers are because they are so secretive about economic data. This comes partly from the twin traditions of family ownership and fear of government controls. Although it is the nation's 10th largest industry, newspaper publishing is the only one whose profit figures are not available in the annual Economic Report of the President or the periodic reports of the Securities and Exchange Commission and the Federal Trade Commission. When in 1968 the chairman of the FTC was asked the reason for the special treatment, he told senators, "I swear I thought they were included. I went and looked and they were not there. . . . I kind of suspect nobody wanted the newspapers mad at them."

After a careful analysis of available information, researchers at RAND Corporation concluded that net profits for American newspapers were averaging 8.8 per cent, or 76 per cent higher than the national average for all industries. Some small- and medium-sized papers were earning the highest returns.

There are those in the investment business, as well as in the newspaper business, who have great confidence in it as a growth industry. The article which follows was prepared by the staff of *Business Week* in that spirit, obviously, but there is more to their case than simply professional market optimism.

WHY NEWSPAPERS ARE MAKING MONEY AGAIN *

Staff of Business Week

John S. Knight, Pulitzer Prize-winning columnist, editorial chairman of Knight Newspapers, Inc., and, at 75, one of the grand, old curmudgeons of American journalism, is a man of many opinions. And these days his one overriding opinion, which may come as a surprise to anyone outside the newspaper business, is that daily newspapers are not only alive and well, but are becoming a full-fledged growth industry.

"Within the last eight or 10 years," Knight points out, "a lot of metropolitan papers disappeared, and everyone was saying that television would be the death of the daily paper." In New York City alone, four dailies suspended operations between 1962 and 1968. "What really happened," Knight says, "is that the industry underwent a long-overdue shakeout, then slowly consolidated. And now it is much, much stronger for it."

Stewart Macdonald, executive director of the American Newspaper Publishers Assn. Foundation, trots out figures showing just how strong: Newspaper advertising revenues are up more than five times since 1946 (to a record $5.8-billion last year), daily circulation is up over 20% (to a record 62-million), and the industry now ranks as the country's fifth-largest employer. Every day, more than 98-million Americans—almost 80% of the adult population—read at least one newspaper. And while it is true that 11 dailies suspended

---

* Reprinted and condensed with permission from *Business Week*, Aug. 29, 1970. © Copyright by *Business Week*, 1970.

publication last year, it is also true that 28 other dailies started up. "That," says Macdonald, "is growth." Perhaps the best proof is KNI itself. Though the company's editorial coverage falls short of a *New York Times* or *Washington Post* and tends toward what one former KNI editor describes as "safe, formula journalism," even rival publishers concede that the Knight papers comprise one of the best-managed, most profitable, and most aggressive chains in the country.

Last year alone, the company added five papers to its collection: the *Philadelphia Inquirer* and *Daily News,* the *Macon* (Ga.) *Telegraph* and *News,* and the *Boca Raton* (Fla.) *News.* Together with other papers in Miami, Detroit, Akron, O., Charlotte, (N. C.), and Tallahassee (Fla.), KNI's acquisitions raised its daily circulation to 2.2-million and its annual level of advertising to more than 340-million lines, while total revenues for the year spurted to a record $162.8-million and profits to a record $12.7-million. Along the way, KNI has also boosted its after-tax profits to nearly 8% of gross revenues, and talks confidently of the not-too-distant day when it will earn 10% to 11% on revenues. That compares with average newspaper profits of 6% to 7% and average magazine profits of 5% to 6%.

Today, as Knight likes to observe, there is not a single KNI paper that—over the long run—has not grown strongly in circulation, advertising, and profitability once KNI took control. Excluding those papers that have expanded through merger, the country's fastest-growing metropolitan daily is now KNI's *Detroit Free Press,* which picked up 42,000 new readers in the last year. And the company's *Miami Herald,* which ranks 12th in circulation among morning papers, is the nation's second-largest daily in total advertising—despite the fact that Miami is the 26th-largest market by population and 19th in retail sales.

There are still plenty of papers that have more troubles than a rusty press. In fact, a few years ago, many publishers in the industry were bearish about the future of all but the best newspapers—and, in some cases, felt it was a business that was becoming increasingly obsolete. But today the industry's broader trend is unquestionably up.

Newhouse Newspapers, Scripps-Howard, Gannett, and the country's other leading chains now account for more than 120 other papers. And nearly all the chains are trolling for more. "There are so many markets," says Gannett President Allen Neuharth, "that you can pick and choose. Some want metropolitan areas, some don't. Knight wants metropolitan. They have Philadelphia. We're in Camden (N. J.) with 120,000 circulation and rapid growth. There is no growth in Philadelphia, but you don't need continued growth to be profitable."

A big reason for the industry's prosperity, of course, is rising newspaper ad revenues. At $5.8-billion (vs. $3.6-billion for television), newspaper ad revenues last year were up more than 11% above the year before. In today's television age, why are advertisers still flocking to newspapers? Simply because newspapers—unlike television, radio, or magazines—are the next best thing to an indispensable medium, if only because of the many service features they provide to their readership.

Besides important local and national happenings, newspapers dish up everything from hometown job, apartment, housing, movie, theater, stock market, and television listings to details on yesterday's garden club luncheon, last night's PTA meeting, and tonight's YMCA squash match, along with A&P's latest prices on sirloin and the department store's close-out bargains on minis. No one, in short, can afford to be without his local paper, especially at today's economy price of 10¢ or 15¢ a copy. As the *New York Times'* Francis Cox pointing to the inflationary trend, puts it: "Most things—even a telephone call for a single item of information—cost a dime today."

Far more basically, there is one other big clincher for newspapers: the long-term shake-out of metropolitan dailies and the virtual elimination of competition among newspapers. While the total number of dailies published today (more than 1,700) is almost the same as in 1945, their distribution has shifted away from major metropolitan areas and toward the suburbs, along with the population and retailers. Right after World War II, there were 117 cities with two or more competing dailies. Today, there are only 45. And in 22 of those cities, a total of 44 papers have pooled their printing and business operations to cut costs. Last month, President Nixon even signed a bill into law, extending antitrust immunity to those joint operations where one of the papers might otherwise fail.

As they fatten up, more and more papers are also able to swing the purchase of big, fancy, labor-saving equipment—computerized typesetters and presses, photocomposition, and so on.

Many publishers are investing in their own paper plants. "Until a few years ago," says Gannett's Neuharth, "there was none of this except in a few isolated examples such as the *Chicago Tribune.*" More papers are also able to afford regional or "zone" editions, thus refining their circulation and luring a few more advertisers. Newhouse's *Long Island Press,* for instance, boasts three geographic editions. "The whole mass numbers game in circulation is fading," says Thomas Vail, editor and publisher of the *Cleveland Plain Dealer.* "The magazine business overstepped itself in this circulation area," adds Brady Black, editor-in-chief of the *Cincinnati Enquirer,* "and some of them got so much circulation they couldn't find enough advertising to pay for it. We don't want to get into that position."

At Knight Newspapers, the top-management thinking is done by four men: John Knight himself, company overlord and chief custodian of KNI's broader editorial philosophy; Knight's younger brother, James 59, board chairman and chief executive officer who presides over the business side; Lee Hills, 64, president and a Pulitzer Prize winner in his own right, who operates just below John Knight on the editorial level; and Alvah Chapman, 49, executive vice-president and the No. 2 man on the financial side, just under James Knight. Oddly enough, the four maintain no central headquarters. John Knight summers in Akron and winters in Miami. Hills spends most of his time in Detroit. James Knight and Chapman operate out of Miami.

Despite management's far-flung nature, KNI's lines of authority and overall operating philosophy—as set down by John Knight—are as fixed and firm as a tray of type. Knight insists on full editorial independence and autonomy among his papers and complete separation of editorial and financial functions. "I'd have to confess," he says, "that every general manager is a frustrated editor. But I don't find too many editors who think they could do a better job of management."

Knight also insists that his editors and managers eschew any political or business alliances, including corporate directorships. "On the two occasions when I violated this rule," he admits, "the bank failed and my candidate faltered." A lifelong Republican himself, Knight proudly points out that many of his critics now call him a "Black Republican" for having supported more than 1,000 Democrats for public office. Other critics call him simply an opportunist who bends with every prevailing public wind. Either way, it keeps the reader guessing, and that is the way Knight likes it. Says he: "In this day of the credibility gap, we think this makes a newspaper believable."

Knight began hammering out his philosophy back in the 1920s when he was managing editor of the *Akron Beacon Journal,* one of three small Ohio dailies then owned by the family. At that time, his father, Charles L. Knight, was the paper's editor and also a political aspirant. This, says Knight, "made every headline suspect in the eyes of our readers. What I learned from c.l.'s era was that newspapering and political involvements are incompatible." When his father died in 1933, Knight took charge of the *Beacon Journal* and four years later launched the company on its current trajectory. In 1937, the Knights bought the *Miami Herald;* in 1940, the *Detroit Free Press;* then in 1944, the *Chicago Daily News,* which was later sold.

As the chain grew larger, Knight saw an increasing need for tighter management and more financial coordination among his papers. So at the suggestion of Lee Hills, then executive editor in Detroit and Miami, Knight formed an executive committee in 1960 to make quarterly reviews of all KNI operations, including labor problems, personnel recruitment, operating costs, advertising, circulation, and acquisitions. "The net of all this," claims Jack Knight, "is that we don't have so many crises now. We're pretty orderly. But it isn't as much fun any longer."

That same year, Chapman joined KNI and brought what Knight describes as "order and business discipline" to the chain. During six years as general manager of the *Miami Herald,* Chapman doubled the paper's revenues and tripled profits. As KNI executive vice-president, Chapman—working closely with Jim Knight—has now introduced budgeting on all KNI papers, a rarity among most small and medium-sized papers. "Some do their budgeting in bits and pieces," says Chapman. "But most of them just don't want to work that hard." Chapman also came up with "management by objective," the use of incentive bonuses for every noneditorial manager. Ad salesmen get bonuses for producing extra business, composing room foremen for rolling more pages on time, accounting managers for beating their deadlines.

Chapman and Jim Knight have wrought similar economies and savings in the composing room. Today, every KNI paper uses a computer not only for administration and typesetting, but to control presses and other equipment, as well. That even includes KNI's *Boca Raton News,* which has a circulation of only 6,169. KNI also uses optical scanners to produce type automatically from a typewritten page; computer-controlled display screens for redesigning ad layouts; and a facsimile system for transmitting ad layouts. KNI's *Miami Herald* even became the first major metropolitan daily to paint its presses white and equip the pressroom with "demisters," making the area as clean as any other part of the plant. "What we did," says the younger Knight, "was turn the composing room into a manufacturing center."

Out in the editorial offices, changes are slower in coming. "The Knight news level is good, though not superior," says one former KNI editor. But there have been improvements, adds one editor in the field, "and the Knight papers are starting to get more of a cutting edge." To hone its blade, Knight is going in for more investigative reporting, adding columnists of almost every political hue, and generally trying to upgrade the quality and quantity of its reporting. Here and there, the results have bordered on the spectacular. In 1968 alone, KNI won three Pulitzer Prizes and ran its total to 12—more than any other single chain. Among KNI's recent winners: the *Detroit Free Press* for its coverage of that city's 1967 race riots, the *Charlotte Observer* for its biting editorial cartoons, and the *Miami Herald* for gaining the freedom of a wrongly-convicted life-termer.

KNI is pouring money, as well, into that staple of every good daily: the service feature. On the *Philadelphia Inquirer,* for instance, KNI has spent more than $200,000 for its page-one "Action Line" column that now requires 12 reporters to handle the more than 1,500 calls and 500 letters that pour in every day. "Our whole approach is to make the *Inquirer* more personal, more down-to-earth," says *Inquirer* Executive Editor John McMullan, a deft, sharp-eyed KNI editor promoted from Miami. "We're trying to be more aggressive in our news coverage, to bring a fresh look to some of the dark corners around here."

Rather than production costs, the No. 1 problem of tomorrow, if not today, shapes up as distribution. It now accounts for some 8% to 10% of the industry's total operating expenses. Growing traffic congestion is slowing up deliveries. Medium-rise and high-rise apartments are swallowing up tenants and making them almost impossible to reach. Metropolitan papers are also losing a favorite, old outlet: the "Mom and Pop" store. In Pittsburgh alone, where circulation and distribution costs are rocketing 12% to 15% a year, 70 such stores closed in 1969. Then there is the problem of ghetto or core-city areas. "The papers can be delivered, but let the boys try to go back and collect," says Michael Tynan, director of circulation for the *Pittsburgh Press* and *Post Gazette*. "They're beaten and robbed. They can never get back with the money." In fact, the *Cincinnati Enquirer's* Brady Black questions whether "anyone is even breaking even in the core areas."

As one possible solution, the *Detroit News, Chicago Daily News,* and several other papers are experimenting with a "block-system" of deliveries and collections. Every one or two blocks, a bundle of papers is dropped off with some enterprising homeowner, and a sign is hung out, indicating that papers can be bought there.

If costs start getting out of hand, newspapers can simply hike their circulation rates. As it is, many publishers feel that rate increases have not kept pace, and that subscribers should be kicking in a bigger share of total revenues. Right now, circulation income accounts for an average 20% to 25% of total revenues compared with 75% to 80% for advertisers. A better balance, some say, would be a 65-35 ratio.

As for his own personal prospects and future, the elder Knight

gives no indication that he plans to step down from active participation in the company. Whether in Miami or Akron, he still shows up
at 9 o'clock every morning and puts in a five-day week. "I'll retire
when I no longer feel I can be effective," Knight vows, giving the
impression that that will not be for some years to come.

The chief difference between the Boyer article and the *Business Week*
piece about the Knight newspapers, in a sense, is the acceptance of change.
The assumption in both selections is that the field will, indeed, tighten,
perhaps to the point at which there are *no* competitive daily newspaper
towns. Just as the "old Hollywood" is gone—a point we shall examine
later—so, perhaps, is the old downtown with competitive newspapers slug-
ging it out.

Furthermore, there is an implied judgment that the best newspapers
will survive—that the shaking-out process has removed papers which were
not only weaker financially but professionally. Certainly New York was
poorer when Pulitzer's old *World* disappeared into a merger in the early
1930's, as was Boston with the departure of the *Transcript,* but it is difficult to contend, other than in terms of abstract principle, that the departure of the *Mirror* or the *World-Journal-Tribune* signified anything at all
to either New York or the nation, or that San Francisco was diminished
by the disappearance of the *Call-Bulletin* and Chicago by the loss of the
Herald-American. Most of the major papers which have failed, to put it
baldly, have deserved to.

In recent times there is one spectacular exception. At the time of its
disappearance into an abortive merger in 1966, the New York *Herald-
Tribune* was not only unquestionably one of the country's great newspapers but also the most innovative and forward-looking.

The marketplace economy which governs all the mass media in this
country stimulates experimentation and new approaches, but sometimes
too late. The market is an organism as well as an institution, and change
is basic. Other media demonstrate this more dramatically than newspapers.

The consumer magazine was the first medium to reach a huge and
relatively disparate audience. The *Ladies Home Journal* reached a circulation of 1 million in 1903. Another Curtis publication, the *Saturday Evening Post,* made it five years later. With them grew a new concept of advertising—national mass marketing of name brands—as well as the owner's
dependence upon advertising, rather than copy sales, as the primary source
of income. The *Journal's* audience was female, but within that limitation
it ranged widely and imaginatively, including everything from advice columns to sheet music and house plans. The *Post,* and the competitive
weeklies which grew in its wake such as *Collier's,* were fat and eclectic. The
Post's great editor, George H. Lorimer, was upset when he received a

letter from a reader who said he read the magazine "from cover to cover." Lorimer felt it was an indication that the editorial scope was getting too narrow.

For more than 20 years the great American consumer magazines were a central element in both the selling system and the popular culture of the country. From that eminence it is difficult to see change, particularly deep structural change, and when it began to come the great magazine men refused to believe it. There still are some who do not, but they are few indeed.

The change was brought about primarily by the networks—first radio and then television. The new medium attracted much bigger audiences (because the mass magazines, for all their honest editorial concern about quality, were essentially time-killers, and radio required less effort of its audience), which meant that those who sought the broadest possible market became convinced that the networks reached it more cheaply and efficiently. Those who sold soap, mouthwash, cereal, soft drinks, cigarettes, and other low-priced essentially universal products began to think about radio first and magazines second, and the pattern which began to reach its culmination in the 1960's was underway.

The most important point is that the change was from one marketing device to another, a classic demonstration of economic factors at work. The actual audience of magazines apparently did not decline. Circulation figures increased much more rapidly than the population. Between 1908 and the year of its death, 1969, the circulation of the *Saturday Evening Post* multiplied seven times while the population multiplied two and a half times. The biggest circulations today, those of the *Reader's Digest* and *TV Guide,* are well over 15 million.

It is necessary to qualify any vast claims about magazine audiences by pointing out that circulation figures are somewhat flawed indicators. Traditionally, advertising rates were pegged to circulation; the magazine sold numbers to its advertisers, and the higher the numbers, the more it charged. As the search for numbers became more aggressive, however, the system began to do itself in. The customer who bought his magazine each week or month at a corner newsstand was less dependable than one who was locked up with a subscription (besides, the number of corner newsstands was skidding).

Many of the big consumer magazines now have more than 80 per cent of their circulation in subscriptions, but many of these have been solicited at fantastically cheap rates in special promotions; frequently they are part of a package deal, bought with several other publications. Advertisers (or, more accurately, the media buyers in the agencies which represent them) have been increasingly unimpressed by such numbers, since the numbers increased circulation costs far more than the advertising gain.

Life was losing 2 cents *on each copy* of the magazine in 1970. Circulation income averaged 12 cents a copy. The costs of production along with editorial expenses came to 41 cents. The per copy advertising income was 27 cents. And each new copy (at great promotion cost, for the old rule of thumb of the magazine business that the cost of a particular subscription promotion should just about balance the income from it has seldom held of late) added another 2 cents deficit.

For this reason the giants, in their hour of agony, have taken to cutting back circulation. Sometimes they do it by drastic surgery, as the expiring *Saturday Evening Post* did when it informed more than a million subscribers that they could not have the magazine any more, but the general practice has been to stop circulation promotion and the soliciting of renewals. The advertiser is then assured that the audience is of higher quality than before, and the action generally has been accompanied by reduced advertising rates. The idea that the bigger the circulation, the healthier the magazine, was true for many years, but after the rise of the networks it was in some cases disastrously false.

The old ways die hard, however. Into the last published issue of *Look* was bound a postage-paid reply card offering a full-year, subscription 24 issues, for $3.00. That was little more than a third of the cost of that many issues at the already-cheap cover price of 35 cents.

The exodus of advertisers from consumer magazines to the networks as the foundation of mass marketing was resisted by the magazines, of course. One of the first responses was a total ban in such magazines as the *Saturday Evening Post* on any mention of broadcasters or broadcasting in either fiction or articles. This marvelously naïve device (paralleled by the refusal of many newspapers for a time to run radio program logs) lasted well into the 1940's.

Once the magazine men decided they could not make broadcasting go away by refusing to admit it existed, they attempted a counterattack with broadcasting's own chief weapon: numbers. The *Post* led the way with complicated research studies of pass-along and repeat readership (how many people read one copy? how many times do they look into it during its stay on the coffee table?) and, through some soaring projections, came up with box-car figures which began to approximate the audience size of routine evening television shows. Other magazines followed the lead, but without much effect on the long-term trend.

In fact, major well-established general appeal magazines were, by their very nature, incapable of fighting back; the significant response had to be a restructuring of the industry. This meant conceding the peddling of toothpaste and beer and cereal and other things which almost everybody uses to the medium which almost everybody uses and delivering instead a special market to a merchandiser who needs just that. In an increasingly affluent and populous society, the special audience magazines thrived, and some of those audiences proved large indeed. Both the growth of the magazine industry and the rise of specialized publications are demonstrated by a simple statistic. In 1964, the total circulation of the top five magazines was about 47 million. Of that total, general interest magazines provided a combined circulation of more than 29 million, or more than 62 per cent. In 1971, the total circulation of the top five magazines was almost 58 million, while the surviving general magazines had 26 million, less than 46 percent. By the same year the list of the hundred biggest circulators included such surprises as *Workbasket* (1.5 million), *Hot Rod* (800,000-plus), and *Hairdo and Beauty* (600,000). The two most sensational cases of growth during that period were *TV Guide* (up to 15.4 million), which, despite a thin slice of solid editorial matter top and bottom, must be classified chiefly as a reference handbook, and *Playboy* (almost 7 million), which has done an astonishing job, at $1 a copy, of attracting a very specialized audience of young men with slight experience but high hopes.

There is one way in which broad-appeal magazines can deliver a specialized audience, and some evidence indicates that its is working. This consists of the construction, with the help of computerized research, of special lists of affluent subscribers and the selling of advertising for an edition which goes only to them. The *Reader's Digest*, for example, has a special edition of about 1 million circulation (out of its total of 18 million) which goes to readers at the upper end of the economic scale—people with incomes of about $15,000 a year, far above that of the magazine's average reader. The rates per thousand readers are four times as high for the special edition, but the investment from the advertisers' point of view is a sound one; most would rather pay something like $12,000 to reach a million well-off homes than $56,000 to reach everybody. *Better Homes and Gardens* and *McCall's,* as well as the *Digest,* have had good results with the scheme—but it was not enough to save one of the first and most elaborate exploiters of special editions, *Look,* which at one time offered 50 different editions.

Generally the magazine business in this country thrives. Combined circulation has gone up steadily; advertising revenue has grown, peaking in 1969 with more than $1.5 billion (1970, in line with the general tendency for advertising to reflect in exaggerated terms any downswing in the economy, was off 5 per cent); the number of titles published apparently has gone up steadily, although any attempt at a hard total disintegrates in the face of the problem of definition. It thrives, but it is a different business from what it was in 1930, when there were 21 general magazines with circulation of more than a million and the *Saturday Evening Post* was the ultimate instrument of mass communication.

Whatever effects television has had on the magazine industry were modest compared with its impact on the theater motion picture business. The dynamics were different, of course. Television took the biggest part of the biggest advertisers from the biggest magazines; in the case of the movies, it simply and directly took away an enormous share of the ticket buyers, which meant that it eventually took away thousands of theaters, demolished both the corporate structure and the star system, and more than halved the number of films produced each year. Since major technological changes also came along while this was going on, it is almost accurate to say that the only thing in common between today's movie industry and the Hollywood foundries of 1940 is popcorn and the fact that the customers still sit in the dark.

Consider some of these figures: during the 1930's and '40's movie attendance in the United States exceeded 50 million a week. Today's audiences are running under 20 million a week, although the population is 40 per cent greater. The greatest year in the history of the movie business was 1948, just before the deluge, with 90 million admissions per week.

Within four years, attendance had been halved (and it continued to decline, although less preciptously, for the next 10 years). Six thousand theaters had been boarded up. Republic, Monogram, and RKO productions had closed down, and the retrenchment and reordering which is still going on among the giants was underway. The number of features produced in the United States had dropped from more than 400 to less than 150.

The simple reason for all this devastation is indicated by the character of the first studios to fold. Both Republic and Monogram were almost exclusively grinding out Westerns; RKO was producing a kind of urban equivalent—cops and robbers, mystery stories, and the like for double feature bills.

The first to go, in other words, were the manufacturers of time-killers, and much of the Hollywood audience had been seeking that when film was a true mass medium. There were literally millions who went to the movies every Saturday afternoon or evening, often without even knowing the name of the feature. It didn't cost very much and it was something to do, a kind of nondemanding company for a couple of otherwise unoccupied hours.

Now television did that just as well and there was far less effort required. Suddenly people were going to the movies only if they wanted to see a particular film (they stayed home in front of the box if they only wanted a little diversion). That meant that the experience had to be meaningful, in one way or another. The old recipes wouldn't work any more, but some of them died hard.

Take the star myth, for example. It was widely believed, and may have been true, that the great American mass audience identified strongly with the top actors in prewar films, that they had a kind of loyalty which brought them to see Gable or Crawford regardless of the film. Around this conviction grew up a whole structure, corporate as well as cultural. Promising young actors and actresses were signed to long contracts—frequently seven years—and their careers carefully nurtured by professional image makers (not only were scandals suppressed, so on occasion were spouses; romances and bright sayings and mythical hobbies were invented and planted) while their professional development proceeded. Only a few ever made it, but never mind, an occasional Carole Lombard, in an era when everybody was making money, made the whole system worthwhile.

Another myth was "the bigger the better." If 40 chorus girls were good, then put 80 in your next movie; if two stars meant box office magic, then cast a dozen. The cost of blockbuster epics and musicals is so high today that few studios will take a chance on them. Gone With the Wind cost $4 million to produce in 1939; no one can guess what it would cost today, but it might exceed the $40 million blown on Cleopatra. GWTW, incidentally, is the most profitable film in Hollywood history. In its first three decades it brought in more than $70 milion, and there were limitless prospects for periodic rereleases.

But the new, chiefly young audience apparently doesn't care that much about extravagant films and big stars. Some of the biggest of the last generation of old-fashioned movie stars bombed repeatedly in the 1950's and '60's. One of the sensationally successful movies of the late 1960's was Blow-up, featuring two then unknowns named David Hemmings and Vanessa Redgrave. By the old reasoning, that success made them stars, and they were promptly cast in Camelot—a lush and gaudy exercise based upon a hit Broadway musical. It proved to be a financial disaster.

With the emphasis upon substance and professional skill, not a plastic culture, different kinds of people came to be dominant in the movie-making process. Directors such as Fellini and John Huston became major figures to the young and purposeful film audience; so did cinematographers, writers, and producers. When Stanley Kubrick went to the banks to borrow money to produce his Paths of Glory, he was told to come back after he had signed a star. He got Kirk Douglas and the money. A few years later when he came to borrow money for 2001: A Space Odyssey he had only a script—and he got the money. The star of that film was a computer named HAL.

Going to bankers for money symbolizes another major change in the industry. Many contemporary films are produced by independents like Kubrick, each financed and produced separately. There are some surviving old-line major studios, but most have moved into the production of television series. The selling of television rights to feature films also has proved profitable, a recent major production costing around $600,000. Studios distribute and occasionally back independents, and, from time to time, still produce their own films. Sometimes these succeed (Universal's *Airport*); sometimes they are economic nightmares (Twentieth Century's *Dr. Doolittle*); however, by the 1970's, the likes of MGM and Twentieth Century's $114 million loss in 1969–70 provoked stormy stockholder fights. Increasingly the conglomerates have moved in. MGM now belongs primarily to a pair of curious bedfellows, Seagram distilleries and Time, Inc.

Few developments dramatize better the switch from intuition to business acumen in the movie business than the revelation in 1972 of a new box office prediction system. The heart of it is computer analysis of scripts. Researchers found that measurements of the emotional response to dramatic situations in the script are the best predictors of ticket sales. Directors, among others, reacted with expected hostility to this finding, but as *Variety,* the trade newspaper, reported, "An advance 'box office predicton' scheme would have evoked peals of laughter a few years ago. Nobody is laughing and some are apprehensive." If moviemakers really could get a good reading on the likely financial return before they started shooting, they obviously could adjust schedules and budgets accordingly.

A sense of all these changes is well conveyed in the article which follows. The great physical monuments of the old Hollywood are the huge pretentious houses in downtown areas of America's major cities. They in their glory represented it all—studio ownership, block booking, the temple of the stars. They have been victims, of course, of more than television. This article provides some insights into the whole world of downtown, of which the movie palace was once such an important part.

DECLINE OF THE DOWNTOWN
MOVIE PALACES *

Robert Kraus

Diane Baker, 50 feet tall, more malevolent and pale than usual, leans slowly toward Peter Cushing apparently unaware that her breasts are mere inches from his rippling nostrils.

* Reprinted with permission from *Detroit* (magazine of the Detroit *Free Press*), Sept. 27, 1970.

Then suddenly something is happening. Her face. Her FACE! The Ivory skin melts away; giant brown warts pop from her pores, and her eyes turn upward until she stands swaying, screaming, and filling the screen like some berserk pecan.

"What a pile of crappo," rumbles a trim, middle-aged Earl Mc-Glinnen, and he puts his foot down on a pedal that makes everything disappear.

For one sub-second all is dark and then the Fox Theater screen lights up anew with screams as Earl, with a master's touch, switches the porno-horror flick to the theater's second two-ton projector while a small matinee audience three stories below notices nothing.

"If I had to watch that stuff all the time," says Earl, "I would go Out . . . Of . . . My . . . Mind. I ignore it and read the New York *Times* instead."

On a recent afternoon, an audience of 50 or so—a typically rack-ity-packity audience of dazed winos, truant high school kids, some-one wearing a cape, and necking couples—watched as a man with eyes several inches too close together set fire to a hotel and 25 men and women screamed and roasted in color.

The Michigan Theater, King of the class shows, first and still handsomest of the giant downtown theaters, is reduced to playing run-of-the-mill flicks and spaghetti Westerns—sadistic, neo-fascistic, pseudo Westerns made in Italy—for a forlorn, off-the-street audience.

To keep its not-too-convincing, but likeable Golden Age French decor in fine shape, the Michigan costs owner Nicholas George about $4,500 a week in overhead. In one week not long ago total gross intake was $267. Pro bets are that this best and finest of the great old theaters will fold soon for good—and become a parking lot.

Still the second largest theatre of any kind in the country, the Fox was built in 1928 for $10 million by international tycoon William Fox, who later *became* 20th Century Fox. With 5,050 seats, it was cannily designed to satisfy the Jazz Age public's eye for elephantine tasteless-ness.

Like a vision brought on by sniffing air wick, the hugely successful lobby was dizzying, artificial and clammy. Red and gold pillars made of hollow, wired plaster climb six stories on either side of a lobby done up in Hindu Cowboy Baroque. For the floor, Fox ordered the largest instant oriental rug in the world ("two tons heavy," he boasted) and two theater organs, one for the lobby and one for inside the great dark dream hall itself.

"The new temple," panted a September, 1928, *Free Press* review, "has 400 employes and a fully equipped emergency hospital with two graduate nurses and a house physician on duty during theater hours."

The Fox opened with Janet Gaynor and Charles Farrell in a piece of silent fluff called "Street Angel," a symphony orchestra of 100, a corps of dancing girls and both theater organs going full blast. A couple of years later, the depression choked off the orchestra and the dancing girls and about half of the 400 employes.

In the '40's, when the Fox went into an all-night policy to handle fun-hungry wartime factory workers, there were two young ushers named Bill Brown and Herman Cohen who met and became good friends.

Things were booming again for Detroit's downtown theaters and the Fox was back on top with a staff of 65 ushers (who had to line up for inspection each day before the show opened), 15 concession stand workers, five usher captains, and five assistant managers. The admission was 95 cents and Hollywood was turning out films at such a clip that the Fox never held a hit movie over two weeks.

For live shows, there was always the touring Kay Kyser Kollege of Musical Knowledge, or radio biggies like Dr. I. Q. ("I have a lady in the balcony, Doctor.")

Herman Cohen became manager of the Fox in 1950 at the age of 24. Bill Brown, also 24, went into the army. In 1951 Cohen went off to Hollywood with fantasies of becoming a successful motion picture producer, and in 1952 Brown came back to manage the Fox.

Cohen became a successful motion picture producer. His first film, which set a trend in the '50s for slightly porno horror flicks, was "I Was a Teenage Werewolf" with the classic neuro-fantasy scene of the teenage werewolf attacking and gobbling up a young erogenous coed caught exercising in her tutu.

Together, in 1963, Cohen and Brown bought the lease on the Fox, which was then already having symptoms of things to come. The gild was fading on the Hindu pillars and stuffing was coming out of half the 5,000 seats. Except for "The Hustler" shown in '62, the second largest theater in the nation lost money almost every week.

Everything hit the downtown theaters at once. The end of the war, television, and the beginning of the move to the suburbs.

"Starting in 1946," says the whitehaired Brown, now 44, "it was all downhill for downtown shows."

Opposites in almost every way, Brown is chubby, happy and disorganized, a born walker; Cohen is lean, sharp-featured and a born flyer.

"Herm's in London right now working on some picture or other," says Brown.

Together the two of them have turned the Fox into the only consistently profitable major downtown show. Whatever else you may think of it.

It's true that to keep it going, Brown and Cohen have had to chain off the big, shadowy balconies most of the time, and 20 seats have to be repaired from knife slashes every week, and obscenities are now carved on the Hindu pillars. But, says Brown: "We love this theater."

In the summer of '69, Brown and Cohen showed "Slaves," a ponderous black and white zombie, and took in $65,000. It was the largest gross since "The Robe."

The secret of the Fox's success is that Brown and Cohen managed to change the theater's image soon enough to establish it for an inner city audience while the others—the class family theaters like the Madison and Michigan—were still angling for the white residential trade.

"Well," says Brown, "primarily we did it by showing one type of movie. The type that's called *exploitation*."

Exploitation is one of those vagaries theater owners use with each other and the public—and you know competition is fierce in a business when insiders say the same things to each other that they use on the public.

Like when showmen bubble that everything is going fine, things are generally going very badly. When they say so-so, they're hiding good news.

So little do they trust each other that it is not uncommon for a theater owner to send spotters to sit outside a rival's show all night and count the number of ticket buyers.

Thus "exploitation" can mean almost anything, depending on the man who's saying it and the current fads. In the '50s an exploitation movie was anything from a moderately spicy Tarzan movie to a porno monster flick. In the late '60s and early '70s, it's something else. It's race and raw sex and any combination of the two.

"It's adult entertainment," grunts Art Weisberg, "and it's not Walt Disney. That's what exploitation is."

If downtown and its theaters are about to become a jungle, Art Weisberg is about to become king of the jungle. The blunt-fingered, carnival-barker-voiced Weisberg was until recently all but unknown in the Detroit theater scene, owning only one respectable residential house, the Palmer Park, and showing no signs of aggressiveness.

But suddenly this year, Weisberg, 50, appeared like an ill-omen comet, formed his own distribution company to handle the rush of new heart-stopping European and American movies that have been made in the wake of relaxed censorship everywhere.

He then bought a couple more neighborhood houses and took over the lease to the Summit Theater, the made over Cass Theatre that was showing Cinerama products and dying.

Next Weisberg was bargaining with the United Artists Corp. in New York to take over the foundering United Artists Theater on Bagley. U.A. wanted to dump the theater but the Automobile Club of Michigan, which owns the building, was worried that Weisberg intended to turn one of the city's most venerable family theaters into a skin-flick grind house.

"It'll be an exploitation house," granted Weisberg. "I'm a born gambler. Things are going so-so. I'm producing my own film in Sweden right now. It's called 'The Night Is Not for Sleeping.' "

While Weisberg talks in the Summit's office, an audience of about 20—who paid $5 each—is watching a Swedish film with English, voice-over dubbed dialog. On the giant curved screen made for Cinerama, three teenage boys and girls strip and make long and carefully photographed love. Someone in the audience is snoring.

Marshall McLuhan, in one of his not-uncommon combinations of insight and overgeneralization, once said that in the age of television all other mass media are art forms. The theater film has become that, certainly; the search to find a product which can still make money has liberated in dazzling fashion the imagination and the daring of filmmakers. Everything is changed; the small movie house, located in the suburban shopping center, has become the first-run showcase. The films it books stay as long as they draw audiences; four- to six-week runs are not uncommon. The credits crawl by, and to all but the buff the names are at best vaguely familiar. But the film is there, the form born out of the chaotic transition of a mass medium into a specialized one, and the product is far better than in any other era.

We have talked about the economic aspects of mass media primarily in terms of financial considerations forcing change—change in content, in format, in distribution, most of all in intended audience. In the case of magazines and theater films, we have particularly discussed the impact of television. That impact is not limited to those two media, of course. We have not even discussed here, for example, the changes wrought in radio, which has been transformed largely (and generally profitably) into a localized producer of analgesic background sounds, or else into the service of remarkably specialized and frequently elite audiences. Television has changed all the media while changing very little itself. A backward look over its first quarter-century reveals a surprisingly simple pattern of development. It has grown in terms of audience, hardware, and earnings; its production costs and advertising rates have grown prodigiously, but along predictable paths. The scales of both money and audience have gradually, increasingly limited experimentation in program-making; there is no longer network "time in which to be bad," as Fred Friendly once put it in explaining the early days of broadcast documentaries. One year the Westerns dominate prime time; another, situation comedies; another, medics and cops; and the prime time shows of a few years before fill the days. There are fewer surprises every year. Professional football turns out to be a good television show, and the number of games on television expands geometrically. The backlog of feature films in the movie studios gets thin, or overpriced, or both, and the networks start making their own. They're cheaper, they draw audiences in the same dimension, and if they do well enough, a whole new series may be built upon them. The essential process is growth and a constant refining toward the ultimate mass appeal.

There is nothing surprising about this. No one wants to fool with a successful formula. An elephant learns slowly, but once he learns, he never forgets.

Or almost never.

SECTION THREE
HOW THE WORK
GETS DONE

Journalists frequently cover in great detail the operations of complex modern organizations—the systems of welfare, medical care, and education and the corporate enterprises of transportation and manufacturing—but almost never the ways in which things are done in their own business. It is hard to find that kind of information, even in the memoirs of journalists.

There are several possible reasons. Perhaps journalists do not want to destroy the faint aura of glamour which others see in media jobs. After all, most jobs in the media (as anywhere) are anchored in routine. Once the integration into the routine of the system is complete, one loses his sensitivity. He does not want to risk boring others, talking about what he does on a routine day, and indeed he may find it difficult to describe. There are newscasters who find that the mind has gone blank when the final commercial begins, and copy editors who have to check their logs to see which stories they wrote headlines for in the edition of the paper which just came off the press.

When you are part of a system, it is especially difficult to sense the changes within a structure. They usually occur gradually, and they occur less frequently in the biggest medium, the one which provides most efficiently mild diversion for the bored. For more than two decades the *Saturday Evening Post* and *Ladies Home Journal* had a commanding domination of all media, and they changed so little during that period that the files of one year look like the files of any other. If you're winning big, you may experiment with little flourishes and shuffle the players a bit, but you don't change the game plan.

Thus there are few long-lived series in television. *Variety* compiled a list of 763 nighttime network series from 1950 to 1965. More than half died in one season (a half-season is becoming increasingly common, with new programs introduced in January). Only 35 per cent lasted three years, 13 per cent five years. But their replacements, and the replacement of the replacements, varied remarkably little. It takes around 40 million viewers to keep a prime time network show on the air, and that leaves little room for seeking the original.

The payoffs for handling the formula properly are prodigious. Interestingly, the networks are not the prime beneficiaries; it is sometimes contended that they do little more than break even. The high profits go to individual stations in good markets. There are stations which have made a net profit *yearly* that is approximately equal to their entire investment. A Philadelphia station with tangible assets of $8 million was sold for $53 million. (The networks make their profits through their station ownership; each owns five major market stations.) To look at another dimension, in 1971 the leading television advertiser spent $128 million; the second-biggest $57 million; even the company in 100th place spent $3.5 million. A single one-minute spot on a highly rated film or football game can cost as much as $60,000.

In terms of both audience and money there is one inevitable outcome to playing for and with numbers like that: the tendency to play it cautious, to imitate rather than innovate, to make decisions by committees rather than give the creative man his head. The article which follows spells out in detail how this worked in one case, but it also says much more. It addresses itself to the *spirit* of mass industry and the commitments forced upon the people who work in it.

It also deals with process—with the way the work gets done—at the very first stage. Inherent in most of the material in this section is highly structured, even mechanically bound process: a television news crew at a national convention, the cameraman-producer-director team setting up the shots for a theater film, a reporter working with the desk on a story against a deadline.

But innovation is a process, too, and in many ways is more demanding than those in which the bones are more visible. The following article is the text of a speech given from notes by Lee M. Rich. At the time he delivered it he had ceased being an independent television producer and had become an advertising man. Here he speaks to fellow ad men—and, in a way, to everybody who watches the most mass of all the media.

"SHERIFF WHO?" *

Lee M. Rich

This is a story of a successful television show that didn't get on the air.

Now that might seem like a contradiction. If it didn't get on the air, where is the "success?"

I might be inclined to wonder that myself—especially when I think of the long effort that went into it. The skull sessions. The all-night meetings. The time it took. The money it took. And most of all, the television shows that got on the air instead! You've seen them.

Be that as it may, I still enter the whole venture on the "plus" side of my own mental ledger.

Nobody has ever accused me of a lack of pride, and my involvement with the tv show I'm referring to certainly won't change that. It may sound strange to hear that somebody in this tough, "show-me" business we pursue could be proud of a show that didn't land a network slot. Strange or not, that's the story.

Why? Because this show had the unmitigated audacity to be a little bit different. Because it was self-confident enough to take some good-natured pokes at a few of the sacred cows of tv. Because it didn't rigidly conform to a lot of moth-eaten, so-called "ground rules." Because it showed some independence of spirit—in the whole creative premise of the show, in the way it was played, in not being afraid to flirt with the danger of being original. And those are pretty unrewarding accomplishments in themselves.

Now, I realize as much as anyone that producing television fare for mass viewing is no business for the self indulgent. Just because a program concept is fun to develop (to those doing the developing), just because it's built around an idea that the producers happen to like, is no reason it should get on the air. Our primary and ultimate concern has to be with the audience that will see it, with *their* tastes, *their* interests, *their* attention. What *I* resist is the assumption that the run-of-the-mill, the undistinguished, the masterpieces of me-tooism that we see all too often on the tube, are really what the public wants.

* Reprinted with permission of the author from *Advertising Age,* Nov. 6, 1967.

And I have a hunch that a few of the "experts" agree with me. To illustrate, let me quote part of a review from a recent issue of *Life*. The review points out that while other networks were premiering their new tv shows, NBC televised eight *pilot* shows . . . of a series it had *not* chosen. The review goes on to say:

"The rejected shows in the main seemed as good or as bad as anything else on television. With one exception. That was a show called 'Sheriff Who?' It was not like the average tv series. 'Sheriff Who?' is falling-out-of-your-seat funny. The premise is absolutely original, the pace unflagging, and the sight gags a delight. The story is laid in Blood, Tex., where Evil Roy Slade rules the roost. Played with malevolent glee by John Astin, Evil Roy elbow-jabs cronies, wears four holsters, grabs old ladies' shawls to lay across mud puddles in his path, and dispatches sheriffs with such speed that the undertaker cannot even remember their names at the funeral . . ."

The review continues in that fashion, and then says: "How network programers could fail to appreciate the obviously superior result escapes comprehension."

I'd like to go on reading from this review, but tears keep welling up in my eyes.

On March 8, 1966, Larry Cohen, a writer, was on the Goldwyn lot in Hollywood visiting Quinn Martin to whom he had just sold an idea called, "The Invaders." While waiting for Quinn, Larry told me that he had an idea for a new comedy western that had been brought to him by a friend named Curtis Sanders.

I had been in Hollywood long enough to know that you always listened to any new idea, because a *good* new idea is a most precious commodity.

Larry told me about a program that he called "Sheriff of Nottingham," and the basic idea, as he described it, was the story of a "villain" who lived in and controlled a little town called Nottingham, Tex. Each week the sheriff would be played by a comedy guest star who would hold office for the length of that particular episode and would be disposed of by our villain and/or hero, as we may call him.

I was extremely interested in the idea and asked Larry for a presentation which was delivered a week later. It was 15 pages long and contained six story lines illustrating the basic show idea.

I was entranced by the concept because it was different, it was new, but most importantly, because it could be a very funny and freshly entertaining television show.

Larry Cohen wanted to write it, but I pointed out to him that he really wasn't a comedy writer and that he should allow me to find a writer or writers who were wild enough to write this kind of material. He agreed, and I immediately thought of Jerry Belson and Garry Marshall, who were the fellas I worked with very closely on an ill-fated series titled, "Hey, Landlord." They had written approximately 20 odd episodes of "The Van Dyke Show," for which they won the Writers Guild Best Writing Award, and they were just zany enough to give the right touch to "Sheriff Who?"

So, we closed the deal with Larry Cohen and Curtis Sanders for the purchase of a property titled, "Sheriff of Nottingham." We paid them $5,000 and a royalty of $2,000 per original episode.

As soon as the deal was consummated, I picked up the phone and made a date for lunch with Belson and Marshall. Now, I had to convince them to write the pilot script.

We had lunch, I told them the idea and they literally "flipped"— their facile minds already starting to work. They didn't like the title and added new ideas with the speed of lightning. By the time I got back to my office, and they to theirs, they called and said they wanted to change the title of the show, with my approval, to "Sheriff Who?" which I thought was a great title, and they also wanted to change the name of the town to Blood, Tex.

Obviously, they were agreeing to write the pilot and the second stage was under way. Belson and Marshall received $15,000 to write the pilot script (plus a bonus of $2,500 if the series sold) plus 10% ownership, plus $1,250 per episode as script consultants.

At this point, I picked up the phone to set up a meeting with Mort Werner, vp in charge of programing, NBC, and Grant Tinker who was then in charge of NBC West Coast programing. I met with Mort Werner and Grant Tinker, told them the idea and gave them a copy of the revised presentation which Belson and Marshall had written and retitled.

They read it, called the next day, and wanted to make a deal for the property. Now, let me take some time off here and tell you about the kind of deals the networks want to make. For shows appearing on the air, they demand an ownership position. They will provide (in this particular case) $7,000 towards the cost of the pilot script, and, dependent upon that script, the casting and all the elements, they will decide whether to go to pilot. Therefore, their investment at the beginning is a very minor one both in time and dollars, and they tie up the property for their network.

I should point out to you that when you make your arrangements with the networks, you are negotiating with the business affairs department, which has absolutely no communication with the programing department. They are negotiating for the amount of dollars that they will give you toward the pilot. They will negotiate for what they will pay for the series, what the mix of originals and repeats will be. Needless to say, they try to keep the prices as low as they possibly can, and they always attempt to get residual rights. By residual rights, I mean syndication, distribution and merchandising. The final deal depends on the desirability of the property and the strength of the seller's position.

By Messrs. Tinker's and Werner's tone, they were, to use a Hollywood expression, "very hot on this property." Under those circumstances, we decided to be as tough as we possibly could in our negotiations—although we really weren't in a position of strength, because we needed them more than they needed us.

At this point, let me make some comments about how difficult it is to get a television show to pilot (let alone on the air) and the various methods used by producers to accomplish this:

The tv production business is a series of steps. It is like an old quiz game whose title will not be mentioned here, where you go from one plateau to another, but you don't go to the higher plateau until you have won the lower level. Anywhere along the line you can get killed. I had now gone past Step 1—to the script stage. Step 2 was the networks' acceptance of the script.

Generally, the producer takes a presentation and sends it simultaneously to the three networks, hoping and praying that one of them will want to go to script.

In this instance, I did that and discovered that CBS thought it was a very funny idea, but really it was a little too different for them. At ABC they thought it was very funny, but after all, who really had the courage to send a Lee Rich presentation to New York? I guess they were still mad at me for some reason or other.

On June 1, three months after the idea was born, the pilot script was delivered by Belson and Marshall, and in turn, to Grant Tinker of NBC.

Meanwhile, our negotiations with the NBC's business affairs department are still going on, and we really don't have a firm deal.

But back in the program department, minor script revisions were made and conversations began as to who should be the lead. The name, John Astin, was agreed on with network approval.

We approached John Astin's personal manager, Mace Neufeld, who told us that John really wasn't interested in doing another television series. He had been pretty much disenchanted with "The Addams Family" because the show only ran two years, and he just didn't know if he wanted to do any more television. I talked to Mace at great length and said, "Fine, but why doesn't he read the script?" I had discovered that actors occasionally will say no to a part until they read the script and visualize themselves in that part. I sent the scripts to Mace Neufeld, who called to say it was the funniest script he had ever read and was sending it on to John Astin.

We waited and we waited and we waited. We called Mace Neufeld practically every 20 minutes for John's reaction. All we wanted was an answer. He said that John had the script but hadn't got round to reading it yet. A week later, Mace called and said John thought the script was the funniest script he had read, but still wasn't sure that he wanted to do any television. Belson and Marshall and I made a date for breakfast with John Astin and Mace at the Bel-Air Hotel. We pleaded, cajoled and begged.

John Astin is a very astute, bright, intelligent man, unlike many, many performers, and he gave us many reasons, all valid, why he didn't want to do television. Primarily, the disenchantment he had was with the medium and the people at the networks. I make this point because this disenchantment exists throughout the industry. But John promised to think it over. He did, and agreed to do the pilot and the series.

After prolonged negotiations, we finally made our deal with NBC for the pilot. They agreed to pay us $125,000 toward production of the pilot, for which they received 45% ownership and agreed to give us a series price of $75,000 per original, $16,500 per repeat. Initial purchase would be 16 shows.

With this finally out of the way, back to Astin for more negotiation. We agreed to pay John $6,000 for the pilot, $3,500 per episode —plus residuals.

Now we needed a director. We settled on Jerry Parris, who received $7,500 to direct the pilot, plus a bonus of $2,500 if the series sold. We then cast the other parts, after several weeks of interviewing. Now came the job of making the pilot.

It was time to take all of these elements and put them on film and attempt to sell it to a network as a series. There were many, many things yet to be done.

First, we had to determine the availability of all of our people, the performers, the director, the grips, the camera men, the crew and try to put a timetable together, so that we could get them all in one place and shoot the pilot in time for delivery to the network.

Next, we had to find facilities. We needed a western street that was available at the same time as all of our people. We had to find a stage that was large enough, and yet while we were looking for all of this, we had to be very flexible because one key element had not been determined. That was the guest sheriff.

The script had been written in such a fashion so as to allow us the greatest latitude in casting the guest sheriff. Our first candidate was Dick Van Dyke, who wanted to do it, but who gave us dates that were impossible to meet. Our next choice was Carl Reiner, but he was busy directing his first picture, "Enter Laughing," and that would tie him up for several months. We then went over a list as long as your arm with our casting people, and many of the people were either not available or they just didn't suit the part.

While all of this was going on, the Mirisch Brothers, my partners, were shooting a picture which they would like to forget—"What Did You Do in the War, Daddy?" One of the leads in that picture was Dick Shawn. We had lunch with Dick. He listened to our description of the show, read the script while he was eating, constantly shoving food into his mouth, and not saying one word . . . not laughing . . . not saying anything . . . just eating! He finished, ordered coffee, then just about the time he was finished with his coffee, he finished reading the script, gulped once and said, "I love it—every word of it—I'll do it."

Our troubles were not over, because we now had to adjust his schedule to our schedule. We paid Dick $7,500 for eight days' work, plus round-trip transportation, first class, between New York and Los Angeles, plus $50 a day for living expenses.

With our cast complete, we now needed a western street and finally made a deal with CBS Studio Center to shoot on their lot using the old "Rifleman" street.

It was determined that we would start shooting the pilot on Monday, Oct. 10, and finish Monday, Oct. 17. Readings and rehearsals would start Oct. 5.

Let me point out that this all started on March 8. Now, in October, we were just about ready to shoot some film.

Meetings were taking place with set designers, property men, costumers, camera men, directors, and they continued, and they continued, and they continued, because as soon as you got something nailed down, something became unnailed. But somehow, things fell into place. There was just one thing that was not tied down, but we were going full steam ahead. We had not decided definitely yet whether to have our "tag" scene indicate who next week's sheriff was going to be. We decided we would wait and make that decision dependent upon whom we could get.

Some coincidences occurred. Our director, Jerry Parris, was in negotiation with Columbia Pictures to direct Jerry Lewis' next movie. We decided to ask Jerry Lewis to play that tag scene.

We paid Muscular Dystrophy $1,000 in Jerry Lewis' name to do this. He was prepared and he did a great job.

I'm going to spend very little time on the days between Oct. 5 and Oct. 17, because everything went just beautifully. The cast was happy. We were on time. Our dailies looked great and there was joy in the world.

The pilot was shot, the cost of the pilot was on budget: $200,000. We saw the first rough cut of the pilot. Keep in mind that you prepare 24 minutes of film for a half-hour of television show. You try to make a pilot as close to that as possible, and perhaps you go five or six minutes over. Our first rough cut was approximately 11 minutes over.

We spent literally hundreds of hours in the cutting room and in the projection room cutting the film down and editing it. It was tedious, but a very important job.

In my opinion, a television show or a motion picture must have three elements to make it successful. An apology to my wife, who is an actress, but I believe the three most important elements are writing, direction and cutting . . . with writing and cutting the most important.

We had the final rough cut on Oct. 28. It was 29½ minutes long, but it was great.

We now needed music and for $1,000 hired Nelson Riddle to compose and conduct the pilot music for "Sheriff Who?"

(At this point, you are probably delightfully surprised that there is some element in a pilot which costs as little as $1,000.)

Finally, on Nov. 16, the final answer print was delivered.

It was eight months since we had started. After eight months and a lot of work and a lot of headaches, I must say that whether the show got on the air or didn't, we were all very proud of what we saw.

Now we come to that part of this saga which has put many gray hairs into the few I have left, which has made me shed many tears and make me cry in my pillow many a night. It is the part of attempting to sell the networks on putting the pilot on the air.

While we were making the pilot, NBC had a change of personnel. Matter of fact, it happened in two phases. Mr. Tinker was transferred to New York and Mr. Herb Schlosser, an old friend who was in charge of public affairs, was put in charge of West Coast tv programing.

Then, Mr. Tinker, after being transferred to New York, decided to resign and return to the sunny climes of California. While we were involved in the pilot, preparing and producing it, we had absolutely no interference from the network. They had the normal rights of approval of casting, which they were just fine about, and the only times we heard from them was when they asked how it was going, and when would it be ready to look at.

Approximately two weeks after the pilot was completed, I received a call from Mr. Mort Werner, vp in charge of programing, asking if he could look at a rough cut. I dislike showing people rough cuts because it takes a very discerning eye to really appreciate and understand them. But after all, he was my partner, and after all, he was the network. So, come morning, at 8 o'clock, on a very unsunny California day, I showed Mort Werner a rough cut of "Sheriff Who?" in the Goldwyn Studios' Projection Room A.

He laughed and said it was just a "great pilot" and asked when I would be delivering the answer print to New York.

If I remember correctly, our date for delivery was set at about Feb. 1. Now, one of the great problems in attempting to sell a television pilot is to determine the most propitious time to deliver the pilot to the network. You don't want to be too early because then they will delay answering until they see the rest of their product, and you don't want to be too late because by that time, they may have their schedule completely locked in.

We now finished the pilot, and on Feb. 6, 1967, NBC tested it. You probably have heard about these tests. The picture was shown under proper research conditions, in front of an audience who, in turn, indicates its preference or dislike. In our case, we have a very acceptable testing score.

On Feb. 10, I showed it to Herb Schlosser and his group of West Coast program executives. After the screening, I was walking on air! They thought it was by far the best and funniest pilot they had ever seen. What I didn't realize was they really couldn't get me arrested. They laughed and enjoyed it, but they weren't going to make the decision. On Sunday, Feb. 19, I brought the show to New York. On Monday, Feb. 20, I showed the film to a group of NBC programing executives in New York. Mr. Werner and Mr. Durgin, the president of the network, did not see the show at this screening.

The executives to whom I showed the picture laughed in the same manner as their counterparts had on the West Coast. They even went a little further. There was no question in their minds that this show was going to be on the air. Needless to say, I was now 50 ft. in the air!

But again, I should have realized that either they would have no opinion or what they said would mean little, if anything.

I took myself off to "21," the 52nd St. rumor factory, and hung around the bar and talked to other producers, told one another that we heard their shows were great, and when they were out of earshot, said to each other, "I hear he has a dog on his hands."

Some of this may be out of context. While all this was going on, you're getting calls from program or media heads from various agencies, asking whether you'll show them your pilot. Not that they want to buy it, or can buy it, but they want to see the film so they then can pick up the phone, call their clients and say, "I just saw this film . . . nobody else has seen it." You, as a seller, are in a quandary as to whether to show them the picture or not.

Let me get on with the story. On Tuesday, Feb. 21, at approximately 4 o'clock, I showed the picture to Mr. Don Durgin. His comments were very guarded. He thought it was very funny, but wondered about whether it wasn't just a little bit violent in several areas. I assured him that the picture was five minutes too long, and any violence could be cut.

I must state at this time, I would have promised him anything. I would have changed the title or anything else. You must remember that I had been working on this pilot for almost one year, and we wanted it on the air.

I left the pilot at the National Broadcasting Co., and from there on, I was in their hands. They assured me that they now would use their discretion to show it to various clients. I told them that I was available and would do anything I possibly could to aid in the sale. They promised to enlist my help.

The two weeks that I spent in New York at that time were the two most demeaning weeks in my entire life. You wouldn't have minded getting an answer of, "No, I'm sorry, it isn't going to make it." But not getting answers and getting statements like, "I think it's a great pilot, but it's too original" . . . "It's never been done before, I'm afraid the public isn't ready for it" . . . "I'm afraid the public won't get it." It's that kind of thinking that made me as unhappy as one human being could ever be.

The weather in New York was typical winter weather, and I ran around and ran around—had lunches, meetings, attempting to get somebody to go along with the show. Attempting to get an answer from the networks as to whether they would take the pilot and put it on the air or not. One of the top executives of NBC told me it was the best pilot that they had seen, but he didn't know whether it was going to get on the air or not because of other commitments that they had made.

I thought I had an ace up my sleeve because purely by error, NBC had a series option on this pilot until March 1, 1967, which really is unheard of, because they usually make sure that their option is for a much longer period of time.

On Thursday, March 2, I showed the picture to the top executives at CBS television. The comment from the head of their program department was as follows: "It was the second best pilot we have seen this year, next to our own, 'He and She,' but our program schedule is locked."

That afternoon, I showed it to the head of programing at ABC who said, "It was a great pilot, but we didn't think it could make a series."

I can only say that these executives are the same people who selected the smashing new programs that are on the air today.

In addition to these network showings, I was taking the picture to various agencies who told me that they thought it was a great pilot but in typical fashion, did nothing about it. On Friday, March 3, I had had it! I felt that there was no more I could do. I took a plane, went back to California, as low as one individual could possibly be. I must say that if I had been told anywhere that it wasn't any good, or somebody didn't like it, or the show wasn't going on the air, I could have understood. But being told by everyone that they loved it and getting no answers because nobody really wanted to make a decision, was about as tough a thing to take as you probably can take.

I arrived home and told my partners in as cheerful a way as I possibly could that we were still in the ball game, but there just was no decision. I really don't think I fooled them.

To end this part of the saga, some months later, NBC decided to pick up another option and ordered three scripts, which are being written, and then came the *Life* article.

Well, here we are.

I maintain that an attitude prevails in network television today that makes everybody so concerned with staying afloat, they don't have time to swim. So much effort goes into trying to stay in the middle of the stream, with avoiding anything that's really unique, with making certain that a decision cannot be attributed to you, they don't have a chance to swim away from the pack and open up some new creative areas. They're afraid of getting in over their heads with shows that have the audacity to be different. They're afraid to get their feet wet in anything that might be "polluted" with originality. They're afraid somebody—an advertiser, a client, an executive—will throw cold water on their innovations. Afraid, afraid, afraid.

In this climate of concern, it's no wonder that the first rule of self-preservation reads: "Don't go near the water."

There is a footnote. NBC later used the concept (and star John Astin) for a new pilot, aired in February, 1972, under the title, *Evil Roy Slade.* Again, it did not make the grade. Rich's name was not in the credits, but it was included as an in-joke in the dialogue. When Evil Roy decided to go straight and change his name, one of those he pondered aloud was Evil Lee Rich. Surely, out of the thousands and thousands of viewers across the land that Friday night, only a handful could appreciate the point of it.

It takes time, months and years of it, to produce television pilots, movies, and books, and that leisurely scheduling is one thing that sets those media apart from news media; nonetheless, the working processes do much to shape any medium.

Magazines make up the most varied group in mass communication, ranging from *Boot and Shoe Recorder,* to *Mad,* from *The Partisan Review* to *Playboy;* it is therefore not surprising that within the magazine field are the widest variations in staff structure and process. Perhaps the system which has been most connected with successful magazines is that of the strong-minded editor who runs the show to please himself, who puts his product on the market and fails, or who succeeds on the basis of how many people share his tastes. Edward Bok, during the years in which the *Ladies Home Journal* was growing into the first genuinely mass magazine, was almost totally responsible for final judgment about what went into the magazine; so was his stablemate (and bitter competitor) George Lorimer of the *Saturday Evening Post.* So was DeWitt Wallace, of the *Reader's Digest,* who has been described as the most sure-fire reflector of mass taste who ever worked as an editor; during the formative years he and his wife were totally responsible for choosing what the *Digest* carried. So, in a quite different league, was the great Harold Ross of the *New Yorker,* who not only conceded to other publications the little old ladies from Dubuque, but also edited almost literally every syllable of his magazine, quarreling in irascible marginalia with the syntax and word choice of some of the best writers alive. Even *Time,* long regarded as a kind of apogee of group journalism, was in its early years marked to an astonishing degree by the idiosyncrasies of a long-dead genius, Britton Hadden. His imprint still is on its pages.

As the physical dimensions of the job became too great for the Wallaces and Lorimers, they delegated decision-making roles to staff members who had demonstrated the faithfulness of their imitations of the great man's ways. By the end of his long editorship, Lorimer had created a whole staff of editors, each of whom was autonomous, a little Lorimer in himself. A promising new writer was assigned to one of these editors, and he seldom had contact with anybody else on the staff; his own editor made all the decisions about use or rejection of material and about rates of pay. These men shared so much a mutual vision of what the magazine should be in the 1930's and '40's that it still read as if it were edited by a single man.

Most magazines, other than specialized business or professional publications, begin with this kind of one-man thrust. An influential political journal, *I. F. Stone's Weekly,* stayed that way; when Stone's age and health made it difficult for him to research, write, and edit it all, he simply closed the magazine down in 1971. Most founders are not like Stone or Lorimer or Ross, however, and the editorial structure changes—sometimes quickly—as acceptance grows. *Better Homes & Gardens,* leader of the chain of Meredith magazines, began with the strong personal stamp of the man who was Woodrow Wilson's Secretary of Agriculture, but moved steadily to a kind of committee system. *Better Homes'* staff is divided into topical sections (for example, food and recipes, gardening, furniture, home repair), each headed by an editor who has a small staff. In issue-planning meetings each editor presents the plans for his section; there is general discussion, suggestions are heard from other editors and the art director, and a general consensus is worked out. There is a chief editor, and obviously the way he plays his role reflects his personality, but there have been successful *BH & G* editors who functioned essentially as committee chairmen, and low-key ones at that.

Magazines which do not have section editors often circulate manuscripts around the editorial staff, and general agreement is required before the piece is used. *Life* at its peak was directed by strong editors; the system gave them a final say after the staff had made preliminary decisions. Closing day was a process of showing proposed layouts and photos to the top man, who either accepted them or improvised changes. *Time* has yet another version of group journalism, in which field investigation is done by a staff of correspondents; library research and general synthesizing by what the magazine calls "researchers," who also have final responsibility for all matters of factual accuracy; and the actual putting of words on paper by a third group, the writers. The system was based originally on the idea that the writer must not get too deeply involved in his story, lest it blur his vision, and there are stories, probably apocryphal, about early-day staff writers who were fired because they went to see an event about which they were going to write. That kind of detachment is breaking down, but the tripartite system still works (and is one of the reasons, incidentally, why there are no bylines in standard *Time* stories; there are too many people involved to credit one of them).

A trend among magazines which has risen along with the committee approach to editing is the rise of total control of content. In an earlier day, a sizable amount of material in general magazines was contributed by freelance writers who lived all over the world. It would be only a slight overstatement to say that Lorimer never knew what the next issue of the *Post* would look like until he opened the mail. The bulk of magazine fiction, in particular, was contributed by freelancers, and a majority of the articles in the general magazines would be proposed in outline form by the writer or his agent and approved by the editor—who might not have even realized, 10 minutes before, that there was a possible article in that particular subject.

The change came as the big magazines lost their mass character and the drive for more definable audiences grew, and as costs made too risky the dickering with whimsical individualists who saw themselves artists. Several years before its death the *Saturday Evening Post* stopped accepting unsolicited manuscripts. The Luce publications never were a freelance market, of course, nor was the *Reader's Digest,* although it does commission original articles which it then plants in such publications as *The Rotarian.*

The common practice in the industry today is planning from the top down. The editor and his staff decide what they want, often in great detail and sometimes including even the fiction (of which there is very little, in any event). Staff writers will prepare some, and proven professionals will be assigned the rest. The day of the free-spirited magazine freelance (perhaps F. Scott Fitzgerald, if quality of work is a consideration, was simultaneously the most typical and the greatest of the lot) is gone. He, too, has been replaced by consensus judgments—and busy research departments which constantly check readership and may even pretest possible articles.

The editing of books and magazines involves less hardware than most processes in the media. Using the mechanical tools—cameras, microphones, telephones, and computers—as effectively as possible is both a limitation and a stimulating challange, and there is one constant requirement: that their use be programed in advance.

In the case of the feature theatrical film, the content is established, the time dimension not so pressing, and the planning more adapted to the situation. Lillian Ross described the "Old Hollywood" process in her now-classic *Picture,* which documented the filming of *Red Badge of Courage* by MGM. The following selection is, essentially, an account of a small group of professionals planning to use the motion picture camera in the "New Hollywood." Author John Gregory Dunne spent most of 1967 observing the activities at Twentieth Century-Fox to gather material for his book.

PLANNING TO SHOOT A MOVIE *

John Gregory Dunne

As the script for *The Boston Strangler* neared completion, director Richard Fleischer and producer Robert Fryer flew back and forth to Boston scouting exterior and necessary interior locations. At the Studio, Stan Hough's production department worked out the final details of the budget. When he was in Los Angeles, Fryer spent hours every day in a Studio projection room looking at footage of actors being considered for parts in *The Boston Strangler*. A few days after Edward Anhalt turned in the final draft of his screenplay, the script was mimeographed and distributed to all the Studio department heads so that they could make a final estimate of the costs their departments would incur on the picture. The correlation of the below-the-line costs was overseen by Hough and Doc Merman. One Thursday afternoon Merman called the *Strangler* production staff and the Studio department heads together for a final budget meeting.

The meeting took place in the conference room of the production bungalow. Fryer, Fleischer and Merman sat at the head of the T-shaped conference table and the rest of the thirty or so conferees sat down on either side of the table. Everyone in the room was given a mimeographed production breakdown of each of *The Boston Stranger*'s 90 sequences and 256 scenes. The breakdown was titled "THE BOSTON STRANGLER—STORY 147—PRODUCER: ROBERT FRYER —DIRECTOR: RICHARD FLEISCHER." Exery sequence in the script had been broken down into its basic elements—set, location, major cast members, bit players, extras and animals (if necessary), special props, special effects and sequence plot synopsis.

Merman tapped his glasses on the table and brought the meeting to order. "The first problem," he said, "is what is the last year in the time sequence of the story?"

"1964," Fleischer said.

"So in any street scenes, we can't have cars later than 1964 models," Merman said. "Right?"

---

* Reprinted from *The Studio* (New York: Farrar, Straus & Giroux, 1969).
© Copyright John Gregory Dunne, 1968, 1969.

"Right," Fleischer said.

"And they weren't wearing miniskirts in 1964," Merman said. "So we're going to have to watch that in the crowd scenes."

Fleischer nodded.

Merman went through the breakdown page by page. Occasionally there was a discussion of potential problems within the individual sequences:

PAGE NO. 7

SET: INT/EXT POLICE CAR—PARKING LOT OF BAR

LOCATION: STUDIO

CAST: JOE

BITS: CLOE

SPECIAL PROP: POLICE CAR, AUTOS FOR PARKING LOT, NEWSPAPER

SYNOPSIS: CLOE INFORMS JOE OF CARR'S STRANGE SEX HABITS

"Let's do that right here at the Studio on the French street," Fleischer said.

"There's not enough room there for a parking lot," Merman said.

Fleischer folded his hands on the table in front of him. He stared straight ahead, quiet, almost dreamlike, not looking at Merman. "It doesn't have to be a parking lot," he said. "We can dress the French street to make it look like a Boston alley."

PAGE NO. 9

SET: INT HOMICIDE SECTION—POLICE HEADQUARTERS

LOCATION: STUDIO

CAST: WILLIS, BRANDY, MC AFEE, JOE

BITS: NEWSMAN #1

SYNOPSIS: WILLIS DISCUSSES CRIME WITH REPORTER—ANOTHER
        KILLING REPORTED

"Is this going to be an exact replica of Boston Homicide?" Merman said.

Fryer shook his head. "No, they wouldn't let us in to get any pictures. The Boston cops didn't like the way they came off in the book, so they're not giving us any help."

"You should go to Boston, get yourself arrested and take pictures with a Minox, Robert," Merman said, his beagle features breaking into a grin. "Isn't that what a creative producer does?"

"Let's just build a set," Fleischer said.

"How about using the standing set we've got for *Felony Squad?*" Merman said. "It's nice and modern."

"Because it's an old police station in Boston," Fleischer said.

Merman threw up his hands. "So who knows from an old police station?"

"Me," Fleischer said.

"Okay," Merman said. "I was just trying to save you some money."

PAGE NO. 24
SET: INT ATTORNEY GENERAL'S OFFICE
LOCATION
CAST: EDWARD BROOKE, BOTTOMLY
SPECIAL PROPS: ICED TEA, SCOTCH
SYNOPSIS: BROOKE TRIES UNSUCCESSFULLY TO ENLIST BOTTOMLY
         IN INVESTIGATION

Merman blanched when he saw the scene was going to be shot on location. "It's an interior," he said. "Why not build a set and shoot it here?"

"No," Fleischer said. "You don't get the same feeling, the desk, the chairs, the mementos."

"We can take pictures," Merman said strenuously. "Duplicate it here."

"Uh-uh," Fleischer said.

"When do you expect to use this office?" Merman said. "When the attorney general's out taking a leak in the men's room?"

"On a Saturday," Fleischer said.

Merman looked down the table at Fryer for assstance. "I don't want to interefere with your creative talents, Mr. Producer, but you've got four and a half pages of dialogue in this scene," Merman said. "That's a long day's work and Mr. Director says you'll be working on Saturday. Well, I've got to remind you, Mr. Producer, Saturday is double time. You build a set here, you're saving money."

"Let's spend it," Fleischer said.

PAGE NO. 43
SET: INT BLUE FALCON BAR
LOCATION
CAST: BOTTOMLY
BITS: LAURENCE SHAW, HAROLD, CEDRIC
EXTRAS: HOMOSEXUALS (MALE, FEMALE), BARTENDERS, WAITERS
SPECIAL PROPS: DRINKS
SYNOPSIS: SHAW EXPLAINS TO BOTTOMLY HIS SEXUAL ARRANGE-
         MENT WITH MISS RIDGEWAY—BOTTOMLY SHOCKED

"Why not build that one here?" Merman said.

"I'd rather use a real location and real faggots," Fleischer said. He smiled benignly down the table at Merman.

"Well, I guess they must have a faggot bar somewhere in Boston," Merman said.

"I want to do as many interiors on location as possible," Fleischer said. "You get a better feeling, a better sense of place. If we have an interior where there's a lot of people, which means a lot of staging and a lot of camera movements, we'll do it here. You can get more control on a stage. Otherwise, if there's just a small group of people, I'd rather use the real thing on location."

PAGE NO. 50
SET: EXT PROVIDENCE AIRPORT
LOCATION
CAST: MC AFEE, BRANDY, BOTTOMLY, JOE, PETER HURKOS, JIM
      CRANE
EXTRAS: AIRPORT EMPLOYEES
SPECIAL PROPS: JET AIRCRAFT, POLICE CARS
SYNOPSIS: AS STAFF WAITS TO PICK UP HURKOS, MC AFEE BRIEFS
          BRANDY ON NEW SUSPECT O'BRIEN—THEY PICK UP
          HURKOS

"We'll freeze our ass off if we shoot this in Providence in the middle of winter," said Buck Hall, Fleischer's assistant director.

Fleischer nodded. "Let's use a local location," he said. "Santa Monica Airport, maybe. We can spread some snow around and make it look like winter." He stared off into space, reflecting for a moment. "What airlines fly into Providence anyway?"

"Eastern and American," Eric Stacey, the *Strangler's* unit production manager, said. "But I don't think Providence was a jet airport in 1964. So Hurkos would have had to come in on an Electra and American isn't using them anymore."

"Eastern still uses them, but Eastern doesn't fly into L.A.," the representative from the prop department said.

"That means we're going to have to find an Electra and paint it," Stacey said. "That gets expensive. It might be cheaper to shoot the scene in Providence."

Everyone at the table looked at Fleischer. He shook his head slowly. "Negative," he said finally. "We use all the same actors in the next scene in the Providence motel room. That's a set we're building here at the Studio. If we shoot the airport scene in Providence, we've got to keep all the actors on the payroll until we fly them out here for the motel room scene. And *that* gets expensive.

So let's find an Electra—I think Western uses them—paint it and use one of the local airports."

PAGE NO. 68
SET: EXT STREET IN FRONT OF TAYLOR'S APARTMENT
LOCATION
CAST: ALBERT, MR. TAYLOR
BITS: POLICEMEN (2), STUNTMAN FOR FALL?
EXTRAS: PEDESTRIANS, MOTORISTS (30)
SPECIAL PROPS: POLICE CAR
SYNOPSIS: ALBERT RUNS THROUGH STREETS, ALLEYS, ETC., PUR-
         SUED BY POLICE AND MR. TAYLOR—IS FINALLY CAP-
         TURED

Fleischer tapped the breakdown with a pencil. "What do you mean only thirty extras, Doc?" he said impatiently. "This is a main city thoroughfare and the shot covers two blocks. Are you trying to tell me that in the middle of the day in Boston you're only going to find thirty people on the street? Come on, Doc. We need 130 extras anyway, and even that's not enough. Make it 150."

PAGE NO. 80
SET: EXT FRONT OF STATLER AND DEPARTMENT STORE WINDOW
LOCATION
CAST: ALBERT, ANNA SLESERS
EXTRAS: PARADE SPECTATORS—MEN, WOMEN
SPECIAL PROPS: CARS
SYNOPSIS: ALBERT RE-CREATES SEEING ANNA SLESERS—FOLLOW-
         ING HER—GOING THROUGH STORE WINDOW AFTER HER

Fleischer pressed his hands against his temples. "I think we've got to shoot that here," he said. "You set up outside a department store at midday, you've got a madhouse. We need control." He thought for a moment. "How about using the New York street at Metro?"

"That's $6,000 a day," Merman said. "Are you sure you can't shoot it in Boston?"

"Sure I can shoot it, Doc," Fleischer said. "But you start tying up a main drag, it will take four weeks to shoot."

"If we're going to spend $6,000 a day, I'd rather build a set here," Merman said.

"Sure, if you can do it, fine," Fleischer said. "I'm not in love with the idea of giving Metro money. But let's keep the idea on the back burner."

When machines came along with their capacity to multiply one man's effort, a whole new level of complexity developed in all production processes. It is not coincidental that the rise of mass-circulation daily newspapers came with the industrial revolution. What is stranger is that newspapers changed so little in their production and circulation techniques. Except for learning how to use such gadgets as a Linotype machine, a colonial printer would have felt fairly much at home in a midtwentieth century newspaper printing plant. Newspapers have recorded the rise of technology, but they have taken little advantage of it until recently.

As in all other businesses, time has come to mean money. Whatever is done has to be done in a hurry, which means a simple but profound change for people: there is no time to argue. This means behavior has to be predictable, which in turn means that the newcomer to a newsroom has to adapt to a consensus which nobody can define but which one learns through experience; it means that news comes in incremental categories, that it must resemble what has already been in the papers; and it means personal relationships must function with a minimum of friction and a maximum of unspoken understanding. All these things taken together, since people are people, have encouraged the development of the authoritarian newsroom, against which is developing some of the rebellion described in the next section of this book.

The details of one aspect of this complicated, fast-moving process is sharply set out in the description which follows. It is excerpted from a book by Theodore Bernstein of the New York *Times.* Bernstein is not only the best-known copy editor of his era but, alas, probably the only one who's known at all. His description is based, understandably, on the *Times,* but the process is not all that different on smaller papers.

HOW THE NEWS GETS INTO THE PAPERS *

Theodore M. Bernstein

In a nebulous sort of way the public knows that newspapers are published in one hell of a hurry. But this nebulous impression comes

* Reprinted from *More Language That Needs Watching* (New York: Channel Press, 1962). © Copyright Theodore M. Bernstein, 1962.

chiefly from movie and television offerings. And what is the picture presented in those offerings? Scoop Smith (in real life his name more probably would be Arnold Dittenhouse) covers the big story, sometimes even taking a few notes. He bursts into the news room and orders the city editor to "hold the front page" (he always knows instinctively that he has the day's lead story). He shucks his jacket, but never his hat. He twists a sheet of copy paper into his typewriter and, never referring to those notes he took, he starts rattling out the story. You see it crawling from his typewriter: "When is District Attorney Sam Shwabisher going to forget politics long enough to go after the real murderer of Pauline Hamilton? When are the corrupt police going to clap the handcuffs on Butch Glonsky? How long will it take. . . ." By this time the city editor, eyes aglow, is looking at Scoop's clattering typewriter. "Great stuff!" he exclaims. "I'll write the head for it." (The implication is that Scoop doesn't need to stop to perform that chore himself.) The next thing you know (without any intervening processes except the snatching of the copy by the blond, toothy copy boy), we are looking over the shoulder of a pressman at a crisp copy of the "Extra," while in the background the papers are cascading off the press. There in big type stretched across eight columns of the front page is the head the city editor wrote: "HAMILTON MURDER STILL UNSOLVED!" (The newspaper that would print that eight-column head is the one that would proclaim, "PRESIDENT McKINLEY STILL DEAD!") Scoop gets a Pulitzer Prize and marries the girl ("SCOOP SMITH WEDS CHILDHOOD SWEETHEART!"). Swelling music. "The End."

If a newspaper were really put out that way, it would have few readers, plenty of libel suits and certainly no Pulitzer Prizes. About the only things true to life in that picture are the typwriter, the presses and the speed. The production of a real newspaper involves a great deal more organization, much more work, much greater care and, above all, editing—the forgotten ingredient in virtually all dramatizations.

Let's get down to earth and see what really happens.

It is mid-afternoon and the office of the morning newspaper is quiet except for the typewriters of a few rewrite men tapping out short stories of routine events. The man covering police headquarters phones the city desk to report a rather large theft of uncut diamonds from a dealer's office—"Looks like a pretty fair story." Should he cover it or does the city desk want to assign another reporter to the story? He is instructed to remain on his beat. Arnold Dittenhouse

draws the assignment. He is told the nature of the story and goes
to work.

From the headquarters man Arnold picks up the basic facts by
phone. A diamond merchant, Gregory Lee, has reported the loss of
$100,000 worth of uncut stones from the safe in his office at 1661
Sixth Avenue. Lee says the stones were there the previous afternoon
but were gone this morning. The police have questioned everyone
in the office except a clerk ("Haven't got his name, but the precinct
cops can give it to you"). The clerk has not been questioned because
he left on a two-week vacation last night and no one seems to know
where he is.

Arnold next travels to the precinct station house and buttonholes
a detective on the case. He learns that the clerk is Julius Feinguy,
22 years old, who rooms with a family named Fickett in Queens
Village. He also discovers that the F.B.I. is investigating because
of a suspicion that the diamonds may have been transported across
state lines. Do the police suspect anything phony about the case—
a staged theft to collect insurance or anything like that? No, they do
not. Was the safe jimmied open or blown open? No, there were no
signs that it had been tampered with in any way. Then it looks like
an inside job, doesn't it? The police are offering no theory about
it just yet.

A visit to Lee's office seems to be in order so that Arnold can
at least get some idea of the physical layout. At the Sixth Avenue
address the reporter is fortunate enough to find Lee in his office.
He thus is able, in addition, to gather a few details about the personal appearance of the distraught, bespectacled, round little man
who has suddenly found himself a figure in the news. Arnold is
curious about how the safe was opened. Lee suggests the possibility
that he may have left it open and unwatched very briefly the previous
afternoon when he stepped into another room to answer a phone
call. He has nothing else to add to what Arnold already knows.

At this point the reporter phones the city desk to report how the
story shapes up and to see whether the office has any further information that would require outside checking before he returns. Time
is getting shorter now, and he is told to come in.

Back at his desk, Arnold knows there are still one or two angles
to be explored. There is also one piece of routine that he senses he
must still perform, but for the life of him he can't recall what it is.
He phones the F.B.I. press officer, but, as he expected, learns nothing except that the investigators would like to question Feinguy.
No, they cannot say where they are looking for him.

Next he searches through the phone book for the Ficketts. (What is that piece of routine he has overlooked?) Mrs. Fickett tells him what she knows about her roomer, Feinguy, which is not much. No, she doesn't know his home town or where he went on vacation.

Ah, yes, that piece of routine. Send to the newspaper morgue to see if there are any clippings on Feinguy. Not very hopeful, but you never can tell. While he is waiting, he organizes his notes. At last the copy boy hands him the slim folder from the morgue. It contains a single small clipping: A five-year-old dispatch from St. Louis relates that Julius Feinguy, 17, won a city-wide essay contest. St. Louis? An angle, perhaps.

It is getting late, but Arnold now has a couple of more phone calls to make. First he checks back to headquarters. Are the police looking for Feinguy in St. Louis? The police won't say. Arnold drags out a St. Louis phone book. There's a chance. Feinguy is an unusual name. He finds a number and puts through a call. Yes, this is Julius Feinguy's mother. No, Julius hasn't been there. No one else has phoned, but a detective did visit her to ask the same question. What is it all about? Thanks, Mrs. Feinguy.

Arnold decides to let his paper's resident correspondent approach the St. Louis police and puts in a call for him. Meanwhile, he has a story and probably an exclusive angle. It is time to begin writing. He checks with the city desk to inform the editors about the story and to get instructions about how much to write. He returns to his desk, feeds some paper into his typewriter and begins. He must hurry, he knows. The deadline is an hour and a half away. But it will take him perhaps an hour to write the story. And it has been drummed into him that every story that is to appear in the paper cannot go to the composition room at the deadline, because if that happened the paper would never be printed. So he writes as rapidly as he can, sending the story to the desk in short sections, or "takes." He pauses only to consult his notes and to take a call from the St. Louis correspondent. Out rolls the story, take after take.

What has happened up to this point is the exercise of the creative faculty of newspapering. The city desk and the reporter combine to bring the story into being. The reporter, now working at top speed, is almost completely preoccupied with his subject matter. Many fine points of writing, of presentation, even of accuracy may escape him. But he is backstopped. The critical faculty is now brought into play on the copy desk. His story is passed to a copy editor. Except for the news editor and his assistants, who oversee in a general way everything that goes into the newspaper but obviously cannot read closely all the thousands and thousands of words, the copy editor exercises final responsibility.

Let's call him Harold Aufseher. The diamond story is now in his hands. He has been told by the city desk how long the story is to be. As a practiced editor, Hal knows that Arnold probably will exceed his limit (most reporters understandably do that) and so he is on the alert to trim out the soft spots as he proceeds. In addition he will try to tighten the wording wherever he can to save precious space. When the reporter writes, "one of the employes," Hal will condense it to "an employe"; when the reporter writes that the police "rushed to the scene," Hal will strike out the phrase as an unnecessary and self-evident detail. In the second paragraph he discovers an involved fifty-word sentence; he breaks it into two short, clear sentences. When he reads that "the tray with its little bags and boxes of stones were missing from the safe," he almost automatically corrects the grammatical error. He sends the lead to the composing room and picks up the next take.

Here he finds that Arnold has inadvertently begun to refer to Gregory Lee as "Mr. Gregory." Rather than interrupt the reporter he checks in the phone book to make sure of the man's name. However, when he notes that there has been no elaboration of the statement in the lead about "$100,000 worth of uncut diamonds, ranging up to nine carats in weight," he decides he will have to interrupt the reporter. "Who made the evaluation—the dealer, the police, the insurance company?" He returns to his desk and inserts the necessary information.

Next he deletes a quotation from Mr. Lee: "I always thought there was something a little shady about Feinguy." Libelous. He also deletes a quotation from Mrs. Fickett: "He was careless personally—fingernails always dirty and that sort of thing." Poor taste and irrelevant.

Smoothly and swiftly, his critical faculties always on the alert, Hal makes his way through the story. As he goes, he writes subheads in the copy—those little headings of boldface type that are inserted to break up long stretches of gray type. And as he goes, he is trying to resolve in his mind what the headline should say. When the story is finished, he tackles the head. His job here is to condense the main news of Arnold's 600-word story into half a dozen words.

Arnold has been writing under pressure; Hal has been editing under pressure. Each has a multitude of things to keep in mind. The story, as it presently appears in the paper, is as accurate as they can make it; it is a smooth, lucid job of narrative and exposition, and it may even have some literary quality. Both have worked hard, if hastily, to make it a finished piece of news writing. For Hal, incidentally, it is only one of a dozen or more stories he has processed before deadline. He has had to switch his attention rapidly from robbery to rocketry, from budgets to bullets, from grand slams to great slums, from racket busters to filibusters. Is it extraordinary, then, that something has eluded him, that he has allowed a mistake to slip into print? It is perhaps not excusable, but it is at least understandable.

Bernstein's reporter and desk man represent a critical part of the process in a big daily, but their interaction is far from all of it. The reporter on the police beat was the first newsman in the chain, and decisions remain to be made after Hal has finished copy-editing and writing subheads and the headline, particularly in terms of placement—what spot on what page. Somebody may even overrule Hal's judgment about how long the story should be and cut it in half when he starts to put the page together.

The prototype reporter in this episode has had almost no chance to put his personal stamp on the jewel-theft story; essentially he is a professional going through a complex, tightly paced series of steps which produce a predictable product. The conventional assignment reporter working off the city desk in many papers is perhaps the most completely structured professional in communications (which is not to say that it is a bad job; there are great satisfactions, both intellectual and psychological, in managing complex routine well).

As a comparison, it may be instructive to look at a quite different kind of reporter, the kind who is potentially most free of the requirements of structure and process.

Consider the foreign correspondent, the most romantic of all journalistic figures. By most estimates, there are 350 to 450 of these knights errant reporting for American wire services, networks, trade publishers (McGraw-Hill has one of the largest teams), and the handful of individual newspapers willing to spend the $50,000 or so a year it costs to keep the correspondent and his bureau going. Assume he is in Belgrade, or Teheran, or Lisbon, or Rio de Janiero, or some city of similar middling newsworthiness, since if he is in Paris or London, he is one of many in a press corps and in a situation much like a reporter back home.

All these media may employ native "stringers" or correspondents to keep them abreast of what might happen in Tirane, Baranquilla, or Addis Ababa. In a similar vein, metropolitan papers, wire services, and stations use stringers to cover outlying towns in the United States.

As the sensory apparatus for one of the world's major distributors of news a correspondent has a prodigious responsibility. It is through his eyes and mind that hundreds of thousands (in the case of the wire services, millions) will see and understand all they know of Iran, Yugoslavia, Portugal, or Colombia. The foreign desk in the home office may direct him to some stories, and there will be others which are automatic because they are of a major importance, but most of the time he will be working under a set of restraints different from, but just as binding as, good old Arnold Dittenhouse.

Begin with the fact that every newsman wants his work to get into print or on the air, the longer and more frequently the better. The material he files has to beat down a lot of competition; his paper or his agency is getting three to ten times as much copy as it can publish.

The first requirement, then, is that he define news as the desk at home defines it. This is not just a matter of ego fulfillment; despite any reassurances, if he sends back material that isn't used over a long period of time, he is bound to worry about his job.

This means, in most cases, that he will send the stories which spell out some kind of conflict (the most common denominator of news), and furthermore conflict that is comprehensible. The business about the Radical Democratic Landholders Coalition being in a life-and-death struggle with the Republican People's Front means little to the desk; a lead that reads "the anti-U.S. opposition party" or "the Marxist-leaning government" has a much better chance. He almost certainly will cover politics more thoroughly than is justified by either the interests of his readers back home or its importance in the life of the country of his assignment; politics was long ago defined as news, perhaps because it is always conflict-oriented.

He also will simplify the story because it must be short. Three hundred to 400 words (a little more than a normal page of double-spaced typing) is the functional limit now for the Associated Press in routine international stories. In a memo to the foreign staff of the New York *Times* in 1969, Seymour Topping, foreign editor, said "a normal spot-news or feature spread will run 300 to 600 words." A Chicago editor once insisted that there was no news story short of the Second Coming that could not be written in 300 words. Although this sounds like idiocy, it is well to remember that few stories on radio or television newscasts get *that* many words.

The foreign correspondent has little choice but to get his story and move it in a hurry, one reason why he makes so much use of local media for his information. The same *Times* memo says "any story that arrives after 5 P.M. has to fight its way into the paper." That is 5 P.M., New York time, which means the early morning or middle of the night in the parts of the world where many correspondents are stationed. It is a cliché of the news business that a mediocre story on time is better than a good one late. Although timeliness is not, logically, a critical factor in many foreign stories, part of the Tradition—or bad habits—of journalism makes most newsmen feel that yesterday's story is second-hand merchandise even though it has never been printed.

The preoccupation with speed is at its most intense in the wire services, which drum into their correspondents that there's "a deadline every minute"—that is, somewhere some broadcast is being readied for the air, some newspaper is closing its forms. A two-minute "beat" on a big story is still cause for buying boastful advertising in the trade press. A sound reason lies behind the agency's point of view—studies show that the media use the story that arrives first, and not only American media. The Yugoslavian news agency Tanjug is a monopoly; it subscribes to almost all the wire services in the world (more than 40 of them) and then distributes the material under a combined slug (Tanjug-Reuters, for example) to the country's papers and broadcasters. This means that for a major story Tanjug has a choice among the versions of the five international giants (AP, UPI, Reuters, Agence France Press, and Tass), plus many smaller ones. More than nine out of ten times it uses the one which comes first.

So our one-man bureau, if he is to interpret a place and a people to the rest of the world, has to do it quickly; he has to be sure it has enough bite to make it all the way through the system, and he has to get it on a single sheet of paper. Once he overcomes the problems of structure and process, he is free to be a great reporter.

The kind of foreign correspondent commonly called a "special" is in a somewhat different situation. A "special" generally works for a single newspaper, magazine, or network, and is based in a news capital. In Moscow in the early 1970's, for example, in addition to the bureaus of the networks, news agencies, and the New York *Times,* there were reporters for such papers as the Los Angeles *Times,* the Baltimore *Sun,* the Washington *Post,* and the Chicago *Daily News.*

With AP and UPI covering the hard news from Moscow (and the other major newsmaking cities), the special can pick and choose the aspects of Soviet life, art, and politics about which he will report. He can do much to fill in the picture for an elite, important group of readers; he can deal in insight and subtlety. In practice, however, he spends much of his time covering hard news. He reads the local papers (in Moscow, he probably has a teleprinter with the Tass service in his office). He covers the May Day parade, the cosmonauts, the visits of important foreigners, and the trials. He races against deadlines, oversimplifies, and triumphantly achieves the predictable.

He works this way because he wants not only to get in print but on the front page. The elegant and subtle backgrounder is likely to appear on page 32, wrapped inelegantly around a supermarket ad, or buried in a mass of prune whip in a Sunday feature section. The way to get on the front page is to cover the breaking news.

His employers like it that way, too. To an editor, "From our special correspondent" looks a lot better than the Associated Press or United

Press International slug line. Similarly, for the radio and television networks, having their own feed, curiously enhanced by the tinniness of short-wave reception, provides the same sense of accomplishment—even though it leaves the newsman weary with frustration from trying to pack a major story into 60 seconds.

Foreign correspondence, outside of major prearranged events such as a Presidential visit to a foreign capital, is not a major concern of broadcast news. The electronic media are better suited to other kinds of coverage, and they are superb at the live reporting of a running dramatic event. The next article is a fine analytical description of the CBS news department during the dramatic Democratic national convention at Chicago in 1968. The article sets out in detail the complex system through which news gets on the air (a process which looks so effortless from the other side of the tube), but it also lets the men in the system speak for themselves. Best of all, it portrays very sharply the things which the system forces the professional to do—and the opportunities it affords him to project his own judgments on the audience.

CORRIDOR OF MIRRORS *

Thomas Whiteside

On the afternoon of Wednesday, August 28, as the Democratic National Convention was called to order by Chairman Carl Albert on the floor of the International Amphitheatre in Chicago, I was sitting at the back of the Central Control Room of the Columbia Broadcasting System convention headquarters several hundred feet away, watching the proceedings on a bank of monitors and listening to the talk on the Central Control intercommunications system among the men who were in charge of various aspects of the CBS coverage. I was there to try to get some sense of the process of communication involved in the portrayal of a modern political convention by a great television network. As it happened, I was to get something else, too: a sense of the problems involved in the television coverage of a confrontation between the myrmidons of established political authority and modern political protestants.

* Reprinted and condensed from *Columbia Journalism Review,* Winter 1968–69. © Copyright *Columbia Journalism Review,* 1968.

Although the television editorial process embraces many stages of preparation and selection, for my purposes Central Control was the best place I could think of to take in both the final televised act itself and the flow of material contributing to it, and to obtain some feeling of the editorial judgment being exercised in the compilation of the stream of images that went out on the air to the tens of millions of people watching CBS on their home screens that day. Network coverage of political conventions is a massive logistical undertaking. For CBS in 1968, it involved the deployment, first to Miami Beach and then to Chicago, of some 800 people—engineers, camera crews, trouble-shooters and expediters of all kinds, news writers, directors and producers, and on-the-air correspondents and commentators—and of perhaps two hundred tons of very complex and expensive equipment, including huge self-contained trailer or mobile van units housing a staggering array of electronic gadgetry, office trailers, and control rooms, as well as mobile electronic camera units. In addition to transporting all this equipment to Chicago and arranging it in a cluster interconnected by a highly intricate wiring system, in a large warehouse-like area forming part of the International Amphitheatre building, CBS News had also erected, within the Amphitheatre itself, two fixed installations that overlooked the convention floor—its anchor booth for Walter Cronkite, the CBS anchor man, and a much smaller booth, very high up on one side of the Amphitheatre, from which the work of the CBS News correspondents on the convention floor could be directed. Also, just outside the convention floor, CBS had erected a large newsroom and another television studio, called the analysis studio, from which Eric Sevareid and Roger Mudd were to make periodical commentaries or to interview political figures.

Besides the Central Control Room, CBS had several other trailer control rooms into which television images flowed and in which editorial judgments were made. These included Perimeter Control, which received the output of cameras placed outside the entrances to the convention floor and from immediately outside the delegates' entrance to the Amphitheatre building, and Remote Control, which, with another trailer control room called Videotape that was served by five videotape recording and storage vans, received the output of electronic and film camera crews at the Conrad Hilton Hotel—the headquarters for the Democratic National Committee—and the Blackstone Hotel in downtown Chicago, and from roving crews on assignment around the city. Because of a long-standing strike of telephone workers in Chicago that made impossible the installation of remote microwave transmission equipment in the city, live coverage of activities in Chicago concerning the convention was limited to the Internatonal Amphitheatre. Thus, whatever images were fed into CBS headquarters at the Amphitheatre from downtown arrived there in the form of videotape or film sent by courier to the Videotape Room, from which it could be fed to the Remote Control Room.

From all the control rooms through which such streams of images passed, after a preliminary editorial straining that might select, say, the output of two television cameras out of eight that were available, tributary streams then flowed into Central Control. There, from a large bank of monitors, the shots that actually were to go on the air could be finally selected. Physically, Central Control consisted of two huge trailers placed side by side, with one wall of each removed so as to produce a large unobstructed area, and this area was further increased by the addition of a fixed enclosure between the two open sides. The focal point of Central Control was the bank of monitoring screens I have referred to. There were five rows of screens and individual monitors identified by such titles as "CAM 1", "CAM 2", "REMOTE A", REMOTE B", "PERIMETER A", "PERIMETER B", and so on. Before this bank of monitors were two long rows of consoles staffed by technicians and production people, including Vern Diamond, CBS News Senior Director; Gordon Manning, a CBS vice-president who is Director of News; and Robert Wussler, executive producer and director of the CBS News Special Events Unit. Wussler, who is in his early 30's, is a round-faced man with a large forehead and rather prominent eyes. He has a controlled manner and a flow of energy that round-the-clock working habits seem in no way to diminish. It was essentially through Wussler's marshaling of subject matter, usually minutes ahead of its actual appearance on the air, that the general pattern of the CBS coverage seemed to merge. Wussler sat in the center of the second row of consoles, wearing a microphone-earphone headset, and in front of him he had an intercommunications box connecting him with each of the producers in the various sub-control rooms: Robert Chandler in Perimeter Control; Bill Crawford in Videotape; Casey Davidson and Sid Kaufman in Remote Control; Paul Greenberg in Floor Control, a small booth high up in the Amphitheatre from which the work of the CBS floor correspondents was guided; Sanford Socolow, the producer attached to the anchor booth; and Jeff Gralnick, an associate producer who sat next to and was the immediate liaison with Walter Cronkite, the anchor man, or, as he was sometimes simply referred to on the intercom, "the Star." Through an extra earphone I was able, while sitting in Central Control and watching the bank of monitors, to hear Wussler's conversations over the intercommunications system with all his producers, as well as with Diamond, who had responsibility not only for the direction of cameras on the convention floor but also for the exacting job of choosing, from among the bank of monitors, shots that actually went on the air. That Wednesday I was able to see and hear how, in this nerve center, CBS News went about the business of informing its audience on subjects that included the debate on the issue of that part of the Administration-backed platform dealing with the war in Viet Nam, and also, later on that evening, the violence that was to erupt between police and anti-war demonstrators, and other events in downtown Chicago.

On that day, CBS had been on the air since 12:30 p.m. Eastern Standard Time. The proceedings at the convention were opened at 1:08 p.m. by Chairman Albert—only eight minutes after the scheduled time. (Three weeks earlier, in Miami Beach, the Republican National Convention had broken all convention records by actually starting exactly on time.) Now Chairman Albert started things off by bringing forward Mahalia Jackson to sing "The Star-Spangled Banner." Between the start of the CBS convention programming and the convention opening there had been a number of interviews with delegates by CBS floor correspondents. Walter Cronkite had told the television audience that the previous day's boom for Senator Edward M. Kennedy had been finished by a statement by Kennedy that he was not available for the nomination. (This alleged boom actually had never got beyond the stage of a few sputtering fuses, most of which had the appearance to me of having been lighted around the place by eager network floor correspondents rather than by Kennedy's men. I have seen how, after these correspondents had been pumping away for a few hours at the notion of a Kennedy boom, a number of hand-lettered "DRAFT TED KENNEDY" signs, got up by people who presumably were not unaware of what the correspondents were saying on television, began to appear on the convention floor. When the signs appeared, the television cameras that were endlessly panning around the hall searched them out as visual confirmation of the so-called boom. It seemed to be a case of Kennedy signs and Zoomar lenses encouraging one another.)

While Mahalia Jackson's image was on the screen marked LINE in the center of the bank of monitors in the control room, showing that it was on the air (this image was a duplicate of another, directly above it, marked POOL, which was the product of one of several cameras operated jointly by the three networks to cover proceedings on the podium), other monitors were showing a variety of scenes being recorded by CBS cameras, but not being fed to the air. On these monitors, there was a great variety of movement—shots in which one camera after another would be panning the convention floor, constantly zooming and searching, homing in now on one delegate and now on another. Sometimes the cameras would be just slewing around in apparently aimless fashion. The effect on me was an extraordinarily dizzying one. It was something like watching the outside world through the windows of a train, except that as seen through adjacent panes parts of the scenery seemed to be moving not in one but in quite different directions. Through some windows, the view was flying to the right, through others to the left. In yet others, it seemed as though the train itself must have suddenly thrown itself off the tracks, moved sideways at express speed, plunged down an embankment, suddenly stopped short within a foot of a man's face. Then, as abruptly, it would reverse its course and pull off in yet another direction.

As I watched this array I could hear, on my earphone, Wussler talking with his producers.

"Next, we'll go to Walter," Wussler told them. "Walter will throw it to a New York commercial and a station break, and out of that if we can fit it in we'll get in that piece on the Illinois caucus—it's on Videotape Number Four."

"Bobby, there's a CND [Columbia news division] story that McCarthy is coming to the convention this afternoon," Gralnick's voice said, as Cronkite, on the air, said a few words that served as a transition from "The Star-Spangled Banner" to a commercial for Zest.

About 1:30 p.m., Kenneth O'Donnell had just finished telling Josh Darsa, a CBS News reporter, that Humphrey might well be better off running against Nixon, whom he called "the super-hawk," on the minority Viet Nam plank rather than on the majority plank. Then Greenberg's voice came in on the intercom. "Are you interested in Charles Evers? He's a dove."

"Mmmm, we just had a dove on," Wussler said. "I'd like to get a—"

"You want a hawk?" Greenberg said. "How about Governor Connally? The biggest hawk that ever took wing."

"Aaah, we've had him on the air so *much,*" Wussler said.

"He's the biggest hawk on the floor," Greenberg's voice said, in eager tones.

On the bank of monitors I could see shots of Roger Mudd and Art Buchwald, who were sitting together rather glumly at the analysis desk, and of Cronkite in the anchor booth, and of Carl Albert on the podium. Alongside the shot of Albert there was a practice zoom-in-and-out shot of Governor Connally, who was standing on the floor with Dan Rather.

"Okay, let's go Rather-Connally," Wussler said.

". . . Dan Rather is with Governor Connally of Texas on the

floor there," Cronkite said, almost after an echo's interval. Instantly, the image of interviewer and interviewee on the monitor multiplied itself and sprang onto the screen marked LINE.

Rather said, on the air: "Governor John Connally of Texas, how do you think this platform vote is going to go?"

On the intercom, Greenberg said, "Bob Wussler, Mike Wallace is offering Burns, the state chairman of the New York delegation, on the possibility of nominating Johnson."

Connally was telling Rather that the minority plank "just does not reflect the feeling of the people of this country."

"I think they're getting down to business on the podium, Bobby. Boggs has the gavel," Socolow's voice warned on the intercom.

"Interested in the possibility of Chairman Burns nominating Johnson?" Greenberg's voice persisted.

"We're getting into Viet Nam, Paul, so we'll cool it for a while," Wussler told Greenberg. Wussler added, referring to the onscreen interview with Connally, "Wrap him up. Wrap him up!"

The order was relayed immediately. "Governor, one last question," Rather said, on camera, within two or three seconds, "How much of this is personal animosity to President Johnson?"

After about an hour and a half of debate I went out of the Central Control Room, picking my way along narrow plywood corridors through a maze of CBS trailers, out of which, at the sides, great bundles of cables spilled, some of them fat like entrails, others finer, with multicolored strands like the exposed nerves in an anatomical drawing. I wandered around to the CBS newsroom, loud with ringing phones, urgent voices, the incessant riffle of typewriters, the line-by-line chugging of news tickers and the sounds of the CBS convention coverage coming from a loudspeaker near a row of three network monitors that also showed what NBC and ABC were putting on the air. From the nearby office of William S. Leonard, a CBS News vice-president who is Director of News Programming, I managed to borrow for a very short time one of the extremely scarce passes that gave the bearer access to the BS anchor booth overlooking the convention floor. After running the gantlet of suspicion through seemingly endless checkpoints of Secret Service and other security men, I reached the doorway of a small producer's booth immediately adjacent to the anchor booth, and overlooking it through two glass windows. Through one of these windows I could see Cronkite, sitting in bright lights at the anchor desk, and behind him, even more brightly lighted and compressed into a garish mosaic, the crowd on the convention floor and galleries. Socolow was there in the little producer's booth. Near him, a couple of people were tapping out, in oversized print on electric typewriters, pieces of copy for Cronkite to read before the cameras.

Socolow took me in to the anchor booth itself, and for a minute or two I stood between two cameras that were trained on Cronkite at the anchor desk. The red lights on the cameras were off momentarily, indicating that Cronkite wasn't on the air. Cronkite's desk was semicircular, faced with teak veneer, and it had set into its top, out of view of the audience, several monitors. Next to Cronkite, three feet or so to his left, was Gralnick, the Star's primary contact with the whole CBS communications machine that was geared to feed information toward him. When Cronkite and his whole anchor desk were visible on the air, Gralnick was out of sight because his seat was down at the floor level, so that he sat with his legs in a small pit sunk into the studio floor; this pit was filled to the brim with monitors, and when I moved over to one side to make a closer inspection of it, I could see that Gralnick's shoes were in a certain amount of debris—crumpled papers blacked with footmarks, an occasional sandwich wrapper. From this nether world, Gralnick's job was to cue Cronkite, to hand him bulletins, brief handwritten notes ("MUDD-SEVAREID NEXT"; "WRAP UP DARSA.") However, Gralnick, as he told me later, didn't have to sit in his hole out of sight too much, because usually the cameras could be trained on Cronkite so as to exclude him. At the moment, Gralnick was standing in his pit. Cronkite, swiveled around in his chair, was scanning the rear of the convention floor area—"eyeballing it" as one of his men described such a direct view. To improve his view, Cronkite picked up a pair of binoculars and focused on a particular area on the floor. Pierre Salinger had just finished a speech for the minority plank, and a demonstration was going on, particularly in the California and New York delegations, with loud chants of "Stop the war!" "I notice there are people down there who seem to be cheerleaders in these delegations," Cronkite told Gralnick and Socolow as he peered through his binoculars. "You ought to pass that on."

"I'll get that to Greenberg," Socolow said.

I left the anchor booth, found my way back to Leonard's office, and after an interval returned to the Central Control Room. Onscreen, Congressman Hale Boggs was making a summation of the majority plank. Off-screen, Greenberg, in Floor Control, was reporting excitedly to Wussler that Mike Wallace had a story that a telegram had been received from Ted Kennedy that Kennedy wanted read to the convention; the telegram said that he supported the minority plank. Greenberg let Wussler know where on the bank of monitors Wallace could be seen: "He's right in that pile of people on Camera Three and he's also on Five. Five is probably a better shot." He added, pleadingly, "Can you go?"

"I can't go during Hale Boggs," Wussler said.

"This is really something. The opposition will have it on the air in a second," Greenberg said. "Dick Goodwin is standing near Mike. And vanden Heuvel. Mike can talk to them about it."

Wussler, for several seconds, was silent. Finally, he said, "We're going to give it to Walter right now." He repeated Greenberg's information for Gralnick's benefit.

On the air, Congressman Hale Boggs was saying, from the podium, "I would turn, too, to another area on God's earth—the Middle East. The Middle East, my friends . . . a powder keg. . . ."

On the bank of monitors, the screen emanating from Camera Five zoomed in closeup on Mike Wallace, standing on the convention floor.

"We've got a clean beat on this—we've got to go!" Greenberg said.

Gralnick's voice said, "Bobby! Bobby Wussler! Walter says he'd rather *Wallace* took it if you want to cut away from Boggs—he doesn't think it's important enough to cut away from the summary."

"It's Teddy Kennedy, supporting the minority plank," Wussler said, in a tone of exhortation.

"I *told* Walter," Gralnick said.

Socolow's voice cut in. "Walter's point is that it's only a matter of another minute or so before Boggs is finished. *Then* we can go," he said.

Greenberg's voice came in, anguished from what he saw on his monitors upstairs. "Here comes NBC, for Christ's sake!" he cried. "Here comes Vanocur!"

"Well, we're moving! We're moving!" Wussler said.

"Yeah, but we're gonna lose it!" Greenberg said.

"Jeff, tell Walter we're going to go to it. We're going to go to it *now*," Wussler said.

"Come *on!*" Greenberg's voice said, agonized.

Gralnick, in a deliberate voice, said, "Walter says you'll have to bring Mike up cold!"

Wussler did not answer immediately. "Did you hear that?" Gralnick said.

"Okay," Wussler said. He went on. "Wallace, stand by. I'm going to you *direct*. Walter will *not* intro it."

Gralnick's voice came on again. "Bobby," he said. "Do you realize you're interrupting a majority summation to deal with the *minority* report?"

Wussler, cutting his microphone off, leaned over and conferred with Manning next to him, and in a few seconds he told Greenberg that "we'll stay with Boggs and *then* throw it to Mike."

CBS did allow Boggs to remain onscreen for the rest of his speech. And then they threw it to Mike. I gathered that the Star was not pleased.

Every camera at the convention, and every producer behind it or reporter before it, might be intended to serve as an extension of some central directorial sense, but I had a strong feeling that if he were such an extension, every man whose person or work was appearing on a monitor in Central Control was there also as an expression of a strong competitive drive—competition not only against the work of other networks, but against his own colleagues at CBS News. ("Believe me, every time that red light on the camera lights up and you're *on,* you're putting your ego right on the line," the CBS News correspondent Hughes Rudd told me later. And Dan Rather told me, "Yes, I'm competitive, all right. When I go out there on the floor, I want to be on camera beating the other guy. I want *in.* I want to be the biscuit company.")

The resulting, final image on the central air screen represented for me a correspondence to reality, but it was an image of reality peculiarly heightened and shaped, particularly by chronological juxtaposition of segments of simultaneously occurring images. It was an effect produced, really, by an editorial process unlike anything we have ever seen before—as different from any other editorial process as tennis is from croquet. Disregarding, for the moment, gross distortions of live actuality that would be apparent to everyone, it seemed to me that the nature of television makes it peculiarly difficult for one to divine its ability to perceive reality by attempting just to separate original action from the series of the electronic images representing it, because what is involved is not merely the subject before the cameras or the instant editorial process but also the immediate reaction of the universal audience. The reality of the televising process consists only of *the whole works*—an entire cybernetic complex of mutually and instantly adjusting elements, in which the act of observation itself inherently tends to modify that which is under observation. The process is something like a man walking down a corridor of mirrors, along which not only his reflections change but the man himself somehow alters as he goes.

On the air monitor, there was a succession of shots following a speech by Governor Harold Hughes of Iowa placing the name of Senator McCarthy in nomination: people cheering, confetti fluttering down, people waving "Peace" signs and McCarthy posters designed by Ben Shahn.

Gralnick's voice, low but enunciating very distinctly, said on the intercom: "Downtown Chicago is blowing up."

"We have videotape in on the rioting," another voice said.

As soon as the McCarthy demonstration was fairly well over (and a total of seven commercials, relieved only by a station break, had followed), a section of videotape showing violence outside the Conrad Hilton Hotel downtown came on the air.

It showed a melee of blue-helmeted police and young people—from the tape, one could not call them demonstrators, because there was really no sign of anything as organized as a demonstration in sight. The police were running about everywhere, in and out of knots of youngsters, and clubbing and dragging them over to patrol wagons. On the accompanying sound track, one could hear a great deal of confused noise, yelling, boos, and an occasional bang, whether from the firing of tear gas grenades, the explosion of firecrackers, or some other cause, one could not tell. Over the videotape, Cronkite's voice provided a commentary that was based partly on a description of the material that had been provided by CBS people on the scene of the disturbance and partly on what he was seeing of the tape on a monitor in front of him. "There seems to be a minister in trouble with the police," he observed. "They're manhandling him pretty severely . . . that cop certainly had his eye on a target"—this over a scene showing a policeman running right into part of a crowd and wildly clubbing and collaring a young man. (Chanting in the background of "Sieg Heil!") "There seems to be a wounded man there, at that point." And again: "The young lady [here, a shot of a girl, in great distress, being led away from the crowd] seems to be quite well dressed." (This in an avuncular tone.)

The scenes, Cronkite said, had been videotaped about an hour previously and represented a situation that now had been restored to comparative calm. He reported that the National Guard had "advanced" into the lobby of the Conrad Hilton, and had cleared the lobby.

Over the intercom: "Dan Rather is with Paul O'Dwyer on the floor. Mr. O'Dwyer is going to say the police used unnecessary brutality on the floor and that real delegates to the convention have been thrown out because that's the way the convention is being stage-managed. Do you want it?"

"Joe Benti up in the stands—he has information that people up there in the stands have been picking up credentials in the mayor's office. We can't do a thing about how it's stacked for Humphrey up there. Are you interested?"

"Alioto is going to nominate Humphrey, and when the demonstration breaks out I suggest cutting to Benti and we can explain how this demonstration got organized."

Forty minutes after the first videotape of the violence outside the Conrad Hilton had been shown, Cronkite, on the air, made a brief introduction of a second section of videotape that had just arrived from downtown. "There has been a display of naked violence in the streets of Chicago," Cronkite told the CBS audience before the film came on. But, he said, there had been no repetition of the worst of the previous violence; he went on to say that National Guardsmen had since reinforced five district lines of police that had pushed antiwar demonstrators half a block from the demonstration area outside the Hilton. Cronkite also reported, before the videotape went on, that "CBS News producer Phil Scheffler, a witness to that Hilton violence, said it seemed to be unprovoked on the part of the demonstrators— the polce just charged the demonstrators, swinging at the crowd indiscriminately."

The videotape, which had a narration by Burt Quint, showed, against a background of great noise and booing, and in the glaring artificial lights of the television network people, columns of National Guardsmen advancing north on Michigan Avenue with bayonet-tipped rifles, a shot of a machine-gun manned by a National Guardsman on top of a car, and other shots of Guardsmen and Chicago police pushing and herding people around.

These shots, I understood, had been made from a CBS mobile unit known as Flash Unit Number One, which had been stationed in Grant Park, directly across Michigan Avenue from the Conrad Hilton. Flash Unit Number One consists of a big, gray-painted truck with a platform on top of it for two television camera rigs, and, inside, a miniature control room manned by a producer, a director, a videotape recording engineer and a couple of other technicians. Normally, it is used for live transmissions by microwave equipment, but during the Chicago convention, because of the telephone workers' strike, it could be used only for producing videotape. The producer in charge of this Flash Unit, a big, gregarious man named Alvin Thaler, later told me that the first two sections of videotape concerning the disorders outside the Hilton that were shown on CBS that evening were taken from at least an hour of continuous electronic-camera photography by two cameramen on top of the truck, using four 1000-watt floodlamps. As the pictures were monitored in the little control room inside the truck, the images were intercut sequentially, in whatever way seemed desirable to the unit director, David Roth, and compiled into one videotape recording. As the tape progressed, parts of it would be cut off, stuffed into a videotape box, and thrown out the back of the truck by Thaler to one of two motorcycle couriers who would dash off with it to CBS convention headquarters at the Amphitheatre. Flash Unit Number One had been in Grant Park since about dusk, and for about half an hour thereafter Roth, watching the monitors in front of him, had his attention focused on the police who were throwing people into a van at the corner of Balbo. Then, he told me, he suddenly saw something on one of the monitors that caused him to be momentarily disoriented; he saw on it a foreshortened shot of a big formation of helmeted troops marching along with rifles and bayonets. He told me that for a moment he imagined that the closed-circuit monitor he was looking at must have been feeding in an actual television broadcast, and that what he was seeing was part of some war movie. He assumed that both his cameras were pointed northward, at the disturbances at Balbo and Michigan Avenues, and sticking his head out of the truck in that direction, he saw no troops there. Still confused, he looked southward, and only then did he realize that one of cameras was pointing south, and that there really were troops with bayonets and gas masks and machine guns and rifles, and jeeps with barbed wire screens in front, advancing north on Michigan Avenue.

In an age when a boy in a ghetto riot who heaves a rock within view of a television camera can do it with a sense that he may be throwing the rock not just across a street but also into the living rooms of tens of millions of homes, the relationship of television cameras to what they are registering at scenes of civil disturbance involves serious problems of judgment. In general, in talking to CBS people before as well as during the Democratic convention in Chicago, I found them quite frank to acknowledge the possibility that the presence of a television crew at scenes where violence might break out might itself somehow help to trigger violence, or, where violence was already occurring, to exacerbate it. In fact, before the start of the convention, Salant called his executives together and briefed them on their manner of any covering of civil disorders that might take place in Chicago. He instructed them to keep all of their reports in reasonable context and to avoid giving publicity to people "desirous only of getting their faces on television by making inflammatory statements." Further, he said, "We must in no circumstances . . . give reasonable ground for anybody to believe that we in any way instigated or contributed to civil disorder." He told them to have their men avoid using lights when shooting pictures, since lights tended to attract crowds, and to obey police instructions instantly and without question. Camera crews were to be instructed that if they found, during any civil disturbance, that but for their presence the disorder would not be taking place, they should immediately cap the lenses of their cameras, regardless of what the crews from competing networks were doing.

As the convention got under way, I found the CBS people in Chicago expressing increasing dismay over what they felt was a deliberate policy on the part of the Daley administration to hamper television coverage of any civil disorders, of any demonstrations taking place within the city against the Johnson administration and American involvement in Viet Nam, of the discussions taking place at delegation headquarters in the downtown hotels, and of the convention itself. The Chicago police were reported to be taking a tough and uncooperative attitude toward television crews working outside the convention hall. The Department of Streets and Sanitation refused to give permits for the networks to park their mobile units on the streets outside the major hotels; when the CBS people attempted to rent space for their mobile units in parking lots adjacent to the hotels, they encountered an extraordinary reluctance on the part of the lot operators to let them have space, even at fees amounting to several hundred dollars a day. Alvin Thaler reported that parking space for mobile units in some places, such as service stations along a projected line of march of a demonstration scheduled for August 28, in several cases could not be obtained at any price mentioned, although usually the owners of such places are delighted to cooperate with television networks and to turn an easy dollar. At the Amphitheatre, the CBS people were informed that "for security reasons" they would not be allowed to put cameras in the windows at the front of the building to photograph any action going on outside; and even at the Conrad Hilton, where on the fifth floor CBS had set up a newsroom to cover the candidates' and delegations' headquarters, the head of the newsroom operation, Ed Fouhy, was warned by security people that the network would not be allowed to use the windows of its suite to photograph events outside—even to train its cameras on Grant Park opposite, where Yippies were expected to gather. At the convention itself, neither CBS nor any other network could obtain an assurance from the Democratic National Committee until the night before the convention as to how many cameras would be allowed on the floor during the proceedings. (In Miami Beach, the Republicans had let the networks know as far back as the beginning of June just how many floor passes they would be allotted.) When at the last moment the decision on floor coverage was made in Chicago, CBS, like the other networks, was allowed passes for only two television correspondents and one miniature portable television camera; the network had been asking for passes for four correspondents and two cameras. (In Miami Beach, CBS had been allowed passes for four correspondents and two miniature cameras.) Eventually, and after many protests, accommodations were made with the authorities over some of these difficulties—for example, parking and the number of floor correspondents, which was increased to four, with the other correspondents getting on to the convention floor with messenger passes. But the CBS people, who in Miami Beach had had the run of the place and had enjoyed quite full co-operation from the Republican National Committee, the city administration, and the police, and had even had a minimum of difficulty with local unions, continued to feel, in Chicago, a sense of official reluctance and resentment. As for the convention itself, the atmosphere was an almost palpably oppressive one, with barbed wire entanglements, masses of helmeted police around the Amphitheatre, the Potemkin-village quality of the approaches through the stockyard slum areas—along which, on block after block, the Daley administration had erected redwood screens that concealed rubble-strewn lots and dingy entrances—the countless security check points, the magnetically coded passes, and the swarms of unrelentingly suspicious plainclothesmen with hips and armpits bulging with weapons. With all this around them, the CBS people, who at the Republican convention had mounted a most elaborate live communications system between Republican headquarters, the delegation hotels, and Convention Hall, were now reduced to keeping in touch with their newsroom downtown by having secretaries continuously dialing the switchboard at the Conrad Hilton Hotel in the hope of getting a line that wasn't busy, so that they could then be connected with the newsroom. On Tuesday, during the CBS Evening News, I had seen on the screen pictures relayed by satellite from three different continents, showing in turn scenes of the Russian occupation of Prague, the visit of Pope Paul to Colombia, and the results of Viet Cong rocket attacks on Saigon. From Chicago that same day, a satellite was relaying to Europe with equal efficiency television coverage of the Democratic convention. The big communication problem seemed to be making a telephone call from the Amphitheatre to a downtown hotel.

All these frustrations had to be coped with by people who had been working for eighteen or twenty hours a day, seven days a week, during the frantic preparatory period at the Amphitheatre. (Casey Davidson remarked to me that the people in his Remote Control unit had "volunteered for service in Czechoslovakia to a man.") But the CBS men had their first really ominous signs of deteriorating relations between the Daley administration and the news media when, on the first night of the convention, at Lincoln Park, Chicago police began beating Yippies and also began to pay physical attention to television cameramen, still photographers, and reporters. One of the cameramen was Delos Hall, of CBS, who had been filming a crowd of young people who were being dispersed on Division Street near Wells by three policemen. "As far as I knew, three policemen were doing a fine job of dispersing the crowd," he later reported. "Then, apparently, a larger group [of police] arrived, running from behind me toward the marchers. Then, without warning, one of the first officers to pass me swung at me and hit me on the forehead with his nightstick, knocking me to the ground. When I got up I continued filming and was pushed and shoved from policeman to policeman, especially when they saw me filming them clubbing or arresting marchers." The clubbing of Hall was witnessed by Charles Boyer, a cameraman for WBBM, the CBS-owned television station in Chicago, who himself had just been beaten by police, and who, at about the same time as he saw Hall being assaulted, saw police attack a third television cameraman, James Strickland of NBC, who is a Negro. Strickland, he said, kept telling two officers who grabbed him that he was from NBC, "but they kept telling him, 'You black mother ———, we'll kill you before the night is over.' He got rapped in the mouth a couple of times and I understand he had a tooth busted off." Besides the scores of young demonstrators and onlookers attacked, about twenty-five newsmen were beaten, Maced, or otherwise severely harassed by the police in or around Lincoln Park that night.

On Wednesday night outside the Conrad Hilton, and in the neighboring streets, newsmen were beaten during the disorders, but the extent of their injuries appears to have been minor compared with those inflicted on other people that night. So far as I know, no CBS people were among those injured. By no means all the CBS network cameramen were sympathetic to the demonstrators. Most of them just aren't made that way; they are people who may earn tens of thousands of dollars a year, have comfortable homes in the suburbs, belong to a craft union that sees to it that they fly first class while the producers of the programs they are shooting are obliged by the network to fly economy. Some of them consider the demonstrators outside the Hilton to have used considerable provocation, ranging from the free use of obscenities to the throwing of bottles at the police. "The Yippies deserved the cops, and the cops deserved the Yippies," one of the cameramen said later in a typical comment. Yet if the cameramen witnessed physical provocations by demonstrators outside the Hilton, they seem, in spite of their generally neutral or even unsympathetic attitude, not to have been able to include shots of these acts in their videotapes or film. (Nor, for that matter, were the undercover police cameramen who provided material for the television film which was later put out by the Daley administration to justify the actions of its police in Chicago.)

On Wednesday night, CBS televised, in addition to the two tapes shot by Thaler's unit that I have referred to, two other sequences of the disorders along Michigan Avenue. The first of these, which was run just before 1 a.m. EST, when the nominating speeches were still going on in the Amphitheatre, was a videotape recording of a film that largely duplicated the scenes shown earlier of arrests and club-bings around the patrol wagons outside the Conrad Hilton. The second sequence was run after the formal close of the Wednesday convention proceedings and the nomination of Hubert Humphrey as the Demo-cratic Presidential candidate. This sequence, which went on the air almost without narration and with only the comment by Cronkite that the pictures seemed to speak for themselves, showd dramatically the predicament of a woman who had picked up a couple of demonstra-tors in her car at a roadblock at about 5 p.m. (These demonstrators, I learned later, were casualties of tear-gassings by the National Guard at Michigan Avenue and Congress Street. As the woman gave the demonstrators a lift, and attempted to drive on, National Guardsmen in gas masks stopped her with guns and bayonets; one guardsman thrust a big-barreled tear-gas grenade launcher through the driver's window and aimed it at her; another, with his rifle pointed downward, motioned as though to bayonet the car's right front tire. (A cry on the sound track, from a bystander: "Come on, CBS, show it all! Show the world!") Then another guardsman discharged tear gas at the car. The sequence, which came through on the screen as though enacted in slow motion, lasted some four minutes.

Much later on, after the Democratic convention was over, and when the initial reaction of shock in the press had abated and an up-roar of criticism by Congressmen of the television networks' coverage of the violence was breaking out, I asked for and obtained an oppor-tunity to take another look at videotapes of these sequences. And it did seem to me that there was a considerable difference, in terms of actual information offered, between reports of the disorders that I had been reading in the press and the sequences I was seeing on the television screen. The television sequences that CBS ran as its version of events on Wednesday night showed far less violence, and far less detail of what took place outside the Conrad Hilton, than reports that appeared in the daily press or those that were compiled by, say, *Time* or *News-week*. And even the still photographers, it seemed to me, provided far more detailed documentation of the violence than the CBS sequences that appeared on television did. The only real violence that CBS documented that night was the clubbing of a few young people as they were being dragged and thrown into the patrol wagons, and that action was later repeated, in a different version, in lieu of other original material from the scene. What the CBS shots televised on Wednesday night did not catch and that press reporters on the scene caught and described in detail included: first, the police charge at Balbo and Michigan Avenues upon a crowd through which, a short time before, a four-mule train of Poor People's Marchers led by the Reverend Ralph Abernathy had been allowed southward; second, a rampage of motorcycle police who drove over the curb on the east side of Michigan and into the crowd gathered on the sidewalk; third, a further charge of police from west on Balbo upon a crowd of onlookers and demonstrators hemmed in around the northeast corner of the Hilton; fourth, the specific acts of police clubbing of individuals among the trapped mass of onlookers and demonstrators; fifth, the panicking of the pushed and beaten crowd (the southerly fringe of which was even assaulted with police sawhorses used as battering rams) so that it backed up against the plate glass windows of the Haymarket Lounge, at the northeast corner of the Hilton, causing the window to break, and people to fall back, some bleeding badly, through the jagged hole to the inside; sixth, the police clubbing, inside the Haymarket, of those who had fallen in, as well as bystanders; seventh, further acts of police clubbing, in the main lobby of the hotel, of young people, some of whom had taken refuge there from the action on the street; eighth, a further charge by the police, with another mass assault with nightsticks on another crowd of onlookers—many of them delegates' wives —on the sidewalk a block north of Balbo at Harrison, and similar indiscriminate assaults on crowds on the side streets off Michigan. In the press, all of this and much more, in detail, was spread over column after column and shown in scores of still pictures. Yet CBS could not show this detail even with a total of something like six television cameras and three film cameras trained on the scene outside the Hilton and north along Michigan Avenue. And when the violence first broke out, the area in front of the Hilton, brilliantly lighted by the television network people, looked, in the words of one CBS man, "like a movie set."

Why the discrepancy in detail between media? I believe part of the answer is that individual reporters and photographers possess much greater mobility in such scenes of disorder than do television crews, burdened with cameras, lights, and sound equipment. (And when the television crews are working with electronic rather than film cameras, their equipment usually is tied by coaxial umbilical cord to a parent truck carrying recording and relaying equipment.) Television people usually need room in which to operate; they work only with difficulty in crowds. The electronic cameras on top of a mobile television unit have an elevated view and are equipped with lenses that can zoom in or out of scenes in a telescopic manner, and this is a great advantage in certain situations, but again not necessarily in crowds, since an overhead telescopic show of part of a dense crowd usually gives such a foreshortened effect that action taking place within the crowd is hard to distinguish—especially during a scuffle, when some of the people involved may be on the ground and out of sight. (A still photographer, using a miniature camera and a wideangle lens, can work very close to his subject and encompass a great deal of action in his field of view.) Further, a press reporter is in a better position to isolate and record the relationship between a particular action and reaction in a crowd or confrontation; when he sees, for example, a provocation such as a taunt that is followed by some reaction on the part of police, he connects the two in his account; but the television cameraman, unless he trains his lens continuously on one spot, is hard put to record the instant when provocation draws police action. He may record the police reaction, but his camera has no memory of *what happened before he pressed the camera trigger;* it has no capacity for generalization, and the cameraman himself is no writer; he usually hands his film on to a courier with a hasty note about the subject matter. I mention this difficulty because often, in disorders, isolated provocations such as stonethrowing occur so quickly that only a cameraman with the quickest reflexes could record them. I was told later by CBS people on the scene that some missiles such as beer bottles were thrown at the police outside the Hilton after the police charged into the crowd. But in the CBS shots shown on the air I could see no flying objects other than young people who were being thrown into patrol wagons.

But what seems to have interfered most with the ability of CBS to televise in detail the disorders outside the Hilton on Wednesday night was the lack of light. The very conspicuousness and drawing power of the television cameras, which, critics say, attracts trouble within camera range, also attracts trouble for the television crews themselves, and it did so, especially in Chicago. Thus, about fifteen minutes after the violence first broke out outside the Hilton, the array of television lights on the second floor of the Hilton that was trained on the area in front of the hotel suddenly went out. This represented nearly all the illumination that had been used by the networks (on a pool basis, with CBS in charge of the pool) to televise the demonstrations and disorders up to that time. When the lights went out, Walter Urban, a CBS man who was in charge of the pooled lighting arrangements, heard a rumor that the cause of the blackout was the police. He went down to the second floor with another CBS man, James L. Clevenger, who had been asked by Ed Fouhy, the chief of the CBS newsroom at the hotel, to get the lights back on. The two men found that the lighting cables had been disconnected. Urban reconnected the cables and turned the lights on again. They had only been on two or three minutes when, according to Clevenger's account, "A policeman wearing a helmet arrived and barreled by me and started pulling the lighting cables. I told him to stop and suggested that he come to the fifth floor and talk to Fouhy. He told me to shut up. I told him he could not pull these cables. He turned, put me up against the wall, waved his night stick at my nose, and said he was giving the orders. I said, 'Yes, sir.' The lights went out."

Then, according to Clevenger, another policeman, wearing a soft hat, arrived on the scene, was asked pointedly by the helmeted policeman if he had his gun and nightstick with him and told him to guard the disconnected lighting cables and to see that they stayed disconnected.

At about the time of the first outbreak of violence outside the Hilton, Herbert Schwartz, a CBS film cameraman, was standing with his crew, an electrician and a sound man, on Balbo Avenue next to the Hilton Hotel, waiting to film Senator McGovern when the senator emerged from the hotel to travel to the Amphitheatre. Schwartz saw a large contingent of police marching east along Balbo toward Michigan Avenue. Schwartz and his men grabbed their portable sound equipment, walked toward Michigan Avenue ahead of the police, and under the marquee of the Hilton on Balbo began to film the advance of the police. Just before Schwartz started his camera, his electrician, Tim McGann, turned on his portable light to illuminate the scene. "Suddenly, a white-shirted police officer charged at [McGann]," Schwartz reported, and he said the officer then yanked the electrical cord from the battery pack the electrician was carrying. According to McGann, he was then pushed back so that he fell against another officer, and then to the sidewalk, and as McGann was falling the second officer hit him on the side of his face with the back of his hand. The electrician never again saw his lamp. All three men wore prominent CBS identification badges, along with Amphitheatre press credentials, which they wore around their necks. Schwartz and his sound man then were pushed by police with nightsticks into a crowd of onlookers and protesters on the corner of Michigan and Balbo, and according to Schwartz the two narrowly escaped being shoved through the windows of the Haymarket, but they managed to get out of the melee by shouting loudly for a police lieutenant who was nearby, thus momentarily distracting the attention of the police who were pushing them against the plate glass. (Schwartz and his sound man then went on to film some of the arrests being made, and they were not further molested. I don't want to convey the impression that the rough treatment they received that night applied to all CBS people on the scene of the disorders; the attitude of the police toward them, by the accounts I have heard, varied from officer to officer and from one incident to another.)

The charge of the police on the crowd near the Haymarket Lounge was observed by a cameraman on top of another CBS mobile unit stationed near the corner of Balbo and Michigan, and the producer in charge of the unit, David Fox, instructed his men to train their cameras on the action. But the unit possessed no lights other than those from the hotel, and since the amount of light shining on the scene was very limited, the unit was unable to get a usable record of this incident. When Fox, sitting before a monitor inside the unit, had a chance to judge the quality of the violence he saw on the screen, he decided, on the basis of instructions issued by Salant not to endanger his men, that the situation might get much worse, and he ordered his men to pull out after the lights from the Hilton were turned off.

At about this time, Ed Fouhy, in the CBS newsroom on the fifth floor of the Hilton, decided that in view of the peremptory disconnecting of the networks' lights by the police he ought to have Urban turn on a limited number of lights in the newsroom and rig them in the windows of the fifth floor CBS suite so that CBS electronic cameras on the floor could record at least part of the scene outside. But as soon as Urban did so a fuse blew and all power in the newsroom was lost. After some delay the fuse was replaced, and the lights were used for a while, but a police officer turned up and requested that they be turned off. Fouhy told me afterward that he had them turned off. (Much later that night, when the Chicago police outside the Hilton were replaced by National Guardsmen, these fifth floor lights were turned on again without objection, Fouhy said.)

When Fox's unit left the area of Michigan and Balbo, Alvin Thaler, across the street from the Hilton on the Grant Park side of Michigan Avenue, continued recording on videotape what his electronic cameras were picking up with the 4,000-watt lights mounted on Flash Unit Number One, but after a while Thaler was told by a police officer to put his lights out. He did so. Some time later, when action broke out on the edge of Grant Park that he felt he ought to be recording, he turned his lights on for a brief period, and then he, too, gave the order for his unit to leave the area. Thaler strongly believes, he told me, that "whenever we put our lights on, we reduced the amount of violence in front of us. You have to realize that cops are far less eager to break heads right out there in front of the TV cameras than they might be somewhere back there in the dark." James Fusca, who was working during the convention at the CBS news desk, was present when the police drove the demonstrators north on Michigan Avenue, well away from what television lights there were outside the Hilton, and he told me that in his opinion police action against demonstrators and onlookers was much more violent out of the lighted area than it was within it. The relationship between turned-on police and turned-on television lights is neatly illustrated by the observations of an assistant U.S. attorney that were reported to the National Commission on the Causes and Prevention of Violence. He was describing the progress of a melee that Wednesday night at State and Jackson:

> I observed the police striking numerous individuals, perhaps 20 or 30. I saw three fall down and then overrun by the police. I observed two demonstrators who had multiple cuts on their heads. We assisted one who was in shock into a passer-by's car.
>
> A TV mobile truck appeared . . . and the police became noticeably more restrained, holding their clubs at waist level rather than in the air. As the truck disappeared . . . the head-clubbing tactics were resumed.

Police action in putting out lights when that suited their purposes was not confined to television floodlights, which the police later claimed had only served to heighten existing disorders; the police also broke or seized the strobe flash units belonging to many still cameramen. Since the duration of a stroboscopic flash averages something like one thousandth of a second, it can hardly be claimed to provide the kind of floodlighting likely to attract crowds. Nor was the dousing of lights by police even limited to the suppression of photographic activity in general. One CBS employee who was present when the police drove demonstrators north on Michigan has described how "One CTA [Chicago Transit Authority] bus had become stranded on Michigan and a number of demonstrators sought refuge from tear gas by climbing on the bus. The police followed them and blocked the exits from the bus while their associates beat those who were on the bus. To avoid being seen, the police turned the lights off. I heard a policeman shout, 'You little long-haired queer. We're going to stomp the ———— out of you and all the other punks like you.' Someone managed to get the bus lights on, and I had someone hold me up so that I could see what was happening on the inside. I observed demonstrators trying to squeeze themselves through the bus windows on the other side and I saw policemen beating one of the demonstrators all about the head and back and one of them had his foot in the kid's groin."

How was it, then, that with such limited coverage, and with all that the CBS people did *not* film or videotape of the more violent episodes in downtown Chicago on Wednesday night, that the sequences that were seen had such a remarkable effect on the audience? In terms of the communications process involved, it strikes me, after having viewed these sequences by themselves, that on Wednesday night the impression of violence in them was greatly heightend by the visual and aural context in which they were shown. And this was true in spite of the fact that the act of taping television shots always robs the audience, in some measure, of the unpredictability inherent in the originally occurring action, and the time lag tends to interrupt and dampen the immediate interactive process so remarkable in viewing live television. By the time the audence saw these tapes, it was already aware of the situation on which they were based, and understood, in effect, that the worst of what it was seeing was already over. It seems to me that the taped scenes appeared so violent because of something resembling what medical men call, in connection with the action of drugs, a potentiating effect—an unusual heightening of the action of some drugs in the presence of others.

How powerfully the interaction of even relatively inert images placed in immediate sequence can affect an audience was pointed out in the 1920's by the Russian film director Pudovkin in his book *On Film Technique:*

> Kuleshov and I made an interesting experiment. We took from some film or other several close-ups of the well-known Russian actor Mosjukhin. We chose closeups which were static and which did not expect any feeling at all—quiet closeups. We joined these closeups, which were all similar, with other bits of film in three different combinations. In the first combination the closeup of Mosjukhin was immediately followed by a shot of a plate of soup standing on a table. It was obvious and certain that Mosjukhin was looking at this soup. In the second combination the face of Mosjukhin was joined to shots showing a coffin in which lay a dead woman. In the third the closeup was followed by a shot of a little girl playing with a funny toy bear. When we showed the three combinations to an audience which had not been let into the secret the result was terriffic. The public raved about the acting of the artist. They pointed out the heavy pensiveness of his mood over the forgotten soup, were touched and moved by the deep sorrow with which he looked on the dead woman, and admired the light, happy smile with which he surveyed the girl at play.

In these cases, almost exactly the same neutral facial expression succeeded in conveying through the process of visual potentiation, quite different and, in two of the sequences, very strong emotions. In the case of Chicago on Wednesday night, it seemed to me that the potentiating effect I have referred to was enhanced by the immediate juxtaposition of the tapes of the disorders in downtown Chicago with the supposedly more orderly scene of a nominating convention, which actually was exhibiting in its own way not dissimilar characteristics of irrationality and violence. It was as though, from widely separate sets of strands, someone were weaving cloth of unique pattern in front of one's eyes.

Of the four tapes relating to the disorders downtown, the one showing the arrival of the National Guard and showing guardsmen pushing people back to the sidewalk near the Hilton probably displayed the least actual violence, although the sight of rows of bayoneted rifles advancing in front of the delegates' hotel and the accompanying boos and crowd noise on the sound track certainly conveyed an air of considerable menace.

While this tape was being played on the air, I was sitting watching it and the bank of monitors (and keeping an ear to Wussler's intercom) in the Central Control Room at CBS convention headquarters at the Amphitheatre. The tape went on the air at 10:13 p.m. EST, and immediately before Cronkite, on camera, made his brief introduction to it, a lot of cheering had been ringing out on the floor and the band had been playing "Will Everyone Here Kindly Step to the Rear," following Mayor Alioto's nominating speech for Humphrey. After a minute or so of the shots of the National Guard advancing on Michigan Avenue had passed, and while everyone was watching the central screen very intently—nobody in Central Control had previewed the images—Gralnick's voice came over on the intercom.

"What are we doing with Daley?" he asked Wussler.

After a second or so, Wussler said, "Greenberg, you got anybody near Daley?"

On one of the side monitors among the bank of screens in front of me, I saw a swiveling, searching, zooming shot that finally closed in on the area where Mayor Daley was sitting in the Illinois delegation, and in another minute or so I saw Dan Rather, wearing his headset and with microphone at the ready, moving in on the mayor.

On the intercom there were other observations:

"Bob Wussler, the McCarthy Wisconsin delegation has walked out to discuss action on Chicago police brutality."

"Wussler, see the New York caucus on Remote D."

Then, as the tape of the scene downtown and of the live shot of Mayor Daley sitting in the Illinois delegation continued on their separate monitors, Vern Diamond, the director, gave a signal that intercut the shot of Daley into the shots of the scene outside the Conrad Hilton.

Throughout the time I had been in Central Control I had watched Diamond at work with increasing interest. In the chain of all the hundreds of CBS people who in some way were interposed, through the exercise of some editorial judgment between reality and the images on the screen serving to represent it, Diamond was the last, and in some instances the most vital link: a surrogate, almost, of the viewer himself in the living room. Diamond was a gentle-faced, gray-haired man in his early 50's who appeared to possess the reflexes of a 17-year-old. For hour after hour, I had seen him in the center of the first row of control consoles immediately in front of and somewhat lower than the bank of monitors, looking up at them so that his eyes never once seemed to stray from the bank as a whole, and, speaking into a microphone on a gooseneck immediately in front of him, giving the instructions that determined exactly what shots, in what sequence, would appear on the central monitor and be fed to the air. Sitting in a forward, intent attitude, always leaning on his elbows, a posture so unvarying that his elbows rested on a foam rubber pad he had provided himself with, he would order shot after shot: "Take *One!*" "Take *Four!*" "Take *Minicam A!*"—the sound of each number called being accompanied by a sharp snap of the fingers. And with each snap, from the bank of monitors images from one row or another would be duplicated and transferred on to the central screen by push-buttons operated by technicians assisting him. By the manner of this instantaneous plucking from the scenes reflected in the rows of monitors and by his particular sequencing and juxtaposing of particular aspects of simultaneously occurring action, Diamond seemed to me to endow the final stream of images with a very special quality, to give the flow of subject matter a certain rhythm and texture. Here, when Cronkite needed to cut into a speech from the podium with a piece of news, he would order a cameraman, "Pull out now for a wide shot —wider—wider," to lessen the abruptness of the transition from one shot to the other; there, when two action sequences would occur simultaneously he would either crosscut between them if the action were sufficiently related, or he would use the image of one scene over the sound of another. In its simplest form, this would involve the voice of Cronkite reporting on progress at a caucus of the Illinois delegation and a long accompanying shot of the delegation's empty seats in the hall. Many of his juxtapositions were made with ironic effect. And sometimes the juxtapositions seemed sharply to distill all of the forces at play in the convention—such as the succession of shots very late in the preceding day's session that showed, among the views of delegates who backed the minority plank attempting to get the attention of Chairman Albert for the purpose of adjourning the Viet Nam debate to a period in prime television time, a telescopic glimpse of Mayor Daley, chin jutting out aggressively, making a wide slashing gesture across his throat at Albert, thus causing to be cut off all floor microphones and all motions for adjournment but his own. (His motion for adjournment was instantly adopted.)

As the taped scenes of the National Guard marching outside the Hilton, and the live shot of Daley on the convention floor remained on the monitors, Wussler's voice, over the intercom in Cenrtal Control, said quietly, "You can intercut as you wish, Vern." Diamond by this time was continuing once more with the taped scenes of the National Guard.

"Rather's ready with Daley," Greenberg's voice said on the intercom.

"Take *two!*" Diamond said.

The shot of Daley was transferred to the central screen. Mayor Daley, bright-eyed, alert, and tough, was looking straight ahead, and then he moved slightly as though he were peering over the shoulder of the delegate in front of him. Dan Rather, standing next to where Daley was sitting, leaned down to talk to him. From the floor, Rather wasn't seeing any of the taped material from downtown of course.

"Mayor? Sir? Mayor Daley, Walter Cronkite is reporting downtown the police have used tear gas and there is considerable turmoil around the Hilton Hotel," he began.

Daley leaned slightly over toward Rather. "The situation is well in hand," he said. "There was a demonstration by people who were violating the law and coming into hotels contrary to the hotel management and were creating acts of violence."

"Did the hotel people complain, Mayor?" Rather asked.

"Everyone has complained. The guests complained, about people being there all night. The police took the proper action, to have them comply with the law," Daley said.

"Well, mayor, so far as you know the police did not respond with undue violence?"

"Our police department is the greatest police department in the United States; and the men in there are all family men, decent men, and they don't respond with any undue violence," Mayor Daley said.

"What about these reports that downtown is strictly an armed camp? For a businessman coming to Chicago tomorrow—should he cancel his reservations—"

"Totally propaganda by you and your station and a lot of Eastern interests, who never wanted this convention in Chicago, and a lot of other people trying to hurt the pure name of this great city," Mayor Daley said.

And throughout this exchange, Diamond deftly intercut, time and again, between Daley and the scenes from downtown of the National Guard and police, and although he as director had no control over the simultaneity of the mayor's words and the unreeling videotapes of the action that had occurred downtown some time earlier, the live shots of Daley seemed to lend to the videotapes the immediate, compelling quality of live television. And the intercutting was not merely from one visual shot to another in straight sequential juxtaposition, but with the sound of one image being made to provide continuity over and to extend emphasis to another image—Daley's assurance that everything was well in hand downtown continued as voice-over accompaniment to scenes of bayonet-flashing troops and milling police. The live shots of Daley increased the scene of violence in the taped scenes from downtown, and the sense of violence in the taped scenes downtown endowed the closeups of Daley's rather blandly obstinate denial that undue force had been used with a sense of heavy villainy that hardly any profesisonal actor could convey.

Daley himself was not privy to the confrontation that viewers were seeing on their home screens. He had no television set in front of him, and he had no way of knowing just what CBS was at the moment showing about what had been happening an hour or so previously. He was in the position of a football coach who was commenting on the behavior of his team without actually looking at what his men were doing on the field. Daley's interviewer, Dan Rather, couldn't see the scenes of the disorders on the screen, either, but at least he knew that the tapes were being played on the air, and when he wasn't actually interviewing the mayor he could hear on his earphones the audio track of the videotaped material. Considering that Daley was unaware of the on-the-air scenes that seemed to belie almost every word he was uttering, it is easy to see how CBS could be accused of playing dirty journalistic pool. And especially so since, on the following day, when Daley appeared in Cronkite's anchor booth to be interviewed at length by the Star, Cronkite was manifestly unprepared for this face-to-face journalistic confrontation with the mayor-unprepared possibly for the change of role from anchor man-host to interrogator; unready, certainly, to produce as evidence the videotapes of the police violence that Daley now might properly have been faced with directly, as the mayor had not been the night before. The Star simply caved in under a Daley handslide of self-justification. The mayor took charge of the interview and, unhindered, denounced the peace demonstrators and extolled the pure name of the city of Chicago and the Chicago police for the better part of half an hour.

But, on Wednesday night, when the videotaped scenes of the disorders downtown and Dan Rather's live interview with Daley were going on the air, it remained for Diamond to juxtapose Daley's words and the disorders as his sense of irony, drama, or truth saw fit at particular moments.

It seems to me that this kind of intercutting is a very risky practice. However, I think that in this instance Diamond's action was justified by the circumstances. It did communicate, in very sharp fashion, the essence of what was going on in Chicago, and the intercutting was carried out by a director who was not only very skilled technically but who also in my opinion showed every sign of being a reasonable and fair man. Rarely does a television director have an opportunity to intercut material that provides such dramatically colliding symbolism. But I think that as time goes on this kind of instantaneous montage, so different in quality from the montage that a film editor in a screening room can labor over almost interminably until he achieves precisely the effect he desires, is likely to loom very large in the television process. For one thing, it is clear that live coverage of events, in which television is at its most fascinating, must increase greatly. For another, this is not an age in which the number of public demonstrations and confrontations of one kind or another is likely to decrease. The intimate quality of this live coverage will be enhanced by the widespread use of portable miniaturized television cameras. To an increasing degree, the images from these cameras will not flow into motion picture or tape screening rooms to be subjected to conventional editing; rather, they will tend to flow through live-image control rooms from which they can be fed directly on to the air. And it is the simultaneity of originally occurring action and the editorial process itself that makes television so potentially powerful in its rendering of the real world. It seems to me quite likely that television will bring forth, sooner or later, its own Pudovkin, a man so skilled at manipulating and juxtaposing, in strong individual style, innumerable fragments of visual and aural reality into a sequential mosaic that he will carry forward the present state of instantaneous electronic-image montage to an altogether new level. It will be an extraordinarily compelling and dangerous journalistic art form.

Whiteside sees the development of a new kind of television newsman. New kinds of print newsmen and other communications professionals are on the way, too. Technology affects the way processes work, and the process affects not only the product but the man who produces it. For that reason it is almost inevitable that this section should end with a look at the future.

During the 1960's, technology had at long last caught up with the newsrooms, and the former bastions of typewriters and pencils added cathode ray tubes and computer terminals. In 1964, at a fairly primitive stage in this evolution, Richard L. Tobin, then communications section editor of *Saturday Review,* set down his thoughts on the future of newsroom technology and what its implications were for the rest of society.

THE MAN WITH
THE PENCIL OF LIGHT *

Richard L. Tobin

What will a newspaper be like in the next forty years? Let's pay a visit to tomorrow's editorial office. It won't be difficult to find the editors, for their chairs will be beside consoles on which are a great number of pushbuttons and a typewriter keyboard. The editors may be completely surrounded by screens similar to television sets, and instead of pencils they'll have slim tubes in their hands—light pencils and erasers that look like pencil flashlights.

The legman, the reporter, and the rewrite man will not have been replaced entirely, and somewhere along the line an original story will still be typed out by someone. Human beings will still be at the core of the newspaper operation. But from that point on, electronic machinery will have taken over. As a rewrite man finishes each sentence, what he has written will be recorded in an electronic morgue where all of the day's news is being stored on computer tapes, along with the tapes of the news of other days. At the same time, the electronic story is also appearing on one of the editor's viewing screens. All the rewrite man and editor will have to do to receive available background material and available photographs on that particular subject is to dial the electronic news library. The material will appear instantly on the editor's viewing screen or, if preferred, it will be electronically printed out for the rewrite man.

The layout department will then begin electronically choosing which story will go in which space on page one and the inside pages; the photographs will be sorted and, after selection, their images projected on the photo editor's screen; and the captions will be written. Headlines will be chosen and the story projected on a screen to a copy editor who will type out his head after reading the material via TV. When the headline is finished, the copy editor will push a button, but the editor may not like the head and flip it back electronically to the copy desk for a revise. Indeed, every transaction, each communication will be done by flicking one switch or another between one editor or another. After a while, all of the news and pictures designed for the front page will have been processed, the top editor will be ready with the heads and makeup, and he will then turn his electronic knob toward the inside pages. When they have satisfied him, he will press a final button that says "Print," for up to this moment nothing in the whole newspaper has actually existed except the original words typed by the rewrite man. Now the button marked "Print" makes those pages a reality.

Not only have the computer and electronic screen taken over in the editorial office, but all copy has been set into lines of appropriate fonts and column widths, words properly split and hyphenated, typographical errors virtually eliminated, loose and tight lines much better spaced than in yesterday's newspapers, and the whole edition delivered in suburban streets dozens of miles away where additional presses have responded to the electronic button marked "Print." In many homes, electronic devices will have acted as their own printing presses.

Is this fantastic hardware far to our future? Not at all. Variations of it already are being used in the assembling, editing, and dissemination of information by intelligence and military headquarters. Will the human being be dropped completely from the newspaper forty years hence? On the contrary, there will be more demand for editing skills and creativity, but considerably diminishing demand for printers, pressmen, compositors, stereotypers, and other mechanical functionaries now prevalent in the relatively unautomated newspaper business of the 1960s.

The chief question is not, however, one of mechanical advancement or automation or futuristic presswork. The morals, the power, and the responsibility of the editor, the reaction of his reader-viewers, their self-control as citizens in a greatly advanced atomic age—these are matters that will count far more than editing with electronic pencil or printing by laser beam. It's what the reader-viewers of mankind do with the information that has been communicated to them that will matter most.

David Sarnoff, chairman of the board of RCA, says that by the year 2000 A.D. our descendants will have the technological capacity to "make obsolete starvation, lengthen appreciably the Biblical life-span, and change hereditary traits." General Sarnoff believes we shall have a limitless abundance of energy sources and raw materials forty years hence, that the moon and other parts of the solar system will have been brought within the human domain, and that machines will have the capacity to multiply thought and logic a millionfold.

But what earthly use will all these advances be to the human race if communication between individuals, between families, and between nations is as obsolete and antedeluvian as it is today? In his fine auto-biography, Raymond B. Fosdick says it superbly well: "We had been undone by technology which came too soon and which found us utterly unprepared in point of religion, ethics, law and philosophy, and politics to meet the problems which it created."

Technically, the year 2004 should see an incredible increase in the facility of communication between individuals and political units. Through communication satellites, laser beams, and ultraminiaturization it should be possible by the beginning of the next century to communicate with anyone anywhere at any time by voice, sight, or written message. From country to country, continent to continent, and from earth and earth's space vehicles to the planets beyond, communication will be relatively simple via satellite telephone, radio, and television. The communicators will be within full hearing and sight of one another through three-dimensional color TV screens. It will be possible for a human being to be equipped with a miniature TV transmitter-receiver with which he can communicate, in color and sound, as he walks along the street, with another human being perhaps on the other side of the world. The system will be quite simply operated from his pocket-size walkie-talkie via radio, switchboard, and satellite. He will use a personal channel and code similar to today's telephone number, but he can talk as he walks along a street in New York to a human being on a street in London. He will be using pushbutton dialing and a form of the new picturephone.

Newspaper and magazine copy written on one continent will be transmitted and set into type instantaneously on another through satellite-electronic means. In fact, forty years from this August, key newspapers will appear in simultaneous editions everywhere in the world, automatically translated and set in type to suit the indigenous language. Television will be able to transmit directly to each home on earth on a world-wide basis, and several billion people may well be watching the same program with automatic language translation to match local comprehension. We may still be sending overseas mail and parcel post by air and ship, but most mail will be transmitted by facsimile reproduction through one of many satellites weighing several hundred tons, floating in the incredibly vast spaces above the habitable world, which forty years hence will of necessity comprise practically all of the land areas, many of which are now considered unfit places to live.

The world will be advanced technically by 2004—that we can forecast—unless it has blown itself sky-high by then, which seems quite possible. If, in Fosdick's words, we have still not brought our philosophical and moral plateau up to the scientific, if we are still unprepared in ethics, law, and self-control to meet the problems that our computer-electronic-atomic world has by then geometrically added to the pressing present, the fact of easy communication between individuals, families, nations, and peoples may be as academic as a monarch's golden boast before the flood.

SECTION FOUR
THE JOURNALIST
AND HIS COMMITMENTS

One major recent change in the mass media unrelated either to technology or to economics has evolved. The perceptions of what a newsman is and should be, both in terms of how he sees his own role and how outsiders perceive him, has become the basis of a continuing debate through a wide spectrum of American society.

The term "new journalism," although it was invented to apply to content and format, has quickly come to refer as much to certain newsmen and their attitudes. Although there is a long history of bitter quarrels between the media and U.S. Presidents beginning with George Washington, not until Richard Nixon's presidency did an American chief executive *openly* take the offensive against the media, sending in his attorney general with writs and requests for injunctions and his vice-president with alliterative accusations of alleged acrimony. "New" journalists debated old ones at almost every professional meeting, while journalism reviews, as much self-analytical as anti-Establishment, sputtered into life across the nation.

The outer edges of the arguments became infinitely complex, but the central issue remained the communicator's—and particularly the newsman's—right to use his skills to bring about change instead of limiting himself to reporting "the facts" and letting others make the decisions. The "new journalists" were seen by their critics as persuaders working with rigged evidence; and indeed many were quite willing to regard themselves as committed to persuasion, but only after a careful consideration of all the evidence.

Newsmen have always had their share of crusaders, of course, and one of the most interesting (and, many would say, most glorious) periods of American journalism was during the early years of this century when Lincoln Steffens, Ray Stannard Baker, and Ida Tarbell were clobbering the Establishment of their own time. Yet there are sharp differences between these muckrakers and today's "involved" reporter.

Look at a contemporary newsman whose work and personality represent a blend of old and new persuasive journalism. Jack Anderson took over from Drew Pearson, whose leg man he had once been, a column conducted in the classic tradition of muckraking—detailed, specific accounts of the seamy underside of activities in business and government. Anderson continued in that tradition of "objective" reporting, laying out his facts as dispassionate verities, keeping his personality essentially invisible except for occasional reports of pressure brought upon him. His day-to-day work, like Pearson's, added up to being profoundly anti-Establishment. He attacked corporations and public figures in all parts of the economic and political spectrum. A continuing inference of his work was that many of the movers and shakers of the society were not to be trusted.

But, in the old tradition, he has never openly stated this in the column. He has never generalized in print about flaws in the system. He has, in a curious way, maintained a sense of not showing personal animus even as he lays out the damning evidence. He won a Pulitzer Prize in 1972 for publishing a series of leaked top-secret memoranda dealing with the government's decision to give tacit backing to Pakistan in that country's brief and disastrous war with India over the issue of independence for Bangladesh. The memos amounted to summary minutes of meetings at the top level of policy-making and gained force by appearing within two weeks of the actual session. The protective rationalization surrounding publication of the so-called Pentagon Papers that the documents were "historical" (some with current implications were never published) was impossible. Anderson was publishing the current grist of policy-making, including injudicious and compromising remarks by powerful presidential advisers, and the instantaneous uproar made Anderson a public figure. He began to appear on television talk shows in addition to his own broadcasts and became much sought after as a speaker. Within weeks he was astride another controversy with the publication of a letter which suggested that the Justice Department had arranged a settlement of an antitrust case against International Telephone and Telegraph after one of the company's subsidiaries made a heavy contribution to the Republican national convention. This one almost immediately became a matter of people calling each other liars; Anderson and his assistants not only testified before a Senate committee, but were interviewed by other newsmen for their reactions after others testified. *Newsweek* summed up what was happening to the man in a piece entitled "A Muckraker with a Mission"; which, after identifying him as a former Mormon missionary, went on to say

> The columnist was also taking his case to any live audience that would hear him. Addressing a mesmerized gathering of fellow Mormons, Anderson did more pacing, finger jabbing, and eye-rolling than Oral Roberts in full cry. "The incestual [sic] relationship between government and big business thrives in the dark," boomed his rich baritone voice. "When those responsible for it get caught in the sunlight, they are like fish out of water. They flip and they flop. They backtrack. They trip over their tongues." His voice soaring, Anderson climaxed his pyrotechnics with a ringing call to action. "Are we going to tolerate this?" he demanded. "Are we going to let them corrupt us? They are not your masters. They are your servants. You have the final decision. You have the final vote!"

That, by any definition, is an involved anti-Establishment journalist, and he may have more permanent influence than all those who see themselves as a new breed.

Yet most observers of journalism, and most working journalists, would not see Jack Anderson as a practitioner of "new journalism" (nor, one suspects, would he). There are several reasons for this. One is the obvious matter of the form itself. Printed Anderson still reads like familiar exposé journalism—"I'm just giving the facts"—and contains none of the self-examining quality of the work of such writers as Nicholas von Hoffman or Gay Talese. It is written lucidly, but without style or nuance or what might be described as personal sensitivity.

More importantly, it contains no elements of criticism of the media or a search for new approaches to the business of being a better journalist working in a more responsive organization. That concern is one of the most important.

Are journalists professionals? It is an old question, the answer to which depends on the definition you select. The Bureau of Labor Statistics lists three requirements for a profession: prescribed educational standards, governmental licensing, and enforcement of performance standards by the profession itself. Such requirements, even if deemed desirable for journalism, would run into First Amendment difficulties. Would anyone really want the government to have the power to say who could and who could not be a journalist? Journalistic codes are strictly voluntary. Forgetting the formal requirements of a profession, however, one could argue that a commitment to service and truth and the sharing of certain ethical standards would qualify journalists as professionals. Perhaps an even more important point is that more and more journalists *look on themselves as professionals.*

Publishers, station owners, and boards of directors can issue broad policy directives, but the actual publications, books, broadcasts, and films are brought into being by vast numbers of talented, creative people, with their own standards of excellence and their own values. These standards and values do more to shape the mass media fare than most members of the audience realize—even more than many executives realize. As in any field, genuinely talented workers are always in short supply. These workers now are demanding more than money and job security to keep them happy.

Here are a few manifestations of the new style demands:

1. Informal cells of workers have organized in many newspapers, magazines, and stations to discuss mutual (largely noneconomic) problems and to channel these complaints and suggestions to management.

2. Cross-media *ad hoc* groups have been organized and financed by working newsmen. For example, the Association of Public Television Producers has lobbied for freedom to select subjects for specials, and the Reporters' Committee on Freedom of the Press has sought advice on subpoena questions from legal scholars rather than from corporate lawyers.

3. Labor negotiations now include more than bread-and-butter issues. Some locals of the American Newspaper Guild (the union which includes reporters) have won a veto over the naming of city editors and similar department editors, representation on the papers' editorial boards, and the right to publish dissenting editorials.

This is not to suggest there is no interest in higher salaries among newsmen, for whom starting salaries for new college graduates in 1972 averaged $130 to $150. Most Guild contracts guarantee at least $300 for those with five years' experience and a few set a $400 floor. Still, newsmen's salaries rose less during the last two decades than did salaries for workers in all production industries. Salaries go up—way up—for the superstars of news. David Brinkley, Walter Cronkite, Howard K. Smith, and Harry Reasoner all earn at least as much as the President of the United States, $200,000 a year. James Reston of the New York *Times* gets about half that amount. The really big money is, as in any industry, in top management: Frank Stanton, vice-chairman of CBS, earns $400,000, and Hugh Hefner of *Playboy* more than $300,000.

What do wages have to do with ethics? Perhaps a great deal. Just as a media owner with money in the bank is less susceptible to advertiser pressure, so is a reasonably well-paid journalist more independent when he is not beholden to news sources for such favors as free drinks and tickets.

Salaries are high enough today that he can, and often does, refuse such favors for fear of a possible conflict of interest. Many employers insist on such scrupulousness by their employees.

Although the activist newsman can hardly resent such policies against accepting favors from news sources, he often does resent attempts by his employers to limit his outside life. We have seen an influx of entertainers and authors into politics, both as candidates and as campaigners; however, most stations and publications prohibit their newsmen from such activities for fear they will cast aspersions on the fairness of the entire news operation. Activist journalists already are murmuring about such restrictions, and that murmur is likely to swell into a roar. Not all the newsmen want to be active in politics, but they want to make that decision for themselves.

Another sign of professionalism is that reporters in more than 50 cities are publishing reviews which explain and often criticize their own publications and stations. Explaining to the public why certain stories were not covered or why they were covered the way they were is not likely to endear an employee to his boss. Publishing any journal takes work, and in the case of reviews there usually is no pay, either for the writers or for the editors. Some of the articles have been mainly sour grapes, but others have given valid and fascinating glimpses into the workings of the media; the long-term goal of the journals is to force their for-pay employers to improve their products.

These journals are particularly healthy in the media business because there is little cross-media criticism published or broadcast in commercial channels. Newspapers and magazines write more about TV stars and gossip than about trends or developments in the industry; even the reviews tend to be of specials, which because they are single-shot offerings, cannot be changed or improved, regardless how insightful the criticism they generate. Stations do even less criticism of the press, although some noncommercial stations offer such programs, and WTOP-TV in Washington has a veteran newsman who regularly broadcasts such material. New York's Channel 13, which has more viewers than any other public television station, regularly attracts half a million viewers for its "Behind the Headlines" program which examines the nation's press.

Articles in the mass-appeal *TV Guide* are far more critical of television than are those in *Broadcasting,* the weekly magazine for those in the industry. *Editor and Publisher,* the parallel trade journal for newspapers, is even more protective of the Establishment elements in its business.

The new activism among journalists is hailed by Professor J. K. Hvistendahl of the Iowa State University Department of Journalism in the following article:

THE REPORTER AS ACTIVIST *

J. K. Hvistendahl

American Journalism is embroiled in its fourth revolution, introduced to the country in the belligerent tones of Vice President Spiro T. Agnew in his Des Moines speech of November 1969. This revolution, like most social revolutions, has even those who are most directly involved in complete chaos and confusion. The revolution is real, those who are involved are in earnest, but the goal is not necessarily the demise of American journalism.

The first revolution was the freeing of the American Press from the threat of control by government. The first and fourteenth amendments to the constitution made it legal, and 18th Century rationalism made it philosophically desirable to criticize actions of the government. The editors of partisan newspapers after the revolution supplied somewhat more criticism than the government wanted.

The second revolution was the growth of the "objective press," brought about largely by the press associations which developed after the invention of the telegraph. Because they served many papers, with many and sometimes violently differing points of view, the press associations had to present the news as objectively as possible, without opinions or evaluations of the authors. The press association made a solid contribution to journalistic writing, and the objective style became the model for journalistic writing.

The third revolution was interpretive reporting, in which the reporter reported the facts objectively, but attempted to explain them or interpret them in a way that would made them meaningful to the reader and listener. Both World War I and World War II contributed to the growth of this type of reporting; readers and listeners wilted before a barrage of objective but totally confusing messages about the war. By interpreting the news to anxious audiences, H. V. Kaltenborn, Elmer Davis, Boake Carter and other "name" commentators commanded audiences of millions. Newspaper columnists like Raymond Clapper, Thomas L. Stokes, Marquis Childs, Walter Lippmann, and Ernest K. Lindley came on the scene for the same reasons.

* Condensed from *The Quill: The Magazine for Journalists,* Feb. 1970, by permission of the author and publisher. © Copyright by *The Quill,* 1970.

Now the fourth revolution is upon us, and the revolutionists are activist reporters. The journalistic activist believes he has a right (indeed an obligation) to become personally and emotionally involved in the events of the day. He believes he should proclaim his beliefs if he wishes, and that it is not only permissible but desirable for him to cover the news from the viewpoint of his own intellectual commitment. He looks at traditional reporting as being sterile, and he considers reporters who refuse to commit themselves to a point of view as being cynical or hypocritical. The activist believes that attempting to describe the events of a complicated world objectively seldom results in the truth for anybody—the source, the reporter, or the reader or listener.

Some of the symptoms of the growing activism:

Some 500 Time, Inc. employees attended anti-war discussions in the company auditorium on Moratorium Day.

The *Chicago Journalism Review,* a publication by reporters dedicated to pointing out the lapses of the very papers for which they work, is now in its second year of publication.

Reporters on at least a half dozen major papers in the country have asked their publishers for a more active role in their paper's policy decisions, as have the employees of *Time.*

Two young women reporters on the New York *Post* were fired for refusing to have their bylines on stories which they thought demeaned women, but were rehired after other *Post* reporters eliminated their own bylines in sympathy.

"Truth-as-I-see-it" reporting, rather than activist reporting, might be a more accurate description of the fourth revolution. The new reporters don't claim that they, or anybody else, have a corner on the truth. But they insist that the reporter, like the scientist, has an obligation to report the truth as he sees it. In the long run, they believe, the reporter who is seeking the truth will serve the reader and listener better than the traditional reporter who attempts to describe an event accurately, reduce it to symbols which fit the news conduits of the various media, and then pipe the product to the consumer who is to make of it what he will.

The activist believes the modern media "lie by sanitation" and sin by omission. The media omit important observations by the reporter because they are "editorial in nature." They clean up and homogenize the news to make it fit the orderly world of the establishment, of which the press is too much a part. Read this excerpt from a letter written by a young journalism graduate after his first job on a large Midwestern newspaper:

In July I went on a walk through ———, the city's worst black ghetto, with the President of the American Public Health Association. We visited homes of five ghetto residents to talk with them about their health problems.

My assignment was to pour out my heart in the story. I did. But by the time the copy desk got through with the material it was unrecognizable. Every reference to tenement was changed to "apartment" and all mention of rat tracks, month-old garbage, and abandoned buildings standing open to kids and arsonists (law requires all abandoned buildings in the city to be boarded up) was edited out.

The reporter thought that he'd been asked to "pour out his heart," but apparently not to the extent that he could describe a ghetto neighborhood in terms which showed his feelings, and might in turn convey similar feelings to his readers.

The truth-as-I-see-it newsman rejects the conduit, or common carrier, theory of the press. The amount that can flow through the conduits is miniscule compared to the totality of available news. The consumer can't possibly be given all the facts about a situation as complicated as, for example, Vietnam. The process of news selection is and always has been subjective; there are no reliable external criteria (first-year journalism books to the contrary) by which anyone can decide with any precision what is news and what isn't news.

If it is indeed true that a news story starts out as a subjective decision on the part of the press service, city editor, or television program director, the question then arises as to whether the story shall be released without further responsibility on the part of the media. Vice President Agnew would probably say yes. But for the activists there are several reasons why the newsman's responsibility should continue. Because only a small part of the totality of relevant information can be presented to the reader or viewer, the situation (as far as truth-as-I-see-it goes) is one-sided and is likely to mislead the reader or listener. The content of a news event within the reporter's own knowledge, may be patently false, exaggerated or misleading but is offered to the reader without comment and with the implication that it is true. "Objectivity" may be served but the truth isn't.

The classic example of "common carrier" reporting, of course, was that of the late Senator Joseph McCarthy. McCarthy made charges on the floor of the Senate which reporters knew were false, but they were obliged to report the stories without comment or warning because the newspapers they worked for were "common carriers." The reporter had no obligation to truth-as-they-knew-it other than to quote the senator correctly, but it was a frustrating experience for those who knew they were spreading false information.

From the viewpoint of communication theory, the "objective" reporter or writer expends most of his responsibility with the source. He is obliged to quote the sources correctly, and accurately describe the news event. Further, he must not in any way permit his own views to provide a warning to the reader if he perceives the information to be false or defective. The reader or listener must be the judge; the writer has no responsibility to the audience other than to deliver the message. The activist reporter with his emphasis on truth-as-I-see-it feels responsibility to the audience. He asks, "If I deliver an 'objective' message to the reader, but that message is likely to take the reader farther from the truth rather than bring him closer to it, who has been served?"

Another area in which the truth-as-I-see-it journalist demands more of the share of the action is in the news selection process. The women reporters on the New York *Post* refused to have their bylines on an interview of Mrs. Gil Hodges. According to their value system, women are people and should appear in the news on their own merit, not on the merit of their husbands. (If this value were widespread in American journalism, Jackie Kennedy Onassis would soon have complete privacy.)

The point is not that one point-of-view is necessarily more valid than another, but there are *multiple points of view* in a diverse society and more of these should surface in the press. For the most part, the "gatekeepers" who make the news decisions in the media are in the bifocal set, and they inevitably make news judgments that reflect their own training and backgrounds, Like all of us, they are victims as well as beneficiaries of all they have experienced. They have "learned" that the public will lap up columns of type on murder cases, so they have given the public columns of type on the Sam Sheppard cases while Lake Erie gets little attention until it is biologically dead. As one young reporter expresses it, "The American press is always last to recognize the disease, but is first to report the funeral."

The activist believes that the base of news judgment should be broadened to include more newsmen with contemporary social conscience, who are actively interested in solutions to social problems, and who might make the press an active partner, rather than a passive chronicler of social change.

Most news executives maintain that objectivity is a worthy goal. Wes Gallagher, longtime general manager of Associated Press, has written, "To the true newsman, partisanship is the original sin, the apple in the journalistic Eden." And consider these words from A. M. Rosenthal to his staff when he became managing editor of the New York *Times* in 1969:

> The *Times* is a newspaper of objectivity. Time was when objectivity was taken for granted as a newspaper's goal, if not always an attained goal. But we live in a time of commitment and advocacy when "tell it like it is" really means "tell it like I say it is" or "tell it as I want it to be."
>
> For precisely that reason, it is more important than ever that the *Times* keeps objectivity in its news columns as its number one, bedrock principle. We are all quite aware that since every story is written by a human being and that the decision on how to play it is made by other human beings, total pristine objectivity is impossible clinically.
>
> But we struggle to achieve the highest possible degree of objectivity. Objectivity is the determination to write and edit with the elimination of as much personal bias as humanly possible, to present facts and situations as close to reality as possible, to avoid our own pejorative phrases or comments, to give accused people or institutions the right of immediate reply, to present all shadings of opinion and counter argument, and most of all, to keep examining ourselves day by day and story by story to see if we are being as objective as we can.
>
> On these things we stand fast, but we do not stand pat journalistically; to do so would be to wither. Our definition of news, and our techniques of handling news, have been changing and broadening.
>
> Spot news—this happened yesterday—and exclusive news—we know about it, nobody else does and we are telling you—remain the foundation of any good paper. They give it immediacy and currency.
>
> But more and more we have to give something considerable in addition to spot news. We have learned that news is not simply what people say and do, but what they think, what motivates them, their styles of living, the movements, trends and forces acting upon society and on a man's life.

Many journalists rejected the premises of the new journalism in more bitter terms. For example, Jim Bormann, director of WCCO News in Minneapolis, told a convention of the Radio and Television News Directors Association:

> It is simply outrageous to think we as modern practitioners have any rights or duties or privileges to deal more lightly with the truth than the journalist of another age may have had. . . . For whatever else the new journalism may be called, the accurate name for it is "dishonest reporting."

More American newspapers are emulating their European cousins in permitting and encouraging staffers to contribute signed opinion articles. During the late 1960's many papers, including the New York *Times,* added an "op ed" page for such disparate opinions, both by staffers and outsiders. *Time* magazine, which pioneered anonymous "group journalism," even added a signed editorial essay. The underground press emerged as a major force, and young filmmakers turned out avowedly opinionated shorts and features.

Broadcasting offers working journalists fewer opportunities for self-expression. Television never developed the commentator tradition that network radio had in its heyday, when many stations carried half a dozen commentators ranging from Elmer Davis on the left to Fulton Lewis on the right. On network TV, Eric Sevareid is almost one of a kind, and he finds himself locked into a short segment at the end of evening newscasts. Even he defended the concept of objectivity in a lecture at Columbia University in 1970:

> Those who would improve our practices in questionable ways come not only from the outside in the form of powerful politicians. Some come from inside. Militant young men and women, in both newspapers and broadcasting who argue that even the *quest* for objectivity is a myth, that the prime purpose of the press is not to report the world but to reform it, and in the direction of their ideas. We have all read the learned articles that tell us objective news accounts in the hard news columns or broadcasts tend merely to deceive the reader or hearer, obscure inner truths that the reporter perceives. He must therefore personalize the hard news, infuse it with his own truth. They would not leave this to the editorial writer, columnist and commentator, whose work is clearly marked away from the hard news. They believe this will give a true integrity to news columns and news broadcasts. I believe it will ruin them. There is nothing new about this idea. In fact, this is the way it was done in the days of the yellow press and the screamers of radio's first, faltering years. This is the way it is still done in many countries. The result there is that one must read many newspapers, hear many broadcasts, then try to piece together what really happened in any given occurrence. Inevitably, this becomes the journalism of polemics.

Objectivity is only part of the debate swirling around the new activist journalism. For example, Ron Dorfman, editor of *Chicago Journalism Review,* sees the central issue as economics: "What the field militants are after is not simply the right to chant a different cotton-chopping rhythm, but a piece of the plantation."

Tom Wolfe is probably the best-known of the new journalists, although he is but one star in a constellation which centers on *New York* and *Esquire* magazines. What they have done is to use many of the techniques of the short story and novel in reporting. Wolfe explains that saturation reporting is much harder than conventional interviewing, in which you talk to the expert, write down his answers, and then try to relay them to readers. In saturation reporting, Wolfe says, you are after more than facts. It means long stretches of time with the people you are writing about, an attention to minute details, and great chunks of dialogue.

"You have to constantly be on the alert for chance remarks, odd details, quirks, curios, anything that may serve to bring a scene alive when you're writing," Wolfe says. "There is no formula for it. It never gets any easier just because you've done it before."

A *Wall Street Journal* staff reporter expressed misgivings about the kind of journalism which Wolfe represented, and he spoke for many in the profession.

THE 'NEW JOURNALISM' IS SOMETIMES LESS THAN MEETS THE EYE *

W. Stewart Pinkerton, Jr.

NEW YORK—Redpants is a hustler from Detroit who wears Gucci shoes. She once worked for a pimp named Sugarman, and she gets a lot of business by hanging around the Waldorf-Astoria here, where a friendly guard looks upon her with fondness and sympathy.

Her story, tragic and absorbing, was told recently in *New York* magazine. Staff writer Gail Sheehy had apparently become as close as a sister to the prostitute, and the resulting story was one of the most readable articles ever to appear in the readable young publication. Readers were given a real insight into a world most don't know.

Miss Sheehy painted a vivid picture. "Leading the john up the warped stairs of the Lindy Hotel, a second-floor fleabag several blocks down from the Waldorf, Redpants looks as awkward as she feels. Behind the desk is a beefy man in a mustard undershirt, his arms blue with tattoos. He smiles at Redpants by way of a welcome into the fold.

* The article is condensed from the issue of August 13, 1971. © Copyright *Wall Street Journal,* 1971.

" 'That's $7.75, pal.' The john fills out a registration card. Half-way up the staircase the couple is stopped by a shout from the tattooed man.

" 'Hey, you're man and wife, right' Redpants giggles. 'Right.' "

The article was filled with such fascinating detail, but there was one detail Miss Sheehy left out:

Redpants didn't do and say a lot of the things Miss Sheehy ascribed to her.

Redpants is what's known as a composite character. Miss Sheehy spent weeks interviewing real hustlers and pimps, and then she combined the salient details of their lives into the characters of Redpants and Sugarman. So the story was true, sort of, but then again it wasn't. The reader, however, was not told any of this.

There are other techniques besides the use of composite characters or the reconstruction of events. Following the Redpants article, Miss Sheehy wrote a piece for *New York* about 24 wild hours in the life of a procurer named David. David was real enough, all right—in fact, he is quite upset by the publicity—and the events in his life are believed to be real. But they didn't all happen within 24 hours. They happened over a period of days, and for storytelling's sake Miss Sheehy telescoped them into 24 hours.

"We're not trying to put anything over on the reader. We're just trying to put a greater degree of reality into it," explains Clay Felker, the imaginative editor who has made *New York* a success. He is clearly concerned about the trend, however, and he says that "we are going to be more careful in the future" about alerting the reader.

Mr. Felker gets much of the credit—or blame—for the development of the New Journalism in the first place. He was an editor at *Esquire* when writers such as Gay Talese and Tom Morgan (now press secretary to John Lindsay) first began trying to write nonfiction in the dramatic style of fiction. (Another early practitioner was Jimmy Breslin.) Mr. Talese, in particular, became expert at both reporting and reconstructing moving or intimate scenes.

It's all part of the New Journalism, or the Now Journalism, and it's practiced widely these days. Some editors and reporters vigorously defend it. Others just as vigorously attack it. No one has polled the reader, but whether he approves or disapproves, it's getting harder and harder for him to know what he can believe. For example:

—*Esquire* some time ago ran a cover showing the reclusive Howard Hughes, but it wasn't really Howard Hughes. And in another issue, right in the middle of a long piece on the war, there was a whole chunk of made-up dialog between the author and a made-up U.S.

general. The reader was never told what was fact and what was fiction, or, indeed, that there was any fiction in the piece at all.

—*Philadelphia* magazine in May 1969 ran an astonishingly detailed account of a burglar named Harry Phillips and his pal, Joey, detailing how they robbed the home of a wealthy Main Line doctor. Harry, the magazine disclosed, has been arrested four times and once served a six-month sentence in Delaware County. One additional fact, which the readers weren't told, is that Harry and Joe are composite characters.

—And, as the world now knows, the *National Review* published some "secret papers" that came not from the Pentagon but rather from the fertile mind of William Buckley, the urbane editor. Newspapers and broadcasters handled the "papers" as if they were news, and Mr. Buckley didn't own up to his prank until after publication.

All this raises some questions that are beginning to trouble practitioners and nonpractitioners alike. To what extent should such techniques as using composite characters be employed? If used extensively, do they edge a story into the fiction category? Is an editor obliged to alert the reader? And to what extent does the New Journalism strain the credibility of the author or the publication or the profession in general? This last question is perhaps the most important.

Some editors aren't too concerned with these questions. "I don't think it really matters" whether a reader can distinguish between a true account and a reconstructed, or probable, account, says Alan Halpern, editor of *Philadelphia.* He says that a true story, such as his magazine's account of how a reporter was approached by a man who was trying to sell a stolen car, and a story such as the reconstruction of the Main Line robbery along the lines it *likely* took place, have the same purpose. "What you're trying to do is understand how a situation works," he says. The reconstruction "is a (literary) convention."

Lewis Bergman, editor of the Sunday *New York Times Magazine,* disagrees. "If there's any question (of credibility) in the mind of the reader, you want to settle it before he starts the story," he says.

Mr. Talese and Mr. Wolfe might have the stamina to stay with a subject for a long time, learning enough about him so it's possible to reconstruct any scene accurately, but critics say there is a whole crop of younger reporters who like the style but don't like the work. (They don't necessarily include Miss Sheehy in this group; while some may question her use of composites or telescoping, she's considered a competent reporter.) Thus, the critics say, the New Journalism is rising but its believability is declining.

Whether it's declining in believability is, of course, debatable, but there's no doubt that it's rising in frequency. In fact, there's a whole new book on the nonfiction shelves that may not belong there. The book, which has been receiving favorable reviews, is titled "U.S. Grant in the City and Other True Stories of Jugglers and Pluggers, Swatters and Whores." It consists of nine portraits of New York characters, including Hector and Louise, two teen-age muggers, and Lamont, a 19-year-old pimp. These two stories originally appeared in *New York* magazine.

New York's Mr. Felker says he assumed Hector and Louise were actual living people and that author David Freeman's portrait of them was yet another straight, well-wrought work. But Hector and Louise, as well as the other characters, are very probably composites. Mr. Freeman doesn't like to talk about it. He will only say: "I set out to create a work of art. I *believe* Hector and Louise to be real." But then he confusingly adds: "It is often possible for the facts to get in the way of real truth."

The New Journalism has become so widespread that editors printing straight articles now sometimes take pains to tell the readers that the articles are fact, not fiction. In the August *Esquire,* for instance, the editors called attention to the vast research that Mr. Talese put into "The Kidnapping of Joe Bonanno," a piece about the life and times of an Italian-American family with links to the Mafia. The article is an excerpt from a book that Mr. Talese has been working on for almost seven years off and on, and it contains intimate glimpses of events that Mr. Talese was not present at.

"I believe Talese wrote the truth," says *Esquire* managing editor Don Erickson, "but I don't know the reader knows that." Thus the squib in the front of the magazine.

Underlying much of the discussion of the New Journalism is what probably can be best described as continuity of credibility. Alfred Balk, editor of the *Columbia Journalism Review,* asks: "If an author or publication jeopardizes its credibility once, can he ever be wholly believed again?"

Many people don't think so. Five newspapers, including the Denver *Post* and Houston *Chronicle,* have dropped William Buckley's syndicated column because of the publication in the *National Review* of the phony "secret" documents. The "documents," Mr. Buckley admitted, were composed from nothing (or, as Mr. Buckley put it, *ex nihilo*) to demonstrate, among other things, "that the Pentagon and the CIA are not composed of incompetents—the unwarranted conclusion to which many Americans and non-Americans were led by the fragmentary revelations of The New York *Times* and the Washington *Post*" in their publication of the Pentagon papers.

Editorialized New Jersey's Bergen *Record*: ". . . It's execrable journalism. . . . The man has destroyed the credibility of his own publication. . . . What could be worse is the impact of his snotty prank on the public's already shaky confidence in the integrity of the news media generally." Indeed, when Mr. Buckley confessed that his secret papers were a hoax, some Americans got the erroneous impression that all the Pentagon papers were a hoax.

For his part, Mr. Balk, in his *Columbia Journalism Review* says he is in favor of "maximum flexibility" of journalistic forms, including traditional spot stories, features, personal columns and mood-type pieces. "But I'm also in favor of truth-in-packaging," he says. "If a story is misleading, it loses credibility. And that hurts us all."

When it comes to commitment, few journalists can match the editors of the underground press. Like ideologues of any age, they have a message to deliver—about drugs, music, racism, sexism, or politics—and the more they are harassed, the more they thrive. While most such publications are as ephemeral and unmemorable as mayflies, a few do survive and exert influence. Their combined circulation probably exceeds 5 million copies a week. Most are opposed to the Establishment and its profit system but soon learn that if they don't adapt to work habits and economic realities, they won't be around long enough to deliver their message. Some adapt too well, at least for their radical staffers and readers. The granddaddy of all undergrounds, the *Village Voice,* was too tame within six months of its founding in 1955 for Norman Mailer, one of its cofounders. Although he continued to own stock in the venture (stock which paid handsome dividends), he stopped playing a role in the management of the paper quite early. A little more than a decade later, the staff of the highly successful Los Angeles *Free Press* (*"The Freep"*) were incensed when the publisher installed time clocks in the editorial offices, and the staff of the Berkeley *Barb* walked out in a huff when they heard about the alleged profits of the publisher of that outrageous tabloid.

There is a story, probably apocryphal, that an underground paper is always founded by three dedicated people, and that inevitably two of them will fire the third because he is the one who shows up on time and is therefore "too bourgeois."

Activist newsmen, both under- and above-ground, are not the only groups concerned with the adequacy of the conventional news media. Some groups have been trying to force the media to publish their opinions. One of the interesting developments in the 1960's was the emergence of the concept of a right of access. When some lower courts held that a citizen or group had a constitutional right to distribute leaflets in bus stations and to purchase advertising card space in subways, Professor Jerome Barron of the George Washington University School of Law extrapolated a more general right of access. He said the media were obligated to sell space and to cover activities of groups seeking to present significant ideas.

It is one thing to insist on access to publicly owned facilities (such as bus stations or subways); it is something else to require privately owned media to do so. There always has been such an obligation in broadcasting, since stations are required under the terms of their licenses to present "balanced coverage" of controversial issues. For the most part, the federal government has allowed the broadcasters to define what was "balanced." In the print media, however, there are no licenses, and owners have enjoyed entrepreneurial rights of making such decisions on any basis they chose. Many constitutional lawyers argue that any government-decreed requirements for content in the print media would be illegal because of the First Amendment.

There is a serious problem of access of another type, namely, the banning by many newspapers of all advertising for X-rated and unrated motion pictures. Large papers in such cities as Phoenix, Cleveland, San Diego, and Detroit have such policies, citing the offensiveness of even the titles of many such films in their "family newspapers."

When the Detroit *News* announced such a policy in 1972, Jack Valenti, president of the Motion Picture Association of America, issued a statement which said, in part:

> If the adult citizens of Detroit are wise enough to choose their mayor, their congressmen, their President, surely adults can make their own choices about films they want or don't want to see, or want or don't want their children to see. When the *News* excludes certain information from its advertising columns, the *News* is withholding useful information from parents.

He defended the industry's rating system and objected to distributors and exhibitors "being indicted and punished through bans on ads because they have willingly joined in a program of information to parents."

Not only is opening access to the media desirable from a freedom of expression standpoint, but it also is good business. Letters to the editor columns always rank well in newspaper readership studies; more recently, the "Action-Line" type column has done even better. Readers like to read what they write better than what the professionals write for them. The same thing is true in broadcasting, where call-in shows have proved extremely popular. WMCA in New York City, which calls itself Dial-log Radio 57, is a 24-hour call-in station, with elaborate facilities which permit the hooking up of as many as eight callers to talk with one another on a sort of urban version of the old telephone party line. Newsmakers appear at regular hours to spur controversy, and the radio host connects the callers directly to the newsmakers. In late 1971, the station ranked sixth in the entire New York City market. (Two of the top four stations at the same time were all-news stations.)

Jerry Williams, who claims he developed the radio-talk-show format in 1950 on a New Jersey stations, has a similar show on WBZ, Boston. "It's a great pure form of broadcasting," he says. "No place in the world has this sort of platform available to people. It's a pure form of democracy, a town meeting." A Chicago talk show host gets 500 to 600 calls a day from listeners.

Sometime during the 1970's the courts probably will have to decide the issue. If Barron's proposal has served no other purpose, it has generated much discussion about the root meaning of the First Amendment.

Protecting one's news sources is looked upon as an almost sacred trust by most journalists. Sometimes the only way they can get certain tips and information is by promising their informants anonymity, and through the years a few newsmen have gone to jail rather than disclose such names. Some states have laws which specifically exempt a journalist from being required to divulge such information to governmental officials, but in 1972 the Supreme Court of the United States ruled that in states without such laws, the newsman had no more right than any other citizen to withhold information from a grand jury. In his dissent in that case, Justice William O. Douglas wrote:

> Forcing a reporter before a grand jury will have two retarding effects upon the ear and the pen of the press. Fear of exposure will cause dissidents to communicate less openly to trusted reporters. And, fear of accountability will cause editors and critics to write with more restrained pens. . . . A reporter is no better than his source of information. Unless he has a privilege to withhold the identity of his source, he will be the victim of governmental intrigue or aggression. If he can be summoned to testify in secret before a grand jury, his sources will dry up and the attempted exposure, the effort to enlighten the public, will be ended.

Certainly most journalists looked on the decision as an ominous one in light of the increased use of subpoenas by federal grand juries, demanding not only identification of sources, but also unpublished notes and records, unused photos, and unedited radio and television tapes. Newsmen insisted that turning over such materials would impair their effectiveness as news gatherers. Frank Stanton, then president of CBS, maintained this same position in 1971 in denying a congressional committee's demands for the footage edited out of the controversial documentary, *Selling of the Pentagon.* Congress, by a narrow margin, voted not to cite the network executive for contempt. NBC, as well as several newspapers and news magazines, also refused to turn over such materials to grand juries.

There are special problems for the black journalist in determining his commitments. Until recent years there were few jobs for blacks on *general* newspapers and magazines. That is changing, but many of the blacks who have gone to work for general publications and stations have felt typecast and thwarted. Some have abandoned these higher-paying jobs for positions on black publications.

The black press always has been an organ of protest and agitation; its editors never accepted the restraints imposed by the goal of objectivity. That is not to suggest that the black press contains no objective reporting; certainly it does. But blacks realized earlier than whites that reporting "facts"—especially from official sources—can distort. They grew skeptical of such "facts" from the police and other Establishment sources long before the other papers. Some black reporters feel more comfortable reporting for black audiences with their unique perspective.

The black papers, themselves, are in a period of change. Many of the established papers are being challenged by more militant new publications, some of them local and some of them organizationally based. Some of these problems are outlined in the article which follows.

THE BLACK PRESS IN TRANSITION *

L. F. Palmer, Jr.

In 1945, whn Gunnar Myrdal's classic study *An American Dilemma* was published, this country had 150 Negro newspapers with a total circulation estimated at 1.6 million, and Myrdal could write: "The Negro press . . . is rightly characterized as the greatest single power in the Negro race." There were three circulation "giants" in the field: the Pittsbugh *Courier* (approximately 257,000); the Chicago *Defender* (202,000); and the Baltimore *Afro-American* (137,000). Twenty-five years later there are 250 to 300 Negro newspapers with a circulation of more than 2 million; they are referred to as the black press; and there is considerable question about the power they wield in black communities. The circulation "giants" are *Muhammad Speaks*

* Reprinted and condensed from *Columbia Journalism Review*, Spring 1970. © Copyright *Columbia Journalism Review*, 1970.

(at least 400,000); *Afro-American* (119,000); and the *Black Panther* (110,000).

Like the readership it serves, the black press is in transition. Characteristically, the field is changing so fast that it virtually defies measurement. Some editions aren't sold, but are given away; large numbers of publications know only a miraculously marginal existence; and small publications come and go in erratic spurts. But it is apparent that the press of, by, and for black people has entered a new evolutionary stage.

The changes in the "big three" of 1945 alone illustrate this. At the close of World War II, the *Courier, Defender,* and *Afro-American* all were national weeklies and could be purchased as easily in Biloxi, Montgomery, or Fort Lauderdale as in Pittsburgh, Chicago, and Baltimore. Today the *Defender* is one of two local black dailies in the country (the other is the Atlanta *Daily World*). The *Defender's* 1969 circulation was 33,320 Monday through Thursday, and 36,458 for its weekend edition. The Pittsburgh *Courier* has dropped to a national circulation of 48,798, plus 15,178 in Pittsburgh only. Of the old "big three," only the *Afro-American* has held its own, showing 1969 ABC figures of 119,902—a quarter-century drop of only 17,789.

Among other great names to have withdrawn from the national field is the Norfolk *Journal and Guide,* consistently credited with being the nation's best-edited and best-dressed black newspaper. Now more of a regional sheet, it has dipped from 61,368 in 1946 to 29,213. Meanwhile, both the Michigan *Chronicle* and Los Angeles *Sentinel* have made dramatic local gains—the *Chronicle* (published in Detroit) from 25,868 circulation in 1946 to 72,776, and the *Sentinel* from 45,892 in 1946 to 41,482. The *Chronicle,* whose editor and general manager, Longworth Quinn, is considered to be one of the best administrators in the field, achieved sizeable increases by winning and holding many readers during Detroit's daily newspaper strikes of 1964 and 1967-68. In Los Angeles, the *Sentinel's* steady gains parallel the city's growth and the migration of blacks westward.

Though copies of the largest black papers can still be found outside their home territories, the end of the national black newspaper is clearly in sight. "Most black papers have to limit their circulation base because it is too costly to maintain far-flung distribution," says John "Rover" Jordan, acting publisher of the *Journal and Guide.* "We can't afford field men any longer, and transportation is too complicated and expensive. It is virtually impossible to provide adequate coverage of the national scene anyway."

Television has made inroads on black newspapers' readership— as it has on that of whites—and, because inner-city blacks are audio-oriented, black-focused radio has hurt, too. As one black editor in Chicago said; "The four black-oriented radio stations here reach more listeners in an hour than the black newspaper has readers in a month."

The limited expansion of black newspapers' advertising bases also is a problem.

Then there is the problem of recruitment. "It's hard getting people who are qualified," says C. B. Powell, seventy-four-year-old publisher of the *Amsterdam News,* "and that goes not only for reporters but in advertising and circulation and management as well. I tried three white advertising managers but it just didn't work out." The *Amsterdam News*, the only black paper with a Newspaper Guild contract, pays the highest average salaries, but even these are below the scale of metropolitan dailies. Echoing Powell, John Murphy of the *Afro-American* says the black press has "become the training ground for the white metropolitan newspapers and radio and television stations ever since they recognized that it is advantageous to have a black reporter or two on their staffs."

The dearth of qualified editorial personnel is reflected in the black press' basic staple—news. Black newspapers, recognizing that they are in no position to compete with the metropolitan press in coverage of black communities, are greedy for handouts. In many instances, the black newspaper seems to have thrown in the towel. The metropolitan press, however, concerns itself largely with the most dramatic and sensational aspects of black life—conflict situations, militancy, unusual achievements of "celebrity blacks," and, of course, crime. Because they have the resources available, white dailies—often with reporters hired from black newspapers—give lengthy coverage to such stories. Thus black readers look increasingly to metropolitan dailies for articles about blacks, even though their treatment may be suspect.

However, when it comes to routine coverage of black communities —social life, church activities, births, marriages, deaths, club and fraternal news, etc.—the black press has an open field and takes full advantage of its monopoly. As one black editor put it: "People like to see their names and their pictures in the paper: Just as sure as day follows night, the average black man or woman will never make the daily newspaper unless he commits a crime, and a serious one at that."

This is why, for example, the Chicago *Courier,* which is rare in that it prints no crime news, in a recent twenty-page issue carried two full pages of business news, a page of entertainment notes, a generous amount of church and social news, and sixty-seven pictures. A sixteen-page edition of the Cincinnati *Herald* included two church pages, two sports pages, and one entertainment page, as well as a full page of pictures, all of different weddings. The *Afro-American* and Pittsburgh

Courier routinely carry two or three pages of women's and society news. It is not unusual for black weeklies to devote two pages to school notes, crammed with names. Once the reader gets off the front page of a black newspaper, he is rarely confronted with hard news.

The front page of most black newspapers, however, are fairly predictable. Banner heads are likely to herald a crime or a racial issue. Typical banners in a recent week: in the Chicago *Daily Defender* weekend edition, E. CHICAGO HTS. RANGER TO DIE IN CHAIR; RAP SCHOOL OFFICIAL FOR STUDENT UNREST; in the *Journal and Guide*, FIRE KILLS 8; FATHER SAVES 3 BEFORE DYING; TROOPS PATROL AT VORHEES; in the *Louisiana Weekly,* COURT HITS RACISM IN ASBESTOS TRADES; INTRUDER SLAIN IN APPLIANCE STORE.

The black press dates to 1827, when John B. Russworm and the Rev. Samuel Cornish went to the editor of the old New York *Sun* and asked him to run a story about a black organization to which they belonged. The editor is reported to have told them: "The *Sun* shines bright for all white men but never for the black man." Rev. Cornish and Russworm walked out and founded the nation's first black newspaper, *Freedom's Journal*. It did not survive long, but the crusading spirit of its founders did.

Early black newspapers cried out against the injustices of slavery and, after emancipation, against the plight of the freedmen. Through the lynching years the black press protested loud and long. Robert S. Abbott and his Chicago *Defender* concentrated on the tortured life in the South with such zeal that he contributed greatly to the northward migration of blacks beginning in World War I. During World War II the black press attacked and exposed discrimination against blacks in the armed forces. This relentless crusade led President Harry Truman to issue an executive order ending Jim Crow in the service. The first historic March on Washington in 1941 was dramatized almost exclusively by the black press. The direct result was President Franklin D. Roosevelt's executive order creating the first declaration for federal fair employment practices.

Today, with the black revolution at its zenith, the question is raised throughout the ghettos: where is the black press? The answer is that the established black press is squarely in the middle of a dilemma. It finds itself trying not to be too conservative for the black revolutionaries, and not too revolutionary for white conservatives upon whom it depends for advertising. Murphy of the *Afro-American* speaks candidly about the tightrope the black press walks: "Newspapers are small businesses and publishers are businessmen. Surely you'd have to describe black publishers as conservatives, I suppose. In earlier years, black newspapers were spearheads of protest. Today we're much more informational."

Powell of the *Amsterdam News* concedes that "we have not kept up with the black revolution as we should have. But you've got to realize that we don't see our role as leaders. We are not out to revolutionize. When the *Amsterdam News* sees issues that are too revolutionary, we speak out against them." Louis Martin, vice president and editor of the Sengstacke Newspapers and the former deputy chairman of the National Democratic Committee, says the black press is "reflecting the rise in black awareness" but admits that "some of the older publishers were a little too slow responding." Now, he says, "even some of our most conservative black newspapers are bowing to the winds of change."

Many black readers wonder if "bowing to the winds of change" is enough. An editor in the Midwest says no. "Playing catch-up is not the name of the game," he declares. "The black revolution has left the black press behind. And one of the reasons is that in the good old days of the black press income came almost exclusively from circulation because there just wasn't any real advertising available. Today, the papers are picking up some pretty good accounts and, aside from wrestling with the increasingly complex economies of keeping a newspaper alive, black publishers have to make sure they don't become too revolutionary in tone for fear of losing those new white accounts."

William Robertson, assistant to publisher Leon Washington of the Los Angeles *Sentinel*, suggests another reason why the black press has relinquished its title of crusader: "I think we have lost much of our penchant for protest because we just don't have the staff to dig out the stories like we used to."

Some reporters on black newspapers, moreover, do not appear to have the dedication to the black cause which characterized black newsmen a couple of decades ago. A former reporter for the *Amsterdam News* was quoted in a New York *Times* Magazine article recently: "You don't feel that you have to stay working there like you do on some jobs because you're doing good works or really helping to change the community around you. It's just a job. . . . You know the publisher's in it to make money, not to reform the black world and that kind of spirit pervades the place. When I was there, my attitude was what the hell, if he's in it for the money, I am, too."

This attitude parallels that of a reporter for a Chicago black newspaper who told this writer: "Look, man, you get tired of brothers and sisters bugging you on the street because your paper just isn't with The Movement. You know, one day our paper looks like it might be getting with it and the next day it sounds like the *Trib* [Chicago *Tribune*]."

Probably the classic example of the black press' ambivalence on militancy is the way it has reacted to the Black Panther Party. At first black papers tried to ignore the Panthers. As the Panthers' brand of activism stepped up to where it could not be overlooked, black newspapers, for the most part, reported their conflicts with police but consciously sought to hew a line that would not identify with the Panther ideology. After the Illinois Black Panther Party served notice that the Chicago *Daily Defender* "will have to become relevant or we will have to deal with it," the *Defender* began carrying more news about the Panthers—their breakfast-for-children program and other activities not tied to police confrontation. But there is a bold new dimension in the black press in the form of the organizational newspaper that in some instances is a profit-making venture but in all instances is a propaganda instrument. These papers are appearing all over the nation, especially in major urban areas, and they are having an impact on their readers and on the established black press. One thing sets them apart—militancy.

Two such papers, national in scope with circulations that outstrip virtually all other black newspapers, are *Muhammad Speaks,* published in Chicago by the Black Muslims, and the *Black Panther,* printed in San Francisco by the Black Panther Party. *Muhammad Speaks*—by far the largest of any black newspaper—has a press run of 498,000, indicating a circulation figure of well over 400,000. It is published in the Black Muslims' modern $1.5-million-dollar offset plant. The Panthers' tabloid, according to Black Panther Chief of Staff David Hilliard, sells 110,000 weekly. Significantly, neither paper depends on advertising for revenue and both are sold enthusiastically by members on street corners. Both are remarkably alike in approach, though not in ideology: each issue of the *Black Panther* carries the party platform and its 10-point program; each edition of *Muhammad Speaks* runs the Muslims' program, also a 10-point platform.

Muhammad Speaks, which sells for 15 cents in Illinois and 20 cents elsewhere, runs stories under such headlines as THE SLAVE TRADE, WHITE EXPLOITERS BUILD NUCLEAR ARSENAL IN AFRICA, LINK STRUGGLE OF U. S. BLACKS, VIETNAMESE, as well as numerous messages from Elijah Muhammad, "Messenger of Allah." There also are reports from various Black Muslim Mosques. Only about half of the editorial staff is Muslim, and most top editors are trained in journalism. The acting editor in Chicago—the base for thirty-two staff members—is a Harvard graduate; the New York editor is an alumnus of the Columbia Graduate School of Journalism. Although the newspaper subscribes to United Press International, it does not use much UPI material, depending more on news contacts in key cities and lifting and rewriting of material from other black newspapers. The paper has an office in Cairo and is opening another one soon in London.

The staff of the *Black Panther*—which sells for 25 cents a copy—

is mostly volunteer, depending heavily on reports from Ministers of Information in Panther chapters. The paper's pages are saturated with Panther police confrontations, progress reports on trials involving Panthers, and activities such as free breakfast and health programs. Typical *Black Panther* headlines scream: BLACK YOUTH MURDERED IN COLD BLOOD BY RACIST S.F. PIG; "RAP" BROWN LAW PUT TO USE BY POWER STRUCTURE; MOZAMBIQUE GUERRILLAS DETERMINED TO CARRY ARMED STRUGGLE TO THE END; THE ANATOMY OF EXTERMINA-TION, A POLITICAL ASSASSINATION.

The fact that these two papers consistently circulate in figures far larger than their memberships affirms that there is a market for the more militant, anti-establishment black newspaper. Indeed, sizeable but unknown numbers of small organizational newspapers are now in existence, with an undetermined but obviously significant aggregate circulation: in Chicago, for example, the bi-weekly *Black Truth* circulates 30,000; the bi-weekly *Torch* 15,000; the weekly *Observer* 25,000; the monthly *Black Liberator* 10,000; and the monthly *Black Women's Committee News* 5,000.

The established black publishers look warily on these militant organs. Sengstacke Newspapers' Martin comments: "It's the same story in every city I've been in. The big weeklies apparently are not able to give these organizations and their points of view the kind of attention they demand." Because they are subsidized by organizations they are less dependent on advertising; and the editors—generally untrained in journalism but committed to the militant black cause—exercise wide freedom in their "news" presentation, which has great appeal to blacks who want action along with words.

Whether the established black press will move more in this direction remains to be seen. But its survival does not appear to be threatened. Publishers, though expressing mixed feelings about their individual futures, agree on that. "As long as there is white racism, we'll have black newspapers," Martin says. "But there is no question about it, we have to change our points of view and presentation of the news as the demands of black people are recognized. We'll have to if we are to be relevant."

In 1950, when network radio was searching frantically for new formats and new audiences to salvage what it could from television, there were a few feeble attempts to program for blacks. Jackie Robinson and Mahalia Jackson were given shows, but when no advertisers appeared, the programs vanished. As radio went local, many stations added black programing, usually a black disc jockey. By 1970, there were more than 100 stations beaming all their programing at blacks and another 300 with at least some such air time. Most of this was soul radio, of course. More important, only 13 of the radio stations were black-owned in 1970.

In 1972, Mutual Broadcasting System and Unity Broadcasting Network both began news and sports programing for black-oriented stations. Mutual made 100 five-minute programs available each week, while Unity had nearly as many. In addition Mutual set up a similar Spanish-language service. The two Mutual nets were particularly interesting, since minorities did all the writing, producing, and broadcasting, but they were able, at the same time, to take advantage of Mutual's worldwide news-gathering operation.

All journalists have become skeptical of comments from official sources; they have learned that policemen and prosecutors can be wrong, and while it is "objective" to quote their wrong opinions, it may not be "right." For example, almost all reporters covering the riot at the Attica (NY) Correctional Facility in 1971 passed along as fact the statement from prison officials that several hostages held by the inmates had their throats cut and that at least one had been castrated. When the riot ended, medical examinations showed these to be lies.

An editorial in *Columbia Journalism Review* pointed out: "Proper attribution—and why, after all the lessons of official news management, reminders about it are needed is a mystery—would only have taken the curse of misstatement off the backs of the reporters. The falsehoods themselves would still have been printed without any real challenge to their veracity."

Withholding information which he considers newsworthy goes against the basic instincts of any newsman. Timeliness is a part of his definition of news, although outsiders often find this emphasis on speed difficult to understand. There is more to the newsman's sense of urgency than the desire for a "scoop"—a term heard more often in late-show movies than in newsrooms. The journalist insists on speed because he sees himself as a representative of the public, with an obligation to get them information which he thinks they need.

Hardest of restraints to swallow, obviously, are those imposed by law or by court orders. It would be hard to find a better example than the Pentagon Papers controversy during the summer of 1971. Here, a federal court ordered the suspension of the series of articles until a judge could determine their importance to national security. The New York *Times* and the Washington *Post* literally were ordered not to publish material which they had in hand. Eventually, by a 6 to 3 vote, the Supreme Court of the United States lifted the suspension, but the specter of such court orders blacken the journalistic horizon.

Only slightly less distasteful are codes and agreements hammered out at the local level among the various media and news sources of a particular kind (such as hospitals or lawyers) about what kind of information may be published and under what circumstances. These have no legal teeth but can block publication of certain news, for whatever reason. An editor of the Milwaukee *Journal* once remarked, "I've never seen one of those agreements that gave the press *more* discretion than it had before," which is true, almost by definition, of an agreement.

Since the mid-1960's, newsmen and lawyers have been working out local codes to implement the recommendations of the American Bar Association's Reardon Report. The report, aimed primarily at attorneys and law enforcement officials, was an attempt to improve the administration of justice. Newsmen were alarmed at proposals to withhold certain information from them, for fear that publication would prejudice a jury. They argued this seldom happened and that strict rules would amount to throwing out the baby with the bath water. Even journalists who agreed with the goals objected to allowing lawyers to determine what was good and bad for them to publish.

The following is an example of a voluntary agreement on guidelines for reporting, adopted in 1968 by the Oklahoma Bar-Media Relations Committee and ratified by all state media organizations:

> Great news interest may be engendered during the pretrial stage of a criminal case. It is then that the maximum attention often is received and the greatest impact may be made upon the public. During that time, when the possibility of dangers to a fair trial may be great, the Bar and the Press must exercise judgment to prevent the release of possibly prejudicial information, especially on the eve of trial. However, these considerations are not necessarily applicable once a jury has been empaneled. It is inherent in the concept of freedom of the press that the Press be free to report what occurs in public proceedings, such as criminal trials. In the course of the trial it is the primary responsibility of the bench to take appropriate measures to ensure that the deliberations of the jury are based upon what is presented to the jury in court.
>
> These guidelines are proposed as a means of assuring both the public's right to be informed and the accused's right to a fair and public trial before an impartial jury.
>
> 1. It is appropriate to make public the following information concerning the defendant:
>
> > (a) The defendant's name, age, residence, occupation, marital status, and similar background information. There should be no restraint on biographical facts other than accuracy, good taste and judgment.
> >
> > (b) The text of the charge, such as the complaint, information and indictment, and, where appropriate, the identity of the complaining party.

(c) The identity of the investigating and arresting agency and the length of the investigation.

(d) The circumstances immediately surrounding an arrest, including, but not limited to, the time and place of arrest, resistance, pursuit, possession and use of weapons, and a description of items seized at the time of arrest.

2. It is the duty of the law enforcement agency to solve and prevent crime. It is the duty of the press to inform, promptly and accurately. It is the duty of counsel, both defense and prosecution, to seek the truth within the confines of a fair trial. It is in the fulfillment of these duties that these professions sometimes may seem to be in conflict.

An editor, who must ultimately make the decision whether to publish or broadcast, should weigh these varying responsibilities, as well as the fact that certain types of information may create dangers of prejudice without serving a significant law enforcement or public interest function. Such dissemination may impose particular risks when it occurs after the filing of formal charges and as the time of trial approaches. It is emphasized that these guidelines must not be used to excuse a law enforcement agency from releasing proper information to the public.

With these considerations in mind, categories of information which may jeopardize the rights of a defendant, if published, include:

(a) Opinions about a defendant's character, his guilt or innocence.

(b) Admissions, confessions, or the contents of a statement attributed to a defendant.

(c) References to the results of investigative procedures, such as fingerprints, polygraph examinations, ballistics tests, or laboratory tests.

(d) Statements concerning the credibility or anticipated testimony of prospective witnesses.

(e) Opinions concerning evidence or argument in the case, whether or not it is anticipated that such evidence or argument will be used at trial.

Exceptions may be in order if information to the public is essential to the apprehension of a suspect, or where other public interests will be served.

Stories reviewing the entire history of a criminal case, disseminated just prior to trial, should be avoided.

3. Prior criminal charges and convictions are matters of public record and are available to the Press through police agencies, court clerks, and the files of the Press. Law enforcement agencies should make such information available to the Press after a legitimate inquiry. The public disclosure of this information may be prejudicial, particularly if it occurs after the filing of formal charges and as the time of trial approaches, and should be carefully considered prior to publication.

4. Photographers, still and film.

(a) Photographs of a suspect may be released by law enforcement personnel in response to a legitimate request by the Press.

(b) Law enforcement and court personnel should not prevent the photographing of suspects or defendants when they are in public places outside the courtroom.

(c) The taking of photographs in a courtroom is governed by rules of court.

(d) The possible effect on the fair trial of a defendant by the dissemination of photographs of the suspect should be considered by editors in the light of these guidelines.

5. The press is free to report what occurs in the course of the judicial proceedings itself, subject to rules of the court.

6. Nothing in these guidelines should inhibit a law enforcement agency from disclosing such information as may be necessary to enlist public assistance in apprehending fugitives from justice. Such information may include photographs, records of prior arrests and convictions, and results of investigative procedures.

The moral problems of the book publisher seldom come to public light, but they did so in rather dramatic fashion in two cases in 1972. The first was the publication of the "autobiography" of Howard Hughes. McGraw-Hill was set to go, and serial rights had been sold to *Life* magazine, when the authenticity of the manuscript by Clifford Irving was questioned. A bizarre plot came to light, the publications were canceled at the last moment, and Irving and an accomplice were indicted for fraud. A few weeks later, the same publisher was caught with its credibility down, when questions were raised about the authenticity of a memoir by an aged Sioux chief who claimed to be a survivor of the Battle of Little Big Horn. The book had been a best-seller in hardback and was then doing well as a paperback. Even after it was established that Chief Red Fox incorporated one entire section from another writer, the publisher insisted the book was otherwise an honest memoir and refused to withdraw it.

Obviously, a book publisher has some obligation to check the authenticity of material it markets. Usually, a book publisher is under little time pressure and therefore can be expected to check more thoroughly than can those involved in media on tighter deadlines. Speed does not excuse misrepresentations, but it does mitigate them.

The Supreme Court of the United States recognized this in handing down two concurrent opinions in 1967. In *Associated Press* v. *Walker* (388 U.S. 130), the court reversed a libel decision against the wire service for erroneously reporting that a retired general "led a charge" during the demonstrations on the University of Mississippi campus to prevent the admission of the first known black student. Walker had been present, but he had not led a charge. The high court did not condone such inaccurate reporting but admitted that in the highly charged atmosphere, such a mistake was understandable; it therefore held that Walker could not collect damages. In the companion case, however, the same court upheld the conviction of

Saturday Evening Post for publishing a story, based solely on what a free-lance writer claimed he heard in a telephone conversation between two major college football coaches. The writer claimed that his connection somehow got crossed with theirs and that he heard them agree to shave the points on their upcoming game for the benefit of gamblers. The *Post* bought the story and hurried it into print. Both coaches collected after the Supreme Court said there was no apparent hurry in handling this story as there had been on the riot-torn campus. With a wire service, deadlines were minutes away; with a magazine, they were whenever they chose to set them. The magazine had an obligation, therefore, to check the facts in the story; by extension, so does a book publisher.

Since 1967, libel has become less and less a threat to the mass media. Courts have held that a public official can collect only if he can show the defamatory matter was published when the publication or station knew it was a lie or with reckless disregard for whether it was true or not. Gradually, this definition was broadened to encompass public figures and even private individuals who became involved in matters of public interest. In short, there was virtually no danger of libeling anyone so long as the newsmen maintained reasonable professional and ethical standards. The vast majority of libel cases always resulted from carelessness, not from editorial crusades, anyway. The social reason for this greater protection from the threat of libel suits has been to promote robust and open discussion of public issues.

But at the same time, the lessening of legal threats only places more responsibility (call it ethics, if you will) on the individual journalist. The fact that he may be able to get by with innuendo or inaccuracy does not justify his knowingly doing so. And no journalist worth his pastepot would do so.

Not every journalist concerns himself with high-flown ethical questions, however. Many simply try to do their job in a comfortable, routine way. But sooner or later, every journalist—by the very nature of his job—is going to face some tough ethical questions.

For example, suppose you were working the newsroom of a big-city radio station on a Sunday morning and you received a telephone call, telling you there were about 100 persons gathered at a certain corner in the ghetto and that 25 policemen were being pelted with rocks. "It looks like the start of a riot for sure," your informant says and hangs up.

What would you do? If you had any journalistic instincts at all you would call the police and try to call some witnesses in the area of the alleged riot to see if such an event was taking place. So you find out that your original informant is right. What now? You call one of the station's newsmen at home, and he says he will get out there; however, it is an hour's drive from his home to the ghetto corner.

You have a newscast coming up in eight minutes. Do you give the facts that you have now, do you wait until your reporter gets there, or do you simply gather information and wait until much later when the situation has clarified? There is no right answer, because all three solutions have something to be said for them. Timeliness is a basic ingredient of news, particularly of news which may have great impact for a large number of citizens. A race riot certainly falls in that category, so perhaps you should broadcast what you have right now. On the other hand, you do not want to go off half-cocked with the possibility of distorting the real situation, so you may want to wait at least until you have a coherent observation from a real newsman you can trust. Broadcasting a news flash may only bring hordes of people to the scene, thereby worsening the situation; for that reason, newsmen in many cities have voluntary agreements to withhold such news for a given length of time.

In a survey conducted by the Detroit *Free Press* after the 1967 riot, it was found that only 30 per cent of the blacks in the riot area first heard about the riot from radio and television. Half heard from friends or relatives, and the rest saw or heard it for themselves. It was young people, 15 to 24, who joined the riot, regardless how they learned of it, and voluntary boycotts on news would have had little effect in containing them. The presence of TV cameras or the cumulative effect of media coverage *might* have other effects, of course.

Such social science data can help the journalist answer some of his ethical questions, but he cannot count on them for most solutions. He will have to resolve such conflicts as advocacy versus objectivity, employer versus employee, legal versus ethical dilemmas for himself, according to his own normative value system. The journalist, like anyone else, plays many roles—often simultaneously. Sometimes he responds as a taxpayer, sometimes as a parent, sometimes as a member of an ethnic or interest group—but hopefully the journalist will respond more and more as a responsible professional. After all, in the last analysis, he is the one who must make the elephant perform.

ADDITIONAL READING

Books on mass communication and the media are appearing at too fast a pace for any short list to do them justice. The following books are *among* the best, and the reader will find that most of them also include bibliographies which can be mined.

Bibliographies

The best bibliographies are Warren C. Price, *The Literature of Journalism* (Minneapolis: University of Minnesota Press, 1959), and its updating volume, Warren C. Price and Calder M. Pickett, *An Annotated Journalism Bibliography 1958–1968* (Minneapolis: University of Minnesota Press, 1970). *Journalism Quarterly* annotates current articles in a wide range of journals.

Introductions

Excellent introductions to the media include John L. Hulteng and Roy Paul Nelson, *The Fourth Estate* (New York: Harper & Row, 1971); William Rivers, Theodore Peterson, and Jay Jensen, *The Mass Media and Modern Society* (San Francisco: Rinehart Press, 1971); Peter M. Sandman, David M. Rubin, and David B. Sachsman, *Media* (Englewood Cliffs: Prentice-Hall, 1972).

History and Law

Edwin Emery, *The Press and America* (New York: Prentice-Hall, 1972) is the best overview. For essays, see Ronald T. Farrar and John D. Stevens, *Mass Media and the National Experience* (New York: Harper & Row, 1971). The definitive history of magazines is Frank Luther Mott, *A History of American Magazines* (5 vols.) (Cambridge: Harvard University Press, 1930–1968), and for broadcasting is Eric Barnouw, *A Tower in Babel, The Golden Web,* and *The Image Empire* (New York: Oxford University Press, 1966–1970). For freedom of the press, see Zechariah Chafee, *Free Speech in the United States* (Cambridge: Harvard University Press, 1941), and William A. Hachten (ed.), *The Supreme Court on Freedom of The Press* (Ames: Iowa State University Press, 1968). Two excellent press law texts are Harold L. Nelson and Dwight L. Teeter, *Law of Mass Communications* (Brooklyn: Foundation Press, 1969), and Donald M. Gillmor and Jerome A. Barron, *Mass Communications Law* (Minneapolis: West Publishing Company, 1969).

Economics of the Media

Start with Bryce W. Rucker, *The First Freedom* (Carbondale: Southern Illinois University Press, 1968), an impressive compilation of facts and figures on all the media. For advertising, see S. Watson Dunn, *Advertising: Its Role in Modern Marketing* (New York: Holt, Rinehart and Winston, 1969).

Criticisms of the Media

A swelling list certainly would include John Hohenberg, *The News Media* (New York: Holt, Rinehart and Winston, 1968); Hillier Krieghbaum, *Pressures on the Press* (New York: Thomas Y. Crowell, 1972); James Reston, *The Artillery of the Press* (New York: Harper & Row, 1967); William L. Rivers and Wilbur Schramm, *Responsibility in Mass Communication* (New York: Harper & Row, 1969). For a unique perspective, see Ivan and Carol Doig, *News: A Consumer's Guide* (Englewood Cliffs: Prentice-Hall, 1972).

Alternate Media

The best one-volume treatment of the black media is Roland E. Wolseley, *The Black Press USA* (Ames: Iowa State University Press, 1971). Robert J. Glessing, *The Underground Press in America* (Bloomington: Indiana University Press, 1970) is an admirable attempt to define the undefinable.

INDEX

Abbott, Robert S., 168
ABC, 50, 51
    television network, 13, 54, 61, 92, 98, 120
Abernathy, Rev. Ralph, 131
A. C. Neilsen Co., 12–13, 65
Adler, Renata, 32
Advertisers:
    impact on audience, 27
    impact on media, 38–43, 46–48, 50, 54, 56, 57, 71, 74, 76–77, 88, 150, 167, 169, 171
    and targeting media, 7–8, 25, 27
Agence France Press, 114
Agnew, Spiro T., 147, 152, 154
Akron *Beacon-Journal,* 72
Albert, Rep. Carl, 115, 118–19, 139
Alioto, Mayor Joseph, 124, 137
American Association of Publishers, 44
American Broadcasting Company (*see* ABC)
American Newspaper Guild, 150, 167
American Newspaper Publishers Association, 9
American Newspaper Publishers Association Foundation, 69
American Press, 29
American Research Bureau (ARB), 65
Amsterdam News, 167, 169
Anderson, Jack, 148–49
Anhalt, Edward, 102

Arnold, Danny, 12
Ashe, Penelope, 45
Associated Press (AP), 53, 113, 114, 155
Associated Press Managing Editors Association, 33
Association of Public Television Producers, 150
Astin, John, 90, 92–93, 99
Atlanta *Daily World,* 166
Atlantic, The, 44
Audit Bureau of Circulation, 166

Baker, Diane, 81–82
Baker, Ray Stannard, 148
Balk, Alfred, 161, 162
Baltimore *Afro-American,* 165–68
Baltimore *Sun,* 114
Bantam Books, 45
Barron, Jerome, 162–64
Bartley, Robert T., 51
BBC (*see* British Broadcasting Company)
Beard, Fred, 36
Belson, Jerry, 91–93
Benti, Joe, 124–25
Bergen (N.J.) *Record,* 162
Bergman, Lewis, 160
Berkeley *Barb,* 162
Bernstein, Theodore M., 107–12
Better Homes & Gardens, 78, 100
Black, Brady, 71–72, 74
Black, Hugo L., 50

181

Black Liberator, 171
Black media and audiences, 26–30, 33–37, 47, 165–71
Black Panther, 166, 170–71
Black Truth, 171
Black Women's Committee News, 171
Block, Carl E., 24–29
Boca Raton (Fla.) *News,* 70, 73
Bogart, Leo, 28–29
Boggs, Rep. Hale, 120–23
Bok, Edward, 99
Bonanno, Joe, 161
Book publishing, 9–11, 39, 43–49, 175–76
  economic health, 2, 15, 44–45, 47, 48
Boot & Shoe Recorder, 99
Bormann, Jim, 156
Boston *Transcript,* 75
Boyer, Brian, 64–68, 75
Boyer, Charles, 129
Breslin, Jimmy, 159
Brinkley, David, 150
British Broadcasting Company, 1, 40
Broadcasting (*see also* Radio; Television)
  advertisers and, 40–43, 46
  impact, 33
  inflexibility, 15
  non-commercial, 20, 39
  quality, 1
  targeting, 9–10
Broadcasting, 151
Brown, Bill, 83, 84
Buchwald, Art, 119
Buck, Pearl, 10
Buckley, William F., Jr., 160–62
Burns, John, 120

Cable television, 2, 13–14, 31, 33–34, 47
Caldwell, Erskine, 10
Caplovitz, David, 24
Carter, Boake, 152
Carter, Don, 33
Cavett, Dick, 45
CBS, 48–49, 54, 94, 150, 164
  television network, 7, 12, 13, 21–23, 40, 52, 54, 61, 92, 98, 115–41
Cerf, Bennett, 44, 52
Chandler, Robert, 117
Chapman, Alvah, 72, 73
Charlotte *Observer,* 74
Chicago *American,* 65
Chicago *Daily News,* 65, 72, 74, 114
Chicago *Defender,* 165–66, 168, 170
Chicago *Herald American,* 75
Chicago Journalism Review, 64, 153, 157
Chicago *Seed,* 67–68
Chicago *Sun-Times,* 64–67

Chicago Today, 65, 67
Chicago *Tribune,* 64–67, 71, 169
Childs, Marquis, 152
Christian Science Monitor, 16, 40
Cincinnati *Enquirer,* 71–72, 74
Cincinnati *Herald,* 167
Citizens Communication Center, 34
Clapper, Raymond, 152
Cleveland *Plain Dealer,* 71
Clevenger, James L., 133
Cohen, Herman, 83, 84
Cohen, Larry, 90, 91
Collier's Magazine, 48, 75
Columbia Broadcasting System (*see* CBS)
Columbia Graduate School of Journalism, 170
Columbia Journalism Review, 52, 161, 162, 172
Columbia Pictures, 31, 95
Congress, 50, 51, 53, 55, 130, 148, 154, 164–65
Connally, Gov. John, 119–20
Conspiracy theory, 2–3, 51
Cornish, Rev. Samuel, 168
Cousins, Norman, 13
Cox, Francis, 71
Cox, Kenneth, 34–37, 51
Crawford, Bill, 117
Crawford, Joan, 80
Credibility, 8, 22, 64, 72, 159–62
Cronkite, Walter, 15, 116–25, 130, 137–40, 150
Curtis Publications, 75
Cushing, Peter, 81

Daley, Mayor Richard, 124, 127, 128, 130, 137–41
Darsa, Josh, 119, 121
Davidson, Casey, 117, 128
Davis, Elmer, 152, 157
Decatur (Iowa) *Democrat,* 19
De Gaulle, Charles, 40
Denoyer-Geppert Co., 48
Denver *Post,* 161
Department of Justice, 50, 55, 148
Detroit *Free Press,* 70, 72, 74, 82, 177
Detroit *News,* 74, 163
Diamond, Vern, 117–18, 137–41
Disney, Walt, 84
Dorfman, Ron, 157
Douglas, Kirk, 80
Douglas, William O., 164
Dow-Jones Company, 42
Dreiser, Theodore, 10
Dunne, John Gregory, 101–6
Durgin, Don, 96, 97

Ebony, 27
Editor & Publisher, 151
Eisenhower, Pres. Dwight D., 49, 65
Emmy Awards, 12
Erickson, Don, 161
Esquire, 158–61
Evers, Charles, 119

Family Circle, 48
Farrell, Charles, 83
Faulkner, William, 10
Federal Communications Commission (FCC), 14, 33–37, 47, 49–54
Federal Trade Commission (FTC), 68
Felker, Clay, 159, 161
Fellini, Federico, 80
Field, Marshall, 68
Field & Stream, 8
Field Enterprises, 64
Fitzgerald, F. Scott, 10, 101
Fleischer, Richard, 102–6
Fortune, 68
Fosdick, Raymond B., 144, 145
Fouhy, Ed, 127, 133, 134
Fox, David, 134
Fox, William, 82
Francis, Arlene, 36
Freedom's Journal, 168
Freeman, David, 161
Friendly, Fred, 85
Fryer, Robert, 102–4
Fusca, James, 135

Gable, Clark, 80
Gallagher, Wes, 155–56
Gannett Newspapers, 70, 71
Gardner, Erle Stanley, 10
Gaynor, Janet, 83
Geneen, Harold, 50
General Motors, 42, 43
George, Nicholas, 82
Goldenson, Leonard, 50
Goldwyn (*see* MGM)
Golf Digest, 48
Goodwin, Richard, 122
Gralnick, Jeff, 117, 119, 121, 122, 124, 137
Greenberg, Paul, 117, 119–23, 137, 139

Hadden, Britton, 99
Hairdo & Beauty, 78
Hall, Buck, 105
Hall, Delos, 129
Halpern, Alan, 160
Hampton, Fred, 170
Hand, Learned, 56
Harper's Magazine, 43, 44

Harris Surveys, 20
Hart, Sen. Philip, 55
Hayes, Chester, 66
Hearst, William R. (Sr.), 49, 68
Hefner, Hugh, 150
Hemingway, Ernest, 10
Hemmings, David, 80
Hilliard, David, 170
Hills, Lee, 72, 73
Hodges, Mrs. Gil, 155
Hoffa, Jimmy, 52
Hot Rod, 78
Hough, Stan, 102
Houston *Chronicle,* 161
Hughes, Emmet John, 40
Hughes, Gov. Harold, 123
Hughes, Howard, 159, 175
Humphrey, Sen. Hubert, 119, 124, 130, 137
Huston, John, 80
Hvistendahl, J. K., 151–55

I. F. Stone's Weekly, 100
Intellectual Digest, 30
International Telephone & Telegraph (ITT), 50, 51, 148
Ireland, Charles, 49
Irving, Clifford, 175

Jackson, Mahalia, 118, 171
Johnson, Pres. Lyndon B., 120, 127
Johnson, Nicholas, 34–37, 48–56, 63, 64
Jordan, John "Rover," 166
Joyce, James, 15, 44

Kaltenborn, H. V., 152
Kaufman, Sid, 117
Kazan, Elia, 9
Kennedy, Sen. Edward M., 118, 121, 122
Kennedy, Pres. John F., 12, 60
Kennedy, Sen. Robert F., 60
Kerner Commission (*see* National Advisory Commission on Civil Disorders)
King, Dr. Martin Luther, 60
Knight, Charles L., 72
Knight, James, 72, 73
Knight, John S. (Jack), 69, 70, 72–75
Knight Newspapers, Inc., 69, 70, 72–75
Knopf, Alfred, 44
Kraus, Robert, 81–85
Kubrick, Stanley, 80
Kuleshov, 136

LaBrie, Henry, III, 30
Ladies Home Journal, 75, 87–88, 99
Leonard, William S., 120–21

Lewis, Fulton, 157
Lewis, Jerry, 95
Liebling, A. J., 63
Life, 7, 40, 48, 77, 90, 98, 100, 175
Lindley, Ernest K., 152
Lindsay, Mayor John, 159
Lippmann, Walter, 19, 152
Lombard, Carole, 80
Long Island Press, 71
Look, 8, 43, 48, 77, 78
Lorimer, George H., 75–76, 99–101
Los Angeles *Free Press,* 67, 162
Los Angeles *Sentinel,* 166, 169
Los Angeles *Times,* 48, 56, 114
Louisiana Weekly, 168

McCall's, 78
McCarthy, Sen. Eugene, 119, 123, 124, 137
McCarthy, Sen. Joseph, 154–55
McCormick, Col. Robert R., 68
Macdonald, Stewart, 69, 70
McGann, Tim, 133
McGlinnen, Earl, 82
McGovern, Sen. George, 133
McGraw-Hill, 112, 175
McKinley, Pres. William, 108
McKuen, Rod, 45
McLuhan, Marshall, 14, 18, 85
McMullan, John, 74
Macon (Ga.) *News,* 70
Macon (Ga.) *Telegraph,* 70
Mad, 99
Mademoiselle, 8
Magazines, 75–79, 99–101 (*see also* Press)
  economic health, 2, 15, 48, 70
  impact, 18, 19, 21–23, 27–28
  targeting, 8, 10, 26, 48, 78, 99–101
Mailer, Norman, 162
Manning, Gordon, 117, 123
Marshall, Garry, 91–93
Marshall, Thurgood, 36
Martin, Louis, 169, 171
Martin, Quinn, 90
Melville, Herman, 10
Meredith Publications, 100
Merman, Doc, 102–6
Metro-Goldwyn-Mayer (*see* MGM)
Metromedia, 54
MGM, 81, 90, 96, 101, 106
Miami *Herald,* 70, 72–74
Michener, James, 10
Michigan Chronicle, 166
Microfilming Corp. of America, 48
Milwaukee *Journal,* 173
Mirisch brothers, 94

Mitchell, John, 147
Mitchell, Martha, 32
Modern Library, 44
Monogram Pictures, 79
Morgan, Tom, 159
Mosjukhin, 136
Motion Picture Association of America, 11, 163
Movies, 39, 46, 79–85, 101–6
  economic health, 2, 11, 15, 79–85
  quality, 1
  targeting, 9
Moynihan, Daniel, 24
Mudd, Roger, 116, 119, 121
Muhammad, Elijah, 170
Muhammed Speaks, 165–66, 170
Murchison brothers, 37
Murphy, John, 167, 168
Mutual Broadcasting System, 52, 172
Myrdahl, Gunnar, 23, 165

Nader, Ralph, 32
National Advisory Commission on Civil Disorders (Kerner Commission), 27, 30, 32
National Broadcasting Company (*see* NBC)
National Commission on Violence, 135
National Review, 160, 161
NBC, 48, 52, 56–63, 165
  news, 56–63
  owned stations, 57, 59, 61, 62
  radio network, 61–62
  television network, 12, 13, 54, 56–63, 90, 91, 93, 95–99, 120, 122, 129
Neilsen Ratings, 12–13, 65
Neufeld, Mace, 92–93
Neuharth, Allen, 70, 71
New American Library, 48
New journalism, 3–4, 147, 149, 153, 156–62
New York, 158, 159, 161
New York *Daily Mirror,* 75
New York *Herald Tribune,* 75
New York *Post,* 153, 155
New York *Sun,* 168
New York Times, The, 4, 10–11, 15, 16, 18, 19, 32, 42–43, 48, 56, 68, 70, 71, 82, 107, 113, 114, 150, 156, 157, 161, 172
New York Times (Sunday) Magazine, 160, 169
New York *World,* 75
New York *World-Journal-Tribune,* 75
New Yorker, The, 8, 63, 99
Newhouse Newspapers, 70, 71
Newsday, 45, 48

Newspaper Guild, 150, 167
Newspapers, 3, 63–75, 107–15, 142–45
  (*see also* Press)
  economic health, 2, 15, 47, 50–52, 55,
    63–75
  impact, 18–19, 22–23, 27–29
  quality, 1, 18
  targeting, 7–11, 15–16, 26, 29, 165–71
Newsweek, 19, 43, 53, 130, 148–49
Nixon, Pres. Richard M., 37, 65, 71, 119,
  147
Norfolk *Journal & Guide,* 166, 168

Observer (Chicago), 171
Ocala (Fla.) *Star-Banner,* 48
O'Donnell, Kenneth, 119
O'Dwyer, Paul, 124
Office of Telecommunications Policy
  (White House), 37
O'Hara, John, 10
Oklahoma Bar-Media Relations Commit-
  tee, 173–75
Onassis, Jacqueline Kennedy, 155
Open access, 14, 34, 162–64

Palmer, L. F., Jr., 165–71
Parris, Jerry, 93, 95
Partisan Review, 99
Paul VI, Pope, 128
Pearce, Alan, 56–63
Pearson, Drew, 148
Philadelphia, 160
Philadelphia *Daily News,* 70
Philadelphia *Inquirer,* 70, 74
Picasso, Pablo, 12, 14
Pinkerton, W. Stewart, Jr., 158–62
Pittsburgh *Courier,* 165–68
Pittsburgh *Press & Post Gazette,* 74
Playboy, 78, 99, 150
Powell, C. B., 167, 169
President's Task Force on Communica-
  tions Policy, 13
Press (*see also* Magazines; Newspapers)
  advertisers and, 40–43, 46
  impact, 33, 49
  non-commercial, 39
Professionalism, 5, 149–51, 177
Psychology Today, 15
Public access, 14, 34, 162–64
Publisher's Weekly, 10
Pudovkin, 136, 141
Pulitzer, Joseph, 75
Pulitzer Prizes, 69, 72, 74, 108, 148
Puzo, Mario, 9

Quadrangle Books, 48

Quinn, Longworth, 166
Quint, Burt, 125

Radio, 57, 61–62, 85, 163–64, 171–72,
  176–77 (*see also* Broadcasting)
  economic health, 11, 15, 47
  impact, 18–19, 27–28
  targeting, 8, 25–26, 30, 47, 171–72
Radio & Television News Directors As-
  sociation, 156
Radio Corporation of America (*see* RCA)
RAND Corporation, 68–69
Random House, 44, 52, 54
Rather, Dan, 119–20, 123, 124, 137, 139–
  41
Rayburn, Rep. Sam, 51
RCA, 52, 54, 144
Reader's Digest, 8, 76, 78, 99, 101
Reasoner, Harry, 150
Red Fox, Chief, 175
Redgrave, Vanessa, 80
Reiner, Carl, 94
Reith, Sir John, 1
Reporters' Committee on Freedom of the
  Press, 150
Republic Pictures, 79
Reston, James, 4, 150
Reuters, 39, 114
Rich, Lee M., 88–99
Riddle, Nelson, 95
RKO Company, 54, 79
Roberts, Oral, 149
Robertson, William, 169
Robinson, Jackie, 171
Robinson, John P., 16–23
Roosevelt, Pres. Franklin D., 168
Rosenthal, A. M., 4, 156
Ross, Harold, 99, 100
Ross, Lillian, 101
Rosten, Leo, 4
Rotarian, The, 101
Roth, David, 125, 126
Rudd, Hughes, 123
Russworm, John B., 168
Ruth, Babe, 11

Salant, Richard S., 126, 134
Salinger, Pierre, 121
Samstag, Nicholas, 42–43
San Francisco *Call-Bulletin,* 75
San Francisco *Chronicle,* 54
Sanders, Curtis, 90, 91
Sarnoff, Gen. David, 144
Saturday Evening Post, 8, 48, 75–77, 79,
  87–88, 99–101, 176
Saturday Review, 13, 142
Scheffler, Phil, 125

Schlosser, Herb, 95, 96
Schulz, Charles, 10
Schwartz, Herbert, 133–34
Scribner's Magazine, 44
Scripps-Howard Newspapers, 70
Seagram, Inc., 81
Securities and Exchange Commission (SEC), 68
Sengstacke Newspapers, 169, 171
Sevareid, Eric, 116, 121, 157
Shahn, Ben, 123
Shawn, Dick, 94
Sheehy, Gail, 158–60
Sheppard, Sam, 155
Skelton, Red, 13
Smith, Howard K., 150
Socolow, Sanford, 117, 120–22
Spillane, Mickey, 10
Spock, Dr. Benjamin, 10
Sports Illustrated, 48
Stacey, Eric, 105
Stanton, Frank, 49, 150, 164
Steffens, Lincoln, 148
Steinbeck, John, 10
Stokes, Thomas L., 152
Stone, I. F., 100
Storer Broadcasting, 54
Strickland, James, 129
Suburban Press Association, 66
Sullivan, Ed, 13
Supreme Court, 11, 50, 52, 164, 172, 175–76
Suzanne, Jacqueline, 9
Swinehart, James W., 16–23

Talese, Gay, 4, 149, 159–61
Tanjug, 114
Tarbell, Ida, 148
Tarzan, 84
Tass, 114
Teaching Resources Corp., 48
Television, 34–38, 56–64, 85–86, 88–99, 115–41 (see also Broadcasting)
  cable, 2, 13–14, 31, 33–34, 47
  economic health, 15, 47, 88
  impact, 17–23, 27–29, 31–32, 136–39
  non-commercial, 41, 151
  quality, 1, 17–18, 49
  targeting, 7–13, 25–26, 29–31
Thaler, Alvin, 125–27, 130, 134–35
Thurber, James, 12
Time, 19, 42–43, 49, 53, 99–101, 130, 153, 157
Time, Inc., 56, 81, 101, 153
Times-Mirror Corp., 48
Tinker, Grant, 91, 92, 95, 96

Tobin, Richard L., 142–45
Topping, Seymour, 113
Torch, 171
Trujillo, Rafael Leonidas, 51–52
Truman, Pres. Harry S., 168
TV Guide, 20, 48, 76, 78, 151
20th-Century Fox, 81, 82, 101
Tynan, Michael, 74

Underground press, 30, 68, 157, 162
Undset, Sigrid, 44
United Artists Corp., 85
United Church of Christ, Office of Communication, 34
United Press International (UPI), 53, 114–15, 170
Unity Broadcasting Network, 172
Universal Pictures, 81
Urban, Walter, 132–33
U.S. News, 53

Vail, Thomas, 71
Valenti, Jack, 163
Van Dyke, Dick, 91, 94
Vanden Heuvel, William, 122
Vanocur, Sandor, 122
Variety, 81, 88
Village Voice, 162
Von Hoffman, Nicholas, 149

Wall Street Journal, 16, 40, 42, 158
Wallace, DeWitt, 99
Wallace, Irving, 9, 45
Wallace, Mike, 120–23
Washington, Pres. George, 147
Washington, Leon, 169
Washington Post, 56, 70, 114, 169, 172
Weisberg, Art, 84, 85
Welk, Lawrence, 13
Werner, Mort, 91, 92, 96
Westinghouse Broadcasting Company, 54
Whitehead, Clay T., 37
Whiteside, Thomas, 115–41
Wiley, W. Bradford, 44
Williams, Jerry, 164
Wilson, Flip, 7
Wilson, O. W., 67
Wilson, Pres. Woodrow, 100
Windom, William, 12
Wolfe, Tom, 157–58, 160
Workbasket, 78
Writers Guild, 91
Wussler, Robert, 117, 119–23, 137, 139

Yankee Network, 54